Having Their Say

Young People and Participation: European Experiences

Edited by

David Crimmens
and
Andrew West

WITHDRAWN

First published in 2004 by:
Russell House Publishing Ltd.
4 St. George's House
Uplyme Road
Lyme Regis
Dorset DT7 3LS

Tel: 01297-443948
Fax: 01297-442722
e-mail: help@russellhouse.co.uk
www.russellhouse.co.uk

British Library Cataloguing-in-publication Data:
A catalogue record for this book is available from the British Library.

ISBN: 1898924-78-3

Typeset by TW Typesetting, Plymouth, Devon

Printed by Antony Rowe, Chippenham, Wiltshire

About Russell House Publishing

RHP is a group of social work, probation, education and youth and
community work practitioners and academics working in
collaboration with a professional publishing team.
Our aim is to work closely with the field to produce innovative and
valuable materials to help managers, trainers, practitioners and
students.
We are keen to receive feedback on publications and new ideas for
future projects.
For details of our other publications please visit our website or ask us
for a catalogue. Contact details are on this page.

Contents

Preface   iv

About the contributors   v

Chapter 1   **Introduction**   1
             David Crimmens and Andrew West

Chapter 2   **Children and Participation: Meanings, Motives and Purpose**   14
             Andrew West

Chapter 3   **The Role of Government in Promoting Youth Participation in
             England**   27
             David Crimmens

Chapter 4   **Connexions: An Example of the Evolution of Young People's
             Participation in England**   37
             David Crimmens

Chapter 5   **Children's Rights in Ireland: Participation in Policy Development** 47
             Nóirín Hayes

Chapter 6   **Many Roads Converge on the Same Hilltop: Children's Rights
             in Scotland**   59
             Judy Furnivall, Andrew Hosie and Meg Lindsay

Chapter 7   **Beyond Rhetoric in the Search for Participation in Youth Work
             in Wales**   70
             Bert Jones

Chapter 8   **The Relevance of a Children's Policy and the Participation of Young
             People in Decision Making in Germany**   84
             Thomas Swiderek

Chapter 9   **Young People as Outsiders: The Italian Process of Youth Inclusion** 99
             Luca Mori

Chapter 10   **Young People Active in Youth Research in The Netherlands:
             An Innovative Approach**   112
             Jan Laurens Hazekamp

Chapter 11   **Participation Rights in Norway**   124
             Ingvild Begg

Chapter 12   **Children's Parliaments in Slovenia**   138
             Bojan Dekleva and Sonja Zorga

Index   146

Preface

Participation is a major principle underpinning the 1989 UN Convention on the Rights of the Child (CRC). During the 1990s participation by children and young people gained momentum as, increasingly, it was recognised by influential adults as both a right in itself and the means whereby other rights enshrined in the CRC could be realised.

The chapters in this book describe and analyse children's participation in the political and policy-making processes in a selection of European states. They address common themes, like the changing status of children and young people in relation to adults and their contribution to the development of more effective services. Each chapter provides a snapshot of work in progress, and illustrates the struggles to establish children's participation as a key element in political life.

The analysis offered here highlights the potential benefits of sharing policies and practices developed in one European state with children, young people, policy-makers and professionals in others. As the European Union enlarges, opportunities for collaboration by both policy makers and practitioners increase. As such, children's and young people's participation within individual states and across the EU will enhance the EU's stated commitment to citizenship and social inclusion.

The new millennium presents challenges to notions of the nation state, citizenship and democracy as well as the realities of an ageing population across much of Europe. To meet these challenges effectively, a recognition of the contribution that children and young people can and do make to defining the future direction of society, is urgently required. This book does not offer a blueprint for children's participation. Instead each chapter details the common and particular struggles that arise from the processes undertaken in individual countries. These processes provide positive learning opportunities for adults as well as for children and young people, reflecting the journey faced by both in moving towards a common future.

David Crimmens and Andrew West, April 2004.

About the Contributors

Ingvild Begg is Senior Lecturer in Law at Lillehammer University College. She obtained a CQSW in 1972 and spent 10 years in professional practice in Scotland before returning to Norway as Head of the Section for Social and Family Affairs in Troms. She was awarded a Law Degree in 1992. Since 1994 she has been teaching law and child care at the University.

David Crimmens lectures at the Hull School of Health and Social Care. His practice experience of over 20 years includes working in pre-school playgroups, adventure playgrounds, detached youth work, adolescent psychiatry, juvenile justice and residential care. He is currently training Personal Advisors for local Connexions Partnerships. Recent Publications include *Positive Residential Practice: Learning the Lessons of the 1990s*, with John Pitts.

Bojan Dekleva, Professor of Theories of Deviance, lectures at the Department of Social Pedagogy in the Faculty of Education at the University of Ljubljana. His research interests include juvenile justice, peer and school violence, and drug use among young people. He has published extensively on these issues in Slovenia.

Judy Furnivall is a lecturer at the Scottish Institute for Residential Child Care. She has spent all her professional life involved in residential child care in a number of roles: practitioner, manager, trainer, consultant and researcher.

Nóirín Hayes is the Head of School of Social Sciences and Legal Studies at the Dublin Institute of Technology, where she lectures in developmental psychology and early education. Her research interests include children's learning, and curriculum and pedagogy in early education. She is a founder member of the Children's Rights Alliance.

Jan Laurens Hazekamp was a senior lecturer at the Vrije Universiteit in Amsterdam in social pedagogy and youth research for more than twenty years. In 1993 he established the Alexander Foundation to develop programmes of youth research in which young people themselves fulfill important roles as youth researchers, inspectors and consultants.

Andrew Hosie is a lecturer in the Scottish Institute for Residential Child Care based at Strathclyde University. He has experience as a residential child care worker, in fieldwork and in training with a special interest in work with young people who offend.

Bert Jones lectures in Community Education at the University of Wales in Cardiff. He also coordinates the Leonardo da Vinci programme at ECTARC in Llangollen for the Wales Youth Agency.

Meg Lindsay is Head of Operations for Care Visions, a private company providing residential care for young people who have suffered significant abuse. She also works as an independent consultant on both child and community care in Britain and overseas.

Luca Mori recently received his PhD from the University of Bologna for a thesis on drug use among Italian adolescents. He is currently working at the University of Verona researching the informal care networks of children with developmental diseases.

Thomas Swiderek works at the Centre for International Studies in Social Policy and Social Services at the University of Wuppertal. He has recently completed his doctoral studies in *Childhood and youth: democracy and participation*.

Andrew West has been living and working in China since 1999, as adviser for Save the Children UK. He has also worked for short periods in Bangladesh, Mongolia and Myanmar, and paid research visits to Thailand, Vietnam and Cambodia. He previously worked in England, as youth worker, youth counsellor, welfare rights worker, researcher and university lecturer. He worked with homeless and unemployed children and young people, particularly on developing children's participation, and young people's own research.

Sonja Zorga is Professor of Developmental Psychology in the Faculty of Education at the University of Ljubljana, where she lectures on undergraduate and postgraduate programmes in Social Pedagogy and Art Pedagogy. She has a particular interest in the supervision of professional staff in pedagogical and social settings and has published extensively on these subjects.

CHAPTER 1

Introduction

David Crimmens and Andrew West

Throughout the 1990s children's and young people's participation once again gained momentum, as it became increasingly taken up as a right in itself, and as a means to realise other rights embedded in the 1989 United Nations Convention on the Rights of the Child (CRC). Participation is a major principle underpinning the CRC, and in November 2002 a group in India declared that 'children's participation is the most important principle and element in CRC that cuts across all other rights, namely: the right to development, survival and protection' (SATFCP 2002). Yet such views are not widespread, and for many people (mostly adults) even the concept of children's rights, let alone children's participation, is contentious. Earlier in 2002 a qualified social worker, with several years experience in a community organisation for a major children's organisation in the UK asked, 'what is this about children's rights? Why should children have the right to stay out late, to go to a disco . . .' (personal comment). This view certainly seems to encapsulate the position of many people, and sums up a misunderstanding and misinterpretation of both the CRC and the notion of rights. Furthermore, the speaker's professional position suggests how acceptance of the notion of rights has a long way to go even with some of those who work with children and young people. But conversely, children's participation, and children's rights are enthusiastically promoted by others, including professional workers, as both framework and practice for the future development of children's welfare and a more equitable and better functioning society. Participation as a means of achieving democracy is discussed further below.

This book looks at children's participation in only one part of the world. The chapters describe and analyse some manifestations of children's participation in relation to policies for children in some places in Europe. The tensions inherent in the realisation of children's citizenship are evident in the battles to establish the practice of children's participation as an element of everyday life. The importance of process in work on children's participation is reflected in the chapters, which provide snapshots of work in progress. The end is not achieved, perhaps not even in sight, but if we take participation as process, then further developments are necessary, reflecting that children's participation is, in essence, a shifting state. Furthermore, the processes of participation are not only under way in various countries, but have also been taken up in pan-European initiatives, and more recently in policy developments of the European Union. Some discussion of recent cross-European initiatives is given towards the end of this introductory chapter, which complements the detail of policy, law and practice developments that are described in individual chapters that focus on different European countries.

Rights and childhood

The inception of the CRC followed the International Year of the Child in 1979 as part of a broader movement of change in perceptions of childhood. James and Prout (1990) discusses the growing interest in sociological perspectives on childhood, and the ensuing decade saw a burgeoning literature on children and childhood not only in Europe and North America, but around the world. They raise the idea of a new paradigm of childhood in a series of points including: an acknowledgement of childhood as a cultural construct with differences around the world; that childhood is a social variable including within it differences of age, gender, ethnicity, ability and the different personal circumstances of children; and finally, that children themselves are 'social actors'. This last point has particular relevance to the theme of children's participation, in recognising that children influence and interact with the social world around them.

Yet, in the discourse on rights, children's participation is probably the most contentious area, perhaps because what it means and what it entails is rarely considered. The idea and practice of children's participation is beset by contradictions. It is not new, nor was it invented by the architects of the CRC. Debate continues over the meaning and practice of participation among its adherents, while others would not countenance such excursions into what they see as radical forms of participation such as children making decisions, say, in community matters. The contentiousness of the idea of children's participation has led some followers to avoid interrogating meaning and content (and therefore issues of quality), because of a perceived need to promote the idea above all else – a position which brings no benefit to children.[1]

In these notions of rights and participation, there is essentially an issue of children's citizenship, denied by some, recognised and assumed to exist by others, and difficult to succinctly describe in a way that fits all societies, cultures and the circumstances of children around the world. But all states (with the exception of the USA and Somalia, the latter having no recognised government) have ratified the CRC and, therefore, the principles of children's participation. The CRC has thus become an important paradigm, and standard for the greater incorporation of children's and young people's involvement in societal decision making, if that is taken as an important indicator both of children's rights and children's participation. But the question remains about how to take forward children's participation?

Although the question of developing *children's* participation is a main theme in this book, the role of *adults* is always open to question, and children can and do take action themselves. The formation of organisations by children is better known from regions outside Europe, but the year 2003 in Europe and North America saw a surge of child-led action, as children ran and took part in demonstrations against the war in Iraq. Some of these involved children taking time from attendance at school, and in England some of them were punished by teachers and school authorities: their participation, and their making a decision to take part were effectively being opposed by adults in power. There have been allegations that some of the prisoners held at Guantenamo Bay are children – picked up when they were under 18, but not officially seen as child soldiers, having therefore entered some sort of limbo. These incidents, including oppression of children's rights, begin to suggest some of the broader problems involved in the realisation of children's rights and especially their participation. Children as 'non-people', or 'not yet human' might be seen in the accusations of witchcraft made by adults against children in Congo, as attempts are made to find explanations for the ravages of war and AIDS, and orphaned, now street children, are easy options (Astill, 2003). But children have also been subject to sexual and other forms of exploitation, which were not seen as important in many social institutions; for example, in order to conceal cases of sexual abuse in one church (Barnett, 2003). Although the inception of an international convention on children's rights gives some recognition to the need for protection of the youngest citizens, implementation of the Convention has a long way to go. Another aspect of internationalism, the increase in global trafficking of humans, especially children, provides additional challenges, as the rights of children continue to be ignored and abused. Children's participation should be seen as a vital aspect in contributing to their protection and to the broader realisation of their rights.

Participation – models, standards and rights

The history of children's participation cannot be discussed here for reasons of space – conventional accounts might include such diversity as Summerhill school in England (Neill, 1970), or the 18th century attempt of children and young people to get arms to defend themselves against the police in France, where police were then over-enthusiastically arresting any children on the street, in order to obtain the bounty per head offered for bringing in homeless children (Mantel, 2003). Even the well-known Children's Crusade of Medieval Europe might be cited. All of these, in context, illustrated the essentially politicised nature of childhood. Different countries have their own symbolic moments and places in the development of experience, practice and policy of children's participation, some of the more recent of which are noted in this book. Much depends on the paradigms and histories of childhood, and the social state and cultural representation and practice. But the current discourse on rights and participation has some common stages and themes, some of which are noted here as introduction to the following chapters.

One of the major issues in the development of policy and practice concerning children's participation has increasingly revolved around the establishment of standards for good practice: essentially that is, in determining what is meant by children's participation. In the 1990s this was seen in attempts to provide typologies of children's participation in order to differentiate the purpose and forms of the variety of activities involving children which were popularly

and professionally seen as falling under the rubric of 'participation'.

Soon after the inception of the CRC, a paper for UNICEF's Innocenti Centre proved extremely influential (see Hart, 1992) partly in raising and formulating issues around children's participation, but especially in the delineation of a set of categories or types of participation in diagrammatic form. The paper is best known for the ladder of participation, drawn from the work of Sherry Arnstein (1969), and which was essentially an attempt to raise debate through the suggestion of a coherent classification of such activities. The ladder took on a life of its own, much reproduced, as a hierarchically structured series of levels of children's participation. The levels included notions of tokenistic and manipulative participation, leading on to what is often seen as 'real' participation. The diagram of the ladder has been much circulated, with intentions apparently unforeseen by the author (personal comment). Instead of seeing a classification, some readers have perceived a series of progressive stages, with a goal of reaching the top, almost an evolutionary paradigm, where the higher rungs or stages are 'better' than the lower. The problem can be seen in some practitioners expressing concerns about 'missing out' rungs, and so taking to be method what is a broad attempt at classification. There is some truth in the idea that some of the types of participation are more meaningful than others especially in terms of children's rights, but the question depends also on the purpose of children's participation, perspectives of children as citizens, and social structures. The problem has remained with the removal of the ladder diagram from its context and its use as an easy tool for evaluating and discussing children's participation. The complexities of practice, it is argued, require different interrogatory approaches (see West (1996) and the chapter below).

The ladder was reworked by some authors in an attempt to address different conditions. For example, Barbara Franklin reworked the classification (1997), Phil Treseder (1997) made it into a wheel, and doubtless it has many other manifestations. Such classifications remain useful starting points in their delineation of what might be identified as 'useful' and 'non-useful' forms of participation, and especially in indicating the preferred goals that are associated with children's rights for many practitioners – of children's involvement in decision making. Subsequent work by Hart and others have focussed on the variety and possibilities of children's participation. But the diversity of practice, the use of classifications and the notions of preferred goals all raise an important set of questions – what do we wish to achieve through children's participation? What is good practice? How is it evaluated?.[2] These questions are of importance to policy makers, youth workers and others who engage with children and young people. It is the experience of children's participation, and how to do it, which is of most concern to many. But the problems of purpose cannot easily be set aside, because to an extent they rest upon issues and ideas of, if not an ideal society, then certainly some vision of a form and structure of society. The idea of children's participation can be enlisted for many practical benefits for children for their protection, development and survival for better organisation, effectiveness and efficiency of services, for the better functioning of communities (see West in this book). These noble aims in turn rest upon ideas of children as citizens, as deserving of a voice at least in their localities, which then opens up larger questions – that have very practical considerations, given for example, the supposed transition of policy into practice in many countries, such as the enactment of legislation for children to have a say in the running of schools in England and Scotland.

These questions are several. Children's competences to participate are often raised in such debates (see, for example, Hart in Verhellen, 1997) but for some the issue is clear – children have a right to participate that is embedded in the CRC. For the latter rights adherents it is not a question of competence nor of evaluation of practice, but of an obligation to ensure children's participation – the world's states have signed up to it. Here the issue becomes not whether, or if, but *how* to ensure that it happens. And again then, we are left with the question of method, wherein children's competence does become an issue, not because they cannot 'do it', but because the diversity of ages alone raises questions of power among children, and the means of incorporating very young children. The question of competence could be seen as a distraction, since children have a right to participate. The competence issue is bound up with older perspectives of childhood, and the notion that a maturity and, therefore, competence in decision-making, arrives at the age of 18 years, or when adulthood is deemed to begin. But the competence of adults as a group can also be questioned. Are all adults competent to make decisions? Who shall judge? Should participation, such as voting, be compulsory? What about issues of power and diversity, including age, gender, ethnicity, and so on? Thus, for some, the participation of children will help to engage younger people and provide for a more inclusive and active society in the future – a broader perspective on rights that offers a challenge to other vested interests.

These themes are both implicit and explicit in the chapters comprising this book. In order to make sense of the possibilities and issues around children's participation, it is necessary to start doing it and to experience and look at practice – just as ideas of children and childhood evolve and change within societies, cultures and localities, so too does practice. Experiential training has been found to be the best way of developing and learning about participation by adults around the world. But it is not the aim of this book to provide a sudden glimpse of best practice, but rather to try and lay out a snapshot of some attempts to develop what has always been difficult, in terms of policy and forms.

Law and policy

The chapters incorporate a diversity of themes, but with a particular focus on the development of state policies for children's participation. This is an important area because, while at the micro-level, children's participation cannot happen in a void but must have a particular vehicle (see West, 1996 and the chapter below), so too at macro-level, if children's participation is to become a feature of children's lives and inherent in existing institutions that affect children, then policy and legislation is needed to facilitate forms of participation. This macro-level is probably especially important in developed Western countries with histories of, and complexities in, structures of governance (and bureaucracies) – but is also required in the South.[3] For countries experiencing economic transition (for example, some countries formerly part of the Soviet bloc, such as Mongolia), or emerging from civil strife, new legislation and welfare forms provide both opportunity and necessity of establishing participation of children. This is not only because states have ratified the CRC, but because of vulnerabilities of children (especially in countries in economic 'transition') and for the practical as well as moral benefits of participation. South Asia in particular has a vibrant discourse and practice on children's participation, not to say that it is not contentious, but with forms of children's own organisations that are not really apparent in Europe. For example, children's labour unions (such as Bhima Sangha in India), and organisations of, and run by, street children in Bangladesh and India. In Africa the African Movement for Working Children provides a vehicle for working children and others. Similarly, South America has well-known organisations *of* street children *run by* street children.

The cultural, social, political and economic context for these developments is important. Europe has its own social and cultural norms (and of course, political and economic unities offered through the spreading European Union), and these are increasingly apparent in such a regional comparison of children's participation. The forms of children's participation in Europe, as evidenced here, are particularly state-institutional, revolving overtly around what adults provide and facilitate, especially through schools and youth work provision, rather than self-supported and facilitated organisations of working children. Age must be raised as an issue, in addition to state practice, given the issues concerning children (that is, under-18-year-old humans) and especially 16–17 year-olds, finding and gaining employment as against them staying at school. Children's 'right to work' is apparently fast disappearing in many parts of Europe (see West, 1997 and Crimmens in this volume).

Given the ratification of the CRC and the responsibilities of states to provide reports to the UN Committee on the Rights of the Child, and the National Plans of Action inaugurated in the UN Special Sessions on Children of 1990 and 2002, it is perhaps not surprising that states' policies for children have taken on new significance. It is here that discussions on children's citizenship are starting to take a wider form. Badham (in Willow, 2002: p.x) maintains that the inclusion of young people, 'will only be advanced significantly when accompanied by wider structural and political change' (p.xi).

Hart (1992) has described participation as 'the fundamental right of citizenship': . . . 'it is the means by which a democracy is built and it is a standard against which democracies should be measured' (p.5). At its simplest level, participation means taking part. White (2001) provides some working definitions, which usefully distinguish participation, from, for example, involvement and consultation. Participation refers to young people taking an active part in a project or process, not just as consumers, but as key contributors to both direction and implementation. By participating, young people are essentially proactive and have the power to shape the project. Consultation means listening to young peoples' voices and views, and giving them appropriate feedback. Its use is largely restricted to mechanisms that bring young peoples' views to adult-led initiatives. Young people are essentially reactive and the power remains in adults' hands – no formal transfer or sharing of power and responsibility (White, 2001: p.7).

Gurumurthy (2001) sees the promotion of young people's involvement in public decision-making as a 'profoundly important change . . . in our understanding of democracy'. He sees participation as: 'producing real changes in the effectiveness of individuals, organisations and communities, and central to social inclusion and the task of building communities' (Cutler and Frost: p.x).

Several writers have claimed that a new kind of political generation is emerging with young people rejecting conventional politics in favour of channelling their attention to single issues such as the environment, human rights, and animal rights. For example, Wilkinson and Mulgan (1995: p.19) conclude that today's young people fundamentally differ from their predecessors in terms of the way they engage with the traditional political process. Cutler and Frost make the point that young people's participation should not be narrowly drawn as to what immediately affects them:

> They should be viewed as active citizens now rather than as citizens-in-waiting and this means that they may well want to speak up about international debt, the cost of care for the elderly in residential accommodation, the size of the state, peace keeping missions or fox hunting.
>
> (2001).

Issues of democracy, often equated with the right to vote, are highlighted by many contributors to this volume, reflecting a tension between participation as process or product. Is the importance of participation to be found in 'learning democratic practice' (an issue raised by Swiderek in his chapter

below) or as a manifestation of children's contemporary citizenship? The issue of voting, and the diminishing rates of adult electoral voting in some countries, is noted below and raises the issue of other forms of participation perhaps having greater significance for citizens who are disappointed with the results of their elected leaders.

In these debates, the possibilities of children's participation takes on a new significance. Given that children, or persons under 18 years, are not generally entitled to vote, the ways in which structures are established for their participation in community or social decision-making, offer new opportunities and forms for a general social participation – in short, what some might call a renewal of democratic forms of governance. However, the barriers to children's participation must first be overcome, and many of the initiatives described below may be seen as tentative steps in experimental processes for greater inclusion of citizens in decision-making. The issues and tensions described for children's participation have far greater implications than for children's lives alone, in effect on social life and as new models of practice for the future. But this may also be a reason why children's participation is so contested. It is, perhaps, also a reason why children's participation is often most readily taken up through the use of existing adult forms (such as parliaments, committees, councils) thus reproducing existing systems. These issues form part of the discussions in the following chapters.

Politics and policy: constructions of childhood

The politicisation of childhood over the past decade is evident in most contributions to this book. New laws have been passed or older legislation reinterpreted in the process of establishing or enabling forms of children's and young people's participation, especially as part of responses to the CRC. The history of participation in some places is noted, often as an aspect of the development of youth policy. In Norway for example, Begg notes that the first school councils were inaugurated in 1919, and in Wales, Jones surveys the issues in the development of a youth work practice since the 1940s, different to that of England although the two countries have, in the past, frequently been regarded as one in policy terms.

Swiderek (below, Chapter 8) notes tensions in the local constructions of childhood and implicitly the politicisation of childhood that has occurred through the adoption of the CRC. The question of childhood, not only as a cultural constraint but also as a social variable where children have distinct cultural processes, is highlighted by Mori (below, Chapter 9) on the Italian experience, where he notes how the development processes of children and young people use different cultural referents to those of their contemporary adults. The cultures of children and young people have been perceived as somewhat separate and as worthy of study at least since the 1960s, and their impact on broader society and representation through media has been much discussed (see for example, Cohen (1972) and Paul Willis (1977)).

Perceptions of the dangers of unregulated children and young people (see for example, West (1999) are part of the different cultural and social constructions of childhood that have also led not only to 'moral panics' but must also have informed policy and legislation. The different state, social and cultural constructions of childhood were evident in the case of the murder of James Bulger in England and the different media and public reaction in Norway to a similar case of children killing a child.

The policy and practice on participation of children would seem to follow a different, opposing line, to that of media panic. But such a statement assumes participation to be liberating and opposed to oppression. West, (Chapter 2 below), notes how participation implicitly asks questions of its purpose and has implications for social and individual change. The notion that political motivations around children's participation might be as much to ensure reproduction of the status quo, as to seek change (much as with different uses of the term 'empowerment'), requires that such assumptions be questioned. The political nature of participation is evident in questions of purpose, and so the development of policy and practice raises issues beyond the problem of how to get children involved. This is exemplified in the Irish development of a National Children's Strategy in 2000 within a vision of children as young citizens. Hayes explores what this conception entails, starting from the vision of a fulfilled childhood where children realise their potential – an example of participation overtly seen as bringing benefits to individuals.

The issue of individual benefits is also raised in Chapter 3, on England, where Crimmens explores the tensions between the possibilities of employment and education and the ambiguities of training. Again this has political implications which also frame the cultural construction of childhood, because of the inherent or implied perception that human beings under 18 years old are necessarily only in some form of preparation for the condition of adulthood. This view questions the idea of children's citizenship. What are the limitations of children and their participation? The possibilities of social change through participation are raised in most chapters and here issues concerning the forms of or vehicles for participation are brought into play.

Forms and vehicles for participation

A diversity of forms and experiences of children's participation are described in this book. These range from formal settings, such as a national children's parliament and local councils of children, to research undertaken by children and organisations involving vulnerable children. The vehicles used for children's participation are part of a process in setting limits to powers of decision-making. The vehicles and the notions of participation are taken up in an overview of motives for adults in undertaking or facilitating work on children's participation, and meanings ascribed to children's participation in Chapter 2 by West.

Schools

Education is one of the best known and discussed rights of the CRC but in many countries around the world the word is synonymous with the institution of school. The institutionalisation of school is well established in Europe, as a site where children spend much of their time, and not surprisingly is a key component in discussions of children's participation in this book. School-based forms of participation are often used as the foundation for wider community participation, as noted here, for example by Swiderek (Chapter 8) Begg (Chapter 11) and Dekleva and Zorga (Chapter 12) although this vehicle for children's participation appears to be struggling to get moving in the British Isles.

Forum, council, parliament

Clearly the most common response to the development of children's participation across Europe is the use of children as representatives to meet and discuss issues, and make recommendations. These forms of participation, forum, councils, and parliaments (or mini-parliaments) are often linked to schools, and tend to reproduce established adult mechanisms. The name and scale of the work, such as parliament or council, seems also related to the size of the state involved. Some countries have comparatively small populations, of several million, where the costs and other issues involved in establishing such councils, fora or parliaments may be different to larger settings. But some of the major questions apply to all, particularly the issue of representation and inclusion. How to ensure minority groups or disadvantaged groups have their voices heard, how to avoid only

the most articulate and better off children taking over the main roles, how to ensure sustainability and interest, how to establish who represents who – the core problems of representative forms of participation. These issues emerge throughout this book. The importance of the role of adults, and other forms of participation, for example, research, may have a particular significance.

Youth work and adults

Many parts of Europe have a long-established out-of-school, 'informal' educational provision, that is, something which is largely unproclaimed or unseen as education by children and young people. What has been emphasised is learning through recreation, often currently described as or falling under the heading of lifeskills. Such work has, in many countries, become institutionalised with a quasi-separate, government-funded service (as in the UK) alongside NGO (or the 'voluntary sector' in the UK) initiatives. Jones (Chapter 7) discusses the difficulties of developing children's participation, demonstrating the problem of adults, even professional workers, inherent in youth work. Such workers have often been linked to education practice and institutions (schools) in the UK, but similar approaches to work might be part of any extra-curricular school activities – which is where children's participation seems currently to be most situated across Europe.

Children in and out of the family

The participation of children in family life has been raised as a vital aspect of children's rights. This is less discussed here, where the focus is more on policies and community structures. But the issue of participation in family life has been little developed in terms of agency practice, except in cases of family breakdown. Countries in Western Europe especially have experienced high divorce rates in recent decades with a consequent impact upon many children. One outcome has been the development of legislation and practice in many states to provide for children's involvement in decision-making when parents separate. Such practice is also linked to the increase in children's participation when taken into the care of the state, and such developments in Scotland form the basis of Chapter 6, authored by Furnivall, Hosie and Lindsay, and forms a part of Hazekamp's Chapter 10 on children's own research in the Netherlands.

Research

Social science research has increasingly focused on children in the past twenty years, and the new interest in children's lives and childhood as a social category in sociology and anthropology disciplines have helped place childhood in a new context. Part of this had been the development of research by children and young people themselves (see Hazekamp below). Much of this is also linked to the rights of 'looked after' children, in that examples from both the Netherlands and England have been of children in care undertaking their own research in the mid-1990s (see Hazekamp below, also for example, West, 1995 and 1999). This work has added to the question of who is responsible for the development of policy, and shown not only the competence of children and young people, but also the importance of their inclusion in consultation and decision-making, especially about services that they use. Research work by children has offered particular interrogation of the scope and possibilities of children's participation, in offering a means of consulting children's views, and forms of practice of decision-making.

Countries

The chapters in this book provide examples of recent developments in children's participation across a few countries in Europe. They provide a diverse description of the state of children's policy and practice from a number of perspectives, focused on participation. The contemporary situation in Germany, Ireland and Italy is examined in relation to the development of law, and issues of legislation and related practice. Norwegian law, policy and practice, and an examination of children's councils form the basis of the chapter on Norway. Tensions in policy and practice following opportunities presented by changes of government are examined by Crimmens in England, and Jones in Wales. Dekleva and Zorga in Slovenia (the development of a children's and young people's parliament), Furnivall, Hosie and Lindsay in Scotland (participation for children in care), and Hazekamp in the Netherlands (children's own research) focus on particular areas and methods.

In providing an account of state policies concerning children's participation rights in various European countries, and the development of practice to implement policy and participation, the benefits of sharing policies and practice must not be forgotten. As the European Union enlarges, and borders become more porous, opportunities for collaboration by policy makers and practitioners increase. The future of Europe lies with its children and young people, and the development of inter-state understanding might be assisted with participation of children and young people within their countries and a collaboration across the continent. Just as children and young people point out that they are not only the future, but are living and involved in society now, so too, we cannot simply wait for a 'good society' to occur: action is needed.

Knutson (1997) maintains that while working to establish a better society, we must pay special attention to children through 'well-considered initiatives' (p.7). So, although this book looks at children's participation in chapters that are focussed on developments in different countries, examples of recent developments in pan-European work on children's policy and practice are discussed below.

Across Europe

The work of the Council of Europe (CoE) provides an example of cross-European activities in promoting children's rights. In 1996 the Council produced The European Convention on the Exercise of Children's Rights, focusing on procedural rights in an attempt to fill in the implementation gap in the international framework of children's rights codified by the CRC, by for example:

> . . . *ensuring that children are themselves, or through other persons or bodies, informed and allowed to participate in proceedings affecting them before a judicial authority.*
> (Article 1, para 2).

In its publication *The Child as Citizen* (Jeleff, 1996) the Council recognises that as the guardian of human rights it has 'a special role to play in promoting the cause of children and placing children's rights among the fundamental values of European civilisations' (p.102).

Knutson (1997) picks up these themes in arguing for the promotion of fundamental human universal values in a world of far-reaching cultural, social, economic and political diversity (p.137), which requires adults to commit themselves to 'the principle of the child not as a noble cause for charitable action but as a worthy citizen' (p.130). He argues for the necessity of a partnership approach – the need for committed and professionally competent initiators, inspirers and facilitators, a partnership between concerned professionals and the community, supportive voluntary organisations and a reasonable positive official structure (p131).

These ideas are evident in the work of EURONET, a coalition of networks and organisations across Europe which campaigns to further the rights and interests of children and young people outlined in the CRC. EURONET developed a project, the 'European Network of Children and Young People', to stimulate and articulate the participation of children and young people as citizens at a European level. NGOs in five European countries – BICE in Belgium, BICE in Italy, Save the Children in England, Focus on Children in Ireland and the Platform of Children's Organisations in Spain – acted as

mediators to provide a democratic way for young people to participate in the project. Through a series of international meetings, the young participants, assisted by their adult facilitators, worked towards the production of *Agenda 2000 for Children and Young People in Europe*. The document was presented to the European Parliament in Brussels at a meeting involving all the young people involved in the project on 22nd November 2000. Among the recommendations which the young participants contributed to the *Agenda* was a demand to 'educate us to participate in society' as a means to securing 'every young persons right to participate as a citizen in his/her community and country of residence regardless of their country of origin'.

At the same meeting another report was launched, *Challenging Discrimination against Children* (Lansdown, 2000). This report reminded Europe's leaders in advance of the UN General Assembly Special Session (scheduled at that time to take place in September 2001), that the continuing disregard for children's rights threatened both the immediate and longer term welfare of Europe as a whole (Lansdown, 2000: p.15). This report built on earlier work by EURONET (Ruxton, 1999) which applauded the sponsorship provided by the European Commission for a unique Children's Forum in the European Parliament, while emphasising that very few activities directly involving children had taken place at EU level (p.72).

It is estimated that there will be 75 million young people (categorised as those aged 15–25 years for European Union (EU) calculations) living in the post-enlargement EU (that is, including the twelve countries negotiating membership at the time of publication of the White Paper in 2001). As part of the process of opening up debate on decision-making processes, the EU has carried out an extensive consultation with young people across Europe. While acknowledging that youth affairs are largely the responsibility of the national, regional and local authorities of the Member States, the European Commission has published a White Paper stating that:

> *It is important that consultations on the way the EU will develop and on its forms of governance should include the people to whom tomorrow's Europe belongs. The European project is itself young, still forming and still to be debated. If it is to make progress, it needs ambition and enthusiasm, and commitment on the part of young people to the values on which it is based.*
>
> (EC, 2001, Foreword p.4).

The White Paper reports on the youth consultations, stating that young people took the view that as well as an investment in greater resources of time and money, an appropriate legal framework was necessary to promote the evolution of structures which would enable meaningful participation to develop. Young people also emphasised the necessity of removing obstacles to participation and to promote participation through citizenship training for all (Annexe 1 results of the consultation) (p.26).

In her introduction to a progress paper on the European White Paper, Viviane Reding, Commissioner responsible for Education, Culture and Youth says that:

> *Political leaders must help young people to become full citizens, in a society in which they will soon be leading players. The debate on the future of Europe is up and running. Young people are the first concerned by this debate which they will soon be leading.*

The White Paper proposals on youth participation include:

- *Promoting participation at local level, including at school, through the widespread use of regional and national youth councils, open to young people who do not belong to any organisations or clubs.*
- *Consolidation of existing mechanisms, for example rejuvenation of the European Youth Forum.*
- *Organising a direct dialogue between authorities and young people on different subjects.*

- *Encouraging young people to participate in the debate on the future of Europe.*
- *Proposing pilot projects to promote participation by young people at every level of government.*

> (EC, 2002: p.11).

These proposals indicate an acknowledgement of the importance of children's and young people's participation. But for that participation to come to fruition, action is needed in individual member states. Perhaps of even greater importance is the practice of participation itself, the methods used to implement policy. The inclusion of children and young people requires that attention is paid to ensure participation is meaningful, does not discriminate, and includes all sections of the population of children and young people in question. The discussions in this book indicate how the development of quality and standards of participation is important, but that this is also a process which is only just beginning. The European-wide dimension offers greater scope and opportunity for the development of practice, just as it also presents greater challenges.

Conclusion

Major themes run through the chapters in this book including the contested nature of children's participation, the role of adults, the struggle to find appropriate forms and to develop meaningful practice, and the problems of theory, implementation, and discourse on children's citizenship. The rights of children underpin contemporary discussion of children's participation, and the widespread ratification of the CRC has brought a new dimension to the importance of policy, law and its implementation. Childhood is a peculiar social category or social variable, in that its members pass out from it – children grow up and become adults, ensuring some degree of change, issues of social reproduction and problems of sustainability in the development of practice. In many countries, such as China, it is common and trite to observe that 'children are the future', but as a child delegate to the United Nations Special Session on Children in 2002 pointed out, children are not the future, but here now. While the Special Session looked to the protection and development of children, other processes of globalisation have increased children's risk of exploitation, through trafficking: the common component in processes of globalisation is inequality. In the context of different incomes, wealth and circumstances, and different perceptions of childhood, recognition of the value of children's participation is not only a step towards protection of the vulnerability of young humans, but also involves a rethinking of other processes of much heralded states of 'democracy'.

Notes

1   A paper examining the need to define children's participation in particular context, as a means of developing quality of practice, was rejected by one journal on children because of a need to promote participation rather than question its purpose. See also Chapter 2 by West, below, on motives for participation.
2   The variety of practice called participation has lead one organisation to develop a set of standards (see CPWG, 2003).
3   The term 'south' has been used by many authors for some years now, in preference to 'undeveloped' or 'underdeveloped' etc. The variety of economies even within a single region, and the increasing inequalities within countries, begin to refute distinctions between states or regions. See West (2003) for an example of disparities within a region.

References

Arnstein, S. (1969) A Ladder of Citizen Participation. *Journal of the American Institute of Planners*. 35: 4, 216–24.

Astill, J. (2003) Congo Casts Out its 'Child Witches'. *The Observer*. 11th May.

Barnett, A. (2003) Vatican Told Bishops to Cover Up Sex Abuses. *Guardian* 17th August.

Boyden, J. and Ennew, J. (1997) *Children in Focus: A Manual for Participatory Research with Children*. Stockholm: Radda Barnen.

Cohen, S. (1972) *Folk Devils and Moral Panics*. London: MacGibbon and Kee.

CPWG (2003) *Standards for Children's Participation*. Child Participation Working Group, Save the Children Alliance.

Cutler, D. and Frost, R. (2001) *Taking the Initiative. Promoting Young People's Involvement in Public Decision-making in the UK*. London: Carnegie Young People Initiative.

European Commission (2001) *A New Impetus for European Youth*. COM 681 final. Brussels.

European Commission (2002) *Europe and Youth: A New Impetus*.

Franklin, B. (1997) Reworked Ladder of Participation, in Boyden, J. and Ennew, J. op. cit.

Gurumurthy, R. (2001) Foreword, in Cutler, D. and Frost, R. op. cit.

Hart, R. (1992) Children's Participation: From Tokenism to Citizenship. Florence: UNICEF Innocenti.

Jeleff, S. (Ed.) (1996) *The Child as Citizen*. Strasbourg: Council of Europe Publishing.

Knutsson, K.E. (1997) *Children: Noble Causes or Worthy Citizens?* Aldershot: Arena.

Lansdown, G. (2000) *Challenging Discrimination Against Children in the European Union: A Policy Proposal by EURONET*. Brussels: EURONET.

Mantel, H. (2003) 'Is it still yesterday?' *London Review of Books*. 25: 8, April.

Neill, A.S. (1970) Penguin.

Ruxton, S. (1999) *A Children's Policy for 21st Century Europe: First Steps*. Brussels: EURONET.

South Asian Task Force on Children's Participation (2002) Notes from second meeting and definition of children's participation. email notice from cwcblr.

Treseder, P. (1997) *Empowering Children and Young People*. London: Save the Children.

Verhellen, E. (Ed) (1997) *Understanding Children's Rights*. Ghent: University of Ghent.

West, A. (1996) *But What Is It? A Critique of Undefined Participation*. Hull and Leeds: Save the Children.

West, A. (1997) A Seven Year Itch: Children's Rights, Sustainability, Citizenship and Work. *Social Work in Europe*. 4: 2, 11–5.

West, A. (1999) They Make us out to be Monsters: Media Images of Children and Young People in Care, With Assessments by Children and Young People in Care, in Franklin, B. (Ed.) *Misleading Messages: The Media, Misrepresentation and Social Policy*. London: Routledge.

West, A. (2003) *At the Margins: Street Children in Asia*. ADB Papers in Poverty and Social Development Series. Manilla: Asian Development Bank.

White, P. (2001) *Local and Vocal*. London: National Youth Agency/Save the Children Fund.

Willis, P. (1977) *Learning to Labour: How Working Class Kids get Working Class Jobs*. Farnborough: Saxon House.

Willow, C. (2002) *Participation in Practice. Children and Young People as Partners in Change*. London: The Children's Society.

CHAPTER 2

Children and Participation: Meanings, Motives and Purpose

Andrew West

Children's and young people's participation has become increasingly popular as an activity in the professional youth and childhood sectors, and as a theme or goal to be promoted and upheld. Yet in many ways it remains a contested concept and practice. First, despite advocacy of the idea, children's participation is still not generally and publicly agreed to be useful, important, nor indeed a right of children. Second, (even among many of those who practice and promote participation) there is disagreement as to what participation implies. What is participation? The essentially contested nature of the term is both beneficial and a problem for its promotion and enaction.

This chapter will first briefly look at some of the practical problems and suggest a means of approaching them.[1] In the second part, the meaning of participation will be discussed further, in terms of the problem of purpose: what is participation for, why is it advocated, how does it fit within broader social paradigms?

Some practical issues

The current popularity of participation is manifested in practice, for example, in the development of youth councils in Britain and elsewhere in Europe in the late 1990s. It is also seen in the growth of published texts, and in the emphasis given to participation practice with children and young people by major non-government organisations, both international such as the Save the Children Alliance, and within countries, such as the Children's Society in the UK. The perception of international importance of the idea and practice was highlighted by a conference/

workshop held in England in 1997, part sponsored by the government Department for International Development, 'Children's participation in research and programming' with some 50 participants from around the world, (see Johnson et al., 1998). A number of texts promoting children's and young people's participation were published in the 1990s (such as Hart, 1992; Lansdown, 1995; de Winter, 1997) and in the second part of the 1990s overviews of work (such as Hart, 1997; Willow, 1997; Wellard et al., 1997), developed from specific projects (such as West, 1995, 1997a; Miller, 1997).

The surge of interest in participation in the 1990s was partly fuelled by its inclusion in the 1989 United Nations Convention on the Rights of the Child, and underpinned by the tenets of the new sociology of childhood, which included the notion of children as 'social actors' (James and Prout, 1990/1997). The focus on participation as a right (see, for example, Cunninghame, 1999) enabled some shift in the practice of participation (which had previously most focused on older children or young people (West, 1999)), toward young children (Miller, 1997; Alderson, 2000).

Yet it would be a mistake to see participation as an entirely new phenomenon. An emphasis on participation practice certainly increased dramatically at the end of the twentieth century, and became linked to ideas of children as citizens (see de Winter, 1997; West, 1997b, 1999), but also there is much work on children's citizenship and governance developing in South Asia). But participation has long been held as a tenet of youth work in Britain, a crucial aspect of informal education, which was formalised in the 1960 Albemarle Report on youth work. Participation has also long been part of community work and community education across Europe, and part of development practice in southern countries. There was an earlier flurry of youth councils in Britain some time in the 1970s. Whether the current rate and weight of emphasis on participation will continue may depend on the development of a critical or analytical approach to practice, in contrast to the more promotional focus adopted to date, which has often concentrated on highlighting benefits for children and society if participation is taken up. The title of an academic conference 'The Tyranny of Participation' held in Manchester in 1998, hinted at a reversionary perspective on the concept and practice: indeed, one of the papers indicated the 'missionary' like beliefs of some adherents. This conference took a critical perspective on participation, and it is clearly time that adherents followed in this.

Process, product and degree

A problem has emerged because participation continues to be elusive in some respects, for it can take many processual forms and make use of, or occur within, a variety of vehicles. There are a number of charts of forms, which list the types of participation, the levels or degree of involvement of children. These range from Hart's (1992) infamous ladder (reworked by Franklin, 1997), Treseder's wheel (1997), and the short list regarding children's consultation by Alderson and Montgomery: 'being informed, expressing a view, influencing the decision-making, being the main decider (quoted in Alderson, 2000: 113). This simple list has many virtues, and although it also refers to 'levels of children's consultation', it does not privilege any. In contrast, Hart's ladder (drawn from the work of Arnstein (1969) on citizen participation) has led many to see it as progressive; the lower rungs include 'decorative', 'tokenistic' participation, while

the upper rungs have 'child initiated' decisions. This has led to many workers emphasising a need to get to the top of the ladder, and an implication that other forms of participation are of less worth: an unfortunate predilection to participation competition has developed among some professionals (personal observation).

The range of vehicles or arenas for participation can include any activity or institution involving children and young people. For example, school is an obvious site, as is the family (discussants at a workshop in China in August 2000 highlighted the importance of children's participation in family decision-making), and other locations such as residential care homes. Other vehicles include youth clubs, research projects, peer education and campaigns. A distinction might be drawn between 'everyday' places for children, such as family, home, school, local community or neighbourhood, and projects established as voluntary leisure activities (youth clubs, out-of-school opportunities or activities for school non-attenders) or to involve children for some purpose (research). Such a distinction indicates an additional problem, in that much of the work involving children has initially occurred in the second, 'voluntary', sector, and children's participation in their everyday life and institutions requires a huge investment to catch up. But the issue of the 'degree' or level of involvement remains.

Partially this issue is a problem of process or product. Is the important element the process of participation, be it in taking part in an activity or decision-making, or is it the product – that is, a goal or outcome of participation? This is not mere tautology: although it is true that to achieve a goal of participation, a participatory process is (or should be) required, the underlying purpose of a project is important. The idea of 'product' appears to be obvious, in the sense of a desired outcome. The notion of process includes the work of 'doing' participation; here that is, the activities involving children themselves, and the interaction between them, and also the interaction between them and any adults involved. These themes may be illustrated by using the example of *child-led* research (see also West, 1998a). Children and young people may be engaged to do research themselves for several reasons. The process itself may be deemed to be important: that is, the activity of carrying out research could be seen as an educational process, and the learning gained in terms of life skills, be viewed as the main component of the project. Alternatively, the product, here that is, research material, might be the most important element. Both elements, of course, might comprise the project. This perspective on process and product emphasises adult controlled or facilitated participation: that is, the adults setting up a project, for benefits which they have decided (here this could be either the personal development of children or the gathering of research results).

As this example of research indicates, the type of participation is important, in terms of why the participatory work is undertaken. But the degree of participation, that is the level of decision-making or consultation is also important. Children's and young people's participation is often led, facilitated or determined by adults. This is not surprising: unlike many other social categories of people, such as women, ethnic minorities, who may have experienced oppression or powerlessness, children grow out of their social group: they may gain skills of resistance or challenge their existing situation, but they still become adults. Thus, it is unusual for groups of children, of their own accord, to challenge the existing balance of power; they need allies, and frequently the stimulus for change comes from those allies – who are adults.[2] Much work needs still to be done on adult's reasons for giving up power (see also below, and West, 1998b). What exactly is offered to children, both superficially or rhetorically, in actuality and in honesty, is important. Is it decision-making, consultation, or a veneer of participation?

Training for participation?

Alongside this problem of the degree of participation, and children's unique position vis-à-vis growing out of one subaltern category, is the issue of children's development or competence, and what some professionals regard as the necessity of *training* for participation. The underlying basis for this is a usually unspoken assumption about the location and form of participation. For example, that children and adults will meet together, but children need training beforehand in order not to waste their or adult's time, because the format of the meeting will use traditional (adult) conventions. Some professionals are explicit about this: 'children cannot just come to a meeting and participate', 'there is no children's participation without capacity building – we must give them information, train them to analyse, and develop decision-making skills'.[3]

The question of 'training' can be especially seen in participation vehicles of young people's councils or forums, and in research. Some young people's councils have been developed to reflect the structures of the local government (see West, 1997a for discussion of this). In these, children and young people need to know and understand the rules and procedures which are applicable, for example, in debate. Here the outcome of participation work looks as though children are involved and representing others, but the process deters many, and a bias in favour of those who are better educated, or middle-class may come into play.[4] The idea of adults changing their format and methods of participation to be more inclusive is less discussed.

Children's and young people's involvement in research has also led to demands that they be first trained in research methods (for example, in some of Save the Children's lottery-funded research in England in 1997, with the training process and materials subsequently published in Kirby, 1999). Here the main purpose of the participation activity rather becomes the research, with an idea that children will gain some benefit in terms of personal development through training to participate. Children's own ideas become less important than a 'professional' outcome (see also West, 1998, for discussion of some of these issues). But it is possible, alternatively, for children to undertake research 'properly' without first doing a programme of formal training (see, for example, Khan, 1997).

The question of 'training' rests not on participation but the privileging of certain procedures and forms of activity and knowledge. It is rather like the process of professionalisation of some practices, with the resulting tension over 'correct' perspectives and activities. The issue highlights the notion of degree of participation from a different angle, for training would be needed to undertake all of the forms of participation listed above: for example, for children to be consulted they would first need to learn how to get and analyse information. Such a strategy negates the idea of participation, *if* the purpose is for the inclusion of a range of different perspectives and opinions, and a greater distribution of decision-making: but might not negate the idea *if* the aim of participation is to bring children within existing hegemonic structures. These questions concerning the purpose of participation are discussed further below.

Along with the issue of training, the vehicles used for participation may be incompatible with each other. Peer education has been identified as an important means of communicating messages to children, especially in the field of health, as in the 'child-to-child' programme. The provision of accurate information is clearly important in this, and some programmes also give training to children on communication processes. However, peer education is largely an information flow in one direction: it does not always encourage the solicitation of children's opinions, because they have learnt that there is a 'correct' answer. For example, a group of children in a village in

Bangladesh had previously participated in a child-to-child programme of health issues. Subsequently, they came to participate in research, identifying what issues were important to the lives of children in their rural area. Such was the success of the child-to-child programme, that they immediately identified 'health' (along with some other issues, such as adult attitudes to children, play space, etc.). But the expression of the health issue was very much in the disease model they had learnt. For children to become researchers gathering the views and opinions of other children, they needed to switch from being an authoritative voice to becoming more of a listener and recorder.

A framework for participation

These issues, such as the degree of participation and the question of training and participation vehicles or arenas, have already indicated that there are some major variables involved in participation work. Just the varieties of forms of participation alone indicate the problem of a ladder or rather a race to the top, as though the issue of degree or form of participation is the same for all – to the detriment of projects and work with children. Instead, projects need to be carefully crafted to take account of the variables possible both in planning and activity – honesty in the power being given away. In developing a participation project, the identification of such variables is essential in building a platform of principles for the practical work to follow and be undertaken. A simple framework based on a set of six or seven questions is given below.[4] The process of determining answers to these questions is also the process of planning and assessing a particular participation project. The questions may appear to be, and are, commonplace. But each project, or phase, in a long term or permanent work of participation, is different. For example, the personnel involved and the social, political and cultural environment do not only differ from place to place, but change over time. Children grow older and gain experience;

new children may join a project. The question most frequently asked about participation work is 'how' to do it; meaning, how adults sit down with children, what do they do. This is a question of technique, and is just one part of the reality of 'how' and much over-emphasised. The answer to 'how' is embodied in the whole of the framework of six questions, who, what, why, when, where and how. Without considering them all, a participation project becomes an activity which may be fun, but is less likely to lead to children's decision-making, or power-sharing with adults: such participation requires a conscious approach, not least in order for adults to be aware of their voices and actions, so as to hold back, check themselves from control.

Although the six questions are not discussed below in any particular sequence, the first three (who, what, why) clearly establish a main part of the framework of any project, but the second three (when, where, how) are also essential. The six questions hinge on a seventh element, the central component of the vehicle or arena used for the project.

Who

This question deals with the specificity of who is to be involved in a project. Which children? What age, gender, class, (dis)ability, experience, location etc. And, which adults? The question of adults is important in terms of facilitation and direction of the project. It is rare for children alone to establish their own participation project,[5] that is, for example in terms of practice of decision-making, or consultation to influence their environment, peers, local community etc. organising themselves to play football or other games, is obviously done. But the type of projects mostly considered here involves local communities or institutions, and are adult initiated.

An additional issue concerning which children is the question of selection of children for a project. How does selection fit in with the idea of participation: should children be self-selecting? If there is a limit to numbers to be involved, who decides the limit, and who selects?[6] Are the children seen as representative of others, and if so, how is it determined that they are representative?

What

What sort of participation will be used? What will children be able to do, for example, decision-making, consultation? Will there be limits to the decisions they can make or the views they can offer? For example, in a research project to be led by children, can they decide the aims, method, questions of the research? Or in a council or forum, what decisions can children make, on what issues can they give opinions? Within an institution, do they have budgetary powers, and are there limits to this? Part of this issue is about power, and about the adult-children relationships in a project. If the project is seeking children's views or advice, what sort of commitment, if any, is there to following their opinions, taking up their suggestions? If there is an idea of joint adult-child decision-making, how are disputes to be resolved?

Why

This question has two forms, pertaining to the purpose of a project, and the motivation of those involved.

Why should children and young people participate – what's in it for them? This is not to suggest selfishness, but rather 'what is the point?' Despite increasing emphasis on participation and social inclusion in many countries, in society generally, children's voices are ignored – there is nothing in it for them, especially those who experience high levels of social exclusion or alienation (such as homeless children). Participation presents a great challenge for motivation as well as for existing power structures. This is one of the reasons projects need to be fun (which cannot be over-emphasised enough), and work at children's pace (see below). Money as motivation (but see note 6) rather invalidates any purpose of participation to lead to a more inclusive society.

The other side to the question 'why', concerns purpose of participation. Is the aim an educative exercise, skill development for children or indeed for adults, with no real structural purpose for the organisation or community involved? Is the participation for process or product? This needs to be made clear from the outset. For example, a theatre group set out to do some participatory theatre with children: an organisation employed them on the basis that their staff would learn from the process, and that the children would be making decisions about the content and nature of the performance. However, the theatre group's idea was that children would learn acting and performing skills, and would enact a play created by the adults. The participation was children acting in a performance.

This question of 'why' is linked to that of the central component of a project: the vehicle used.

Vehicle or arena

This rather clumsy expression concerns the setting for the participation work: not the place, nor the process, but the means of participation. For example, each of the forms of participation noted above (being informed, expressing a view, decision-making) can be carried out through a forum, council, theatre work, research, education, school, residential care, youth club etc. In some cases the vehicle is most important, since the participation concerns its control, such as in the case of a school governing body; in other cases, the vehicle is a means to solicit children's opinions and contributions to decision-making in a community or neighbourhood.

Where

The issue of where the participation occurs is not always the same as a vehicle. For example, a school governing body does not have to meet at the school. Projects involving children's views about their neighbourhood may be at least partially undertaken away in a residential setting. Here participation is taken to mean children's views, consultations, decision-making, rather than involvement in an activity without the purpose of children having some social influence. Thus, participation in communities, neighbourhoods, institutions, organisations is a focus.

What is important about the question of 'where', is the feelings of comfort or ownership in the environment selected. Is it child or adult friendly? Who is most familiar with the space, feels most at ease there? An official meeting room may seem comfortable enough for adults, but a new and possibly unnerving experience for children. Also, how is the space laid out? On what do participants sit? Where do they play? The question of where participation takes place might also be extended to include the facilitating organisation. Many organisations now promote children's participation, advocating that children should give their views and have a say in decision-making in communities and government, but children's participation on decision-making within such organisations is often sadly limited or non-existent.[7]

When

The question of 'when' is most under-rated. It often seems simple – setting a date and time, but the issue of who is controlling this process is fundamental to the participation work. Because of the involvement of adults, the question of 'when' is frequently timed to fit in with their schedules, and their commitments. Yet, children also have not only preferences but commitments, especially those who are working. The principle of working with children, and jointly deciding how much time to allocate to the work, and when, is one most easily lost, or decisions over-ridden in favour of the agency or adults involved. For example, an agency or group of adults may insist that they only have a particular set time to carry out the participation work with children – with all the implications that it must be completed within that period. Such a position also conflicts with another element involved in the question of 'when' – that is the principle of working at children's own pace. Working in this way may lengthen the initial period conceived as necessary by adults. These processes of timing set an important framework for participation work and it is important to be honest about any limitations on children's decision-making in this area – but there is also a need for consistency with other elements in a project. For example, children are not real partners in decision-making about a project and its organisation, if the timing is not at their disposal to choose. Children may also differ among themselves about their preferred time: for example, boys in one project in Bangladesh wanted a different time of day to meet than girls, due to different work commitments.

For adults to let go of the power to fix time, is a challenge many find unexpectedly fearful. For example, one project set up meetings with children to gauge their ideas on the law and legal processes. The adults scheduled five days for the work. They planned a morning session of participatory consultation with the children on their ideas of law and how the week should be planned: but had already planned the rest of the week in detail, including visits and role play activities. The adults were fearful that otherwise they may not get through their intended schedule. In deference to some criticism of this practice, they invited in some of the children, put their proposals to them, secured their agreement to the plan, and so progressed on the basis that children had participated in setting up the meeting. However, the adults subsequently changed the starting date three times in order to fit in with their own schedules.

How

Finally the question of 'how' concerns the techniques to be used in engaging children, and in adults and children working together. These need to be appropriate to the personnel involved (such as the age and gender of the children), to the type of participation intended, the purpose of the project, the vehicle etc. The means to be used should be relatively simple to design, and books of games and activities exist which can be used. Conventional elements of adult participation, such as small group discussions and role play, all can be used effectively: the major difference is the element of fun, not often taken into consideration in adult participation. The project should be enjoyable, and games, serve also to break up, relieve and provide energy and stimulation for the serious parts. There is no reason why this principle should not also be pre-eminent for adults, and include for example, some of the drawing games (which have been used to great effect in working with adults in China).

These six questions provide a framework for creating a participation project; note the large number of variables to be taken into account, which ensure that each project is different, and cannot be repeated exactly – the change of time and experience ensures that. There are other issues not covered in the questions above, most of which concern the need for adults to be wary and to stick to their agreements and responsibilities. For example, the need for adults to be consistent, to turn up regularly; for adults not to interfere and answer on behalf of children, or tell children they are stupid if they have nothing to say; for language used to be clear and jargon free; flexibility, and so on. Many of these points may seem too obvious to be worth setting down, but the frequency, with which supposedly professional, participatory or empowering workers intervene and, for example, answer on behalf of children, is alarming.

The purpose of participation

The question of training for participation, raised above, and the rationales about process or product, open up the issue of children's participation in society, and the underlying question of, what is it for? Is the inclusion of children's views and perspectives, and their involvement in decision-making, about social change or social stability? Why do adults, or at least some adults, want children to participate, and promote the idea and practice of participation? Some of these questions are considered below.

It was noted above that participation is a contested term. Participation is also associated with a diverse range of largely political concepts, such as citizenship and empowerment, many of which are also contested. Such terms tend to be favoured by all parts of a political spectrum, with both right and left wings and centre groups each defining or making its own interpretation. This activity increases the problems associated with defining participation, especially in terms of children's participation in consultation or decision-making in communities, neighbourhoods, organisations.

Participation in these arenas is essentially about power. The idea of participation also implies marginalisation, exclusion and powerlessness – here of children and young people. Participation is sometimes thought of as a way of addressing these problems, but what does it entail? Is the goal of participation to achieve change (for example, shift the realm of power) or no-change (that is, to enable children to be content or even happy with their lot).[8] One way of exploring the various purposes of participation projects is to plot them on a framework taking the form of a grid. The two axes here are borrowed and adapted from sociological theory (see Burrell and Morgan, 1979) and have also been used in theorising positions in social work in the UK (Howe, 1987) and youth work in Ireland (Hurley and Treacy, 1993).

The two axes were:

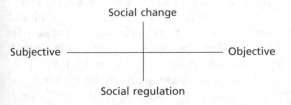

In the work of Howe (1987) and Hurley and Treacy (1993) they became:

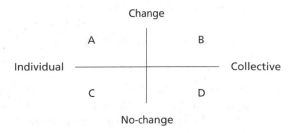

For children's participation, the framework might look something like:

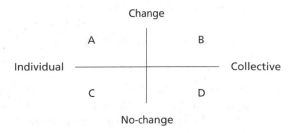

This framework is not suggested as a fixed grid, but as a starting point for further analysis of the purpose and place of children's participation.

The two axes are vertical – from *no change* to *change*. That is, in the lower part of the framework, children's participation is aimed at maintaining social institutions, while in the upper part the goal is to achieve social change. The left-hand side focuses on the role of responsibilities and opportunities for the individual child, and the right hand for children as a whole, or specific groups of children. This cross framework produces four sectors which can be broadly characterised as follows:

- In the lower part of the grid, the aim of participation is to maintain social institutions and relationships as they are.

- The emphasis of participation in the lower right-hand quadrant is on ensuring children's basic welfare (which might include the development of participative and thus responsive services).
- The lower left-hand quadrant aims to use participation to develop children's understanding of individual responsibility and to be able to undertake roles within existing social networks and status.
- The upper left-hand quadrant again focuses on personal development of the individual, but here in a critical vein in order that they may acquire skills to challenge existing institutions and look for change, or to make full use of or even seek personal opportunity.
- In the upper right-hand quadrant existing social institutions themselves change to bring in and involve children, for the benefit not only of children but new perspectives and a form of society that gives weight to the voices of children, and especially those experiencing poverty and social exclusion.

We might see in this framework, that there is an implicit emphasis on more marginalised and excluded children, although in quadrant A, above, where organisations change their working practices from adult monopolies to involving children, any group of children would probably have impact. But the issue of participation for wealthy, well-educated or well-connected children surely raises other questions. However, some participation projects (even involving NGOs) have aimed at a 'general' constituency of children – which almost inevitably means that the voices and views of the poorest will continue to be excluded.

These framework characteristics are not intended to be as arbitrary or fixed as they appear in the brief outlines given above. Most children's participation is necessarily fluid and dynamic if it is to last, but it can also be stifled and restricted or guided (for example, to a type of activity, of doing, rather than deciding). Children themselves vary (as do adults): some are conservative in

their views, others more liberal or radical – some change their ideas, others keep to a particular viewpoint. For example, children have suggested rather drastic forms of physical punishment for law breakers and other transgressors of social *mores*. Children do not form a constituency with one voice: one child cannot represent the views of all others, even those of the same age (or birthplace etc.): forms of representative participation need to pay attention to the inclusion of the weakest and those with less social and financial capital.

Such variety adds further dimension and complexity to the processes and goals of children's participation. It means that while adults can set out with a particular purpose, children may challenge that purpose – for example, they may demand a greater say in decision-making *or* alternatively may prefer more conservative options than adults. But it is important to remember that the power generally continues to lie with adults – who may permit children to do something, or may simply follow the path they have already chosen.

There are comparisons to be made of participation with other concepts such as citizenship and empowerment within this framework. For example, empowerment has been advocated by politicians of both right and left as learning for young people. On one hand it concerns young people[9] learning to make use of opportunities for themselves, for example, for homeless young people, how to seek a home, how to gain access to welfare benefits (if they exist). On the other hand, empowerment, giving power, means changing social institutions, such as housing allocation and welfare systems, in order for all children and young people to benefit.

Citizenship is also currently much emphasised in a variety of forms in popular discussion regarding young people. In one reading it entails individual responsibilities and on the other, individual rights. These different interpretations of the meaning and purpose of citizenship can imply, for children and young people, changes in current social institutions, relationships and practice vis-à-vis children and young people, or simply legitimise a restriction on their social performance that is, by a focus on their social responsibilities, subaltern status and 'correct' moral behaviour.

The complexities of purpose mean that it is difficult to place individual types of participation project rigidly in the framework outlined above: projects define themselves formally (in their planning) and in practice, as they develop. But having a sense of purpose is important for many organisations facilitating children's participation. Individual children's participation projects can demonstrate some various characteristics of the framework. For example, a youth council project might seek to maintain existing social relationships through acting as a safety valve; or it might aim to change social institutions to develop different forms of democratic involvement; or it might be a means of personal development for children, to enable them to understand how local government works and their own responsibilities; or personal development to enable them to challenge and change aspects of their social situation for their own benefit. How it works will depend upon both the adults and the children involved, in addition to the formal boundaries set at the initiation of the project, and how these are, or are not reinforced, as the project progresses. Similarly, a research project might articulate the views of a group of children – and might reinforce or change ideas of existing social relationships.

It is clear that such a 'purpose' framework might offer aspects of an analytical tool, but for organisations and individuals concerned with children's rights, achieving particular purposes, something else is required to formulate a coherent, logical and consistent strategy. This framework of purpose can incorporate ideas of participation, citizenship and empowerment which include and emphasise children's responsibilities. But for participation as children's right, then another layer needs to be placed over the framework in order to plan purpose. This is because many would

argue that children's rights are not linked to responsibilities (for example, freedom from torture does not depend on moral behaviour), so in order for children's participation to move beyond the immediate activity, and lead to a societal level of change as would seem to be intended by the Convention on Children's Rights. There is a danger in this, for it rather suggests that adults do need to take some control of the situation, or at the very least, to recognise the reality of their control at the moment, of most arenas, vehicles and forms of children's participation. There is a crucial question: what are adults' intentions regarding children's participation? This question should not be asked in general, but specifically – what are your intentions, what are my intentions? Is it to do with a move to end child exploitation, or a realisation of the Convention on the Rights of the Child, or what? We might ask, what is there in participation that might engage children, but we need also to ask, what is it that engages adults? Of course, the answer might simply be that it is fun, engaging, and the learning and adjustment gained from the communication of other people's (children's) perspectives, provides sufficient reason. But this is really not enough: participation cannot escape its connection with power and thus with politics.

Conclusion

While children's participation has become more discussed in recent years, there is a need to set it in the context of an increasing debate on the participation of all people, especially adults, in both Western/Northern and in 'developing' countries. In the West/North this has often taken the form of participation in elections, that is, voting, and the apparent disillusion of potential voters with this right as a means to achieve change, or to have a 'voice'; in developing countries, participation has been especially articulated by external (read donor or West/North) countries as a formulation of human rights. It is apparent that such participation poses problems – those adults who have the right to vote appear to be using it less, because it apparently fails to exercise the influence they wish (this is of great concern in local government elections in Britain, while in the US, the amount of money apparently required in reality to stand for high office, means that politics is professionalised – the ordinary individual cannot really offer themselves to represent fellow citizens with even the remotest chance of success).

Therefore, what hope is there for children's participation? Perhaps this question should be reversed: that children's participation offers a longer-term hope for increased involvement of adults in social decision-making. But the concept must be critically employed, and the specificity of culture, society, and opportunity be considered. Childhood is constructed differently in societies around the world, and no recipe can be offered to fit all. Instead, children's participation must deal with local moral, social, cultural and political circumstances, and begin with individual projects: the variety possible must be a joy to anyone who recognises and delights in diversity. For those who prefer a rigid, singular perspective on social life, children's participation can only be concerned with stability and a correct point of view – yet even these perspectives rejoice in difference, and that, probably, is another core of participation work with children, whatever its purpose.

Notes

1   This chapter builds on work undertaken in the mid-1990s, originally circulated as a discussion paper in 1996 (West, 1996). However, it remains work in progress, especially the final section on the 'purpose of participation'. Because participation is dynamic, and both the children involved and their circumstances, and the environment necessarily changes, this paper will hopefully develop further responses to the questions posed.

2   Children, particularly 'street children' and working children are forming their own organisations and unions in South America, Africa, South Asia and elsewhere. These are becoming powerful in protecting their peers and raising issues of exploitation and rights. Not all of these have been started by adults.

3   These quotes are from an interview with the head of a major agency developing children's and young people's forums in Thailand. Elsewhere, of course, the idea of children's participation is not really accepted at all. A conference on 'youth' held in England in 1995 advertised that young people would be welcome, but in the event virtually none came. One of the main speakers, discussing this, said that actually the conference was 'unsuitable' for young people, and that in any case, young people were present since the papers presented included their words. Interestingly, a short article on the issues raised in this debate at the end of the conference was turned down by two 'radical' social policy journals, on grounds that the issue of participation and presence was not really important.

4   At a meeting of Manchester Youth Council in 1997, where each school sent one pupil per class to represent others, it was clear that the schools had selected their 'best' pupils, to use the Council meeting as a showcase. The Council meeting was chaired by the Mayor, who permitted each delegate to speak just once on each issue. Since each pupil came with a ready prepared speech on every issue, there was no real debate. Only the delegate from the Manchester Young People's Forum was able to improvise and speak, taking in some of the comments made by others.

5   These questions were originally devised as part of a critique of the loose and often vague way in which the term 'participation' was used in work with children and young people (see West, 1996). They were subsequently used in training for and in participation work with children in Britain, Bangladesh and

China, and found to be a useful tool and framework for establishing and assessing projects.

6   An example of older children (14–15 years) establishing a project is the *Youth Support Group* which was set up in Manchester in 1997, by a group who had been involved in Manchester Young People's Forum (see West, 1997a).

7   There is an additional issue, which is not explored here, on the question of payment to children for participating in a project. Part of the answer lies in the purpose of participation, for example, if children are used as researchers for the sake of the research. There is also the question of expenses – children and young people are not usually given expenses for attending a youth club, but should they receive expenses for attending a youth council or school council meeting? Is participation work or leisure? Some children in some countries need payment if they are to participate in a project, because they would otherwise be working: for example, the street children in Bangladesh who undertook their own research, needed payment since they would otherwise be out working during the time of the project.

8   Similarly the hierarchies involved in many such organisations mitigate against participation of their staff in decision-making or real consultation, which does not facilitate a good environment for the staff to model participation for children.

9   The final part of this chapter owes much to the invigoration of Joachim Theis. He may not agree with its presentation, but thanks are due to him for making his thinking available.

10   Examples here use the term *young people* because the discussions of empowerment and citizenship are usually couched in terms of these older children in Western Europe. For example, while homeless children are both visible and invisible in the West, the term young people seems most frequently employed in order to disguise or make that fact more palliative.

References

Alderson, P. (2000) *Young Children's Rights: Exploring Beliefs, Principles and Practice.* London, Jessica Kingsley.

Arnstein, S. (1979) Eight Rungs on the Ladder of Citizen Participation. *Journal of the American Institute of Planners.*

Burrell, G. and Morgan, G. (1979) *Sociological Paradigms and Organisational Analysis.* London, Heineman.

Cuninghame, C. (Ed.) (1999) *Realising Children's Rights: Policy, Practice and Save the Children's Work in England.* London, Save the Children.

De Winter, M. (1997) *Children as Fellow Citizens: Participation and Commitment.* Oxford, Radcliffe Medical Press.

Franklin, B. (1997) Reworking of the Ladder of Participation, in Boyden, J. and Ennew, J. *Children in Focus: A Manual For Participatory Research with Children* (p.53). Stockholm, Radda Barnen.

Hart, R. (1992) *Children's Participation from Tokenism to Citizenship.* Florence, UNICEF.

Hart, R. (1997) *Children's Participation: The Theory and Practice of Involving Young Children in Community Development and Environmental Care.* London, Earthscan/ UNESCO.

Howe, D. (1987) *An Introduction to Social Work Theory.* Aldershot, Wildwood House.

Hurley, L. and Teacy, D. (1993) *Models of Youth Work: A Sociological Framework.* Dublin, Irish Youth Work Press.

James, A. and Prout, A. (Eds.) (1990/97) *Constructing and Reconstructing Childhood: Contemporary Issues of the Sociology of Childhood.* London, Falmer Press.

Johnson, V., Ivan-Smith, E., Gordon, G., Pridmore, P. and Scott, P. (Eds.) (1998) *Stepping Forward: Children and Young People's Participation in the Development Process.* London, Intermediate Technology Publications Ltd.

Khan, S. (1997) *A Street Children's Research.* Dhaka, Save the Children/Chinnamul Shishu Kishore Sangstha.

Kirby, P. (1999) *Involving Young Researchers.* York, Joseph Rowntree Foundation.

Lansdown, G. (1995) *Taking Part: Children's Participation in Decision Making.* London, Institute for Public Policy Research.

Miller, J. (1997) *Never too Young: How Young Children Can Take Responsibility and Make Decisions.* London, National Early Years Network/Save the Children.

Treseder, P. (1997) *Empowering Children and Young People: A Training Manual for Promoting Involvement in Decision Making.* London, Save the Children/Children's Rights Office.

Wellard, S., Tearse, M. and West, A. (1997) *All Together Now: Community Participation for Children and Young People.* London, Save the Children.

West, A. (1995) *You're on Your Own: Young People's Research on Leaving Care.* London, Save the Children.

West, A. (1996) *But What Is It? A Critique of Undefined Participation.* Leeds, Save the Children.

West, A. (1997a) *Having Our Say: The First Three Years of Manchester Young People's Forum.* London, Save the Children/Manchester Youth Service.

West, A. (1997b) Citizenship, Children and Young People. *Youth & Policy.* 55: 69–74.

West, A. (1998a) Young People as Researchers, in Banks, S. (Ed.) *Ethical Issues in Youth Work* (pp.181–99). London, Routledge.

West, A. (1998b) Different Questions, Different Ideas: Child-Led Research and Other Participation, in Johnson et al., op cit. (pp.271–7).

West, A. (1999) Children, Young People and Citizenship, in Cuninghame, op cit. (pp.19–39)

CHAPTER 3

The Role of Government in Promoting Youth Participation in England

David Crimmens

The election of a 'New Labour' government in May 1997 marked a change in the direction of social policy. The previous neo-liberal conservative government was committed to free market-based solutions for the alleviation of social problems, and were against using the state as an instrument for creating social change. By comparison the New Labour government is overtly committed to active interventionist social policies to achieve its social objectives.

This chapter will examine the contribution of the New Labour government to recent developments in young people's participation. The state as 'party' to the United Nations Convention on the Rights of the Child (CRC) must be overtly committed to facilitating the change processes that are required across society in order to implement the range of articles of the CRC. This is particularly the case with Article 12, which provides a legal framework for the participation of children and young people in the decisions that impact on their daily lives.

Under New Labour the development of children and young people's participation is linked to economic growth and the future prosperity of the wider society. Participation has moved to the centre of policy agendas because it is linked explicitly with government imperatives of social inclusion and citizenship. Participation therefore becomes part of a political equation that links the needs of the economy with young people as scarce social capital, and young people's citizenship and participation with commitments to social inclusion and social justice. The government's commitment to the participation agenda is evident in a raft of reforming social policy.

One illustration for this assertion is in the 'double dividend' that the Prime Minister spoke of in the Foreword to *Bridging the Gap* in July 1999, (SEU) which gives young people 'more opportunity to make a better life for themselves' while increasing 'their capacity for making a bigger contribution to society'. The report maintains that in an economy based on knowledge there are fewer unskilled jobs for young people. Consequently 'staying at school or in training until 18 is no longer a luxury. It is becoming a necessity'. The key mechanism for achieving social inclusion is seen to be through employment, which for many young people requires them to be better educated, trained and experienced:

> *Getting this right offers the prospect of a double dividend. A better life for young people themselves saving them from the prospect of a lifetime of dead-end jobs, unemployment, ill-health and other kinds of exclusion. A better deal for society as a whole that has to pay a very high price in terms of welfare bills and crime, of failing to help people to make the transition to becoming independent adults.*
>
> (SEU, 1999)

Social Exclusion among young people emerged as an issue in all the reports from the Social Exclusion Unit (SEU). The SEU research acknowledged that while some young people face a long–lasting combination of problems and require particular support if they are to achieve their potential, many more young people simply go through vulnerable periods and circumstances. Consequently there is a major task to confront the risk factors which many young people face as they move in and out of vulnerable stages that can put them at risk of social exclusion. Recognition that young people face new risks and challenges was reflected in the White Paper *Learning to Succeed* (June, 1999) in which the government announced its plans to create a 'single new advice and support service, in charge of steering young people aged 13 to 19 through the system (SEU, 1999).The strategy for confronting the barriers that impede young people from making effective transitions from childhood to adulthood was to be 'Connexions'. The evolution and contribution of Connexions to the social inclusion of young people will be evaluated in detail in the following chapter.

The report by the Policy Action Team 12 (PAT 12) on young people in March 2000 (SEU, 2000) provided another policy landmark in focussing on how Government can improve policies and services for young people. Importantly for the current purpose of understanding and evaluating Government's contribution to the evolution of youth participation, the so-called 'Champion Minister' highlighted the importance of 'designing policies around the needs and priorities of young people – not least through involving them in thinking about policies and services and in their delivery'. The report identified existing good practice and the underlying principles which lead to good practice with young people. It is significant in addressing the question of 'what can be done?' The first principle highlighted is:

> The best programmes are thought through from the perspective of young people, including the most marginalised.
>
> (SEU, 2000).

An emphasis is placed on the importance of choice for young people who are 'quick to spot where they are being asked to conform to someone else's agenda or are being put through a pre-ordained process'. While acknowledging that effective mechanisms for involvement and consultation already exist in the voluntary and local government

sectors, the report recognised that central government 'has been comparatively uninvolved', with the exception of the 'Quality Protects' initiative targeted particularly at young people in state care (see Crimmens, 2003). The report recommended that:

> ... all Government departments and agencies whose work has a significant impact on young people should have a policy of consulting them in policy development and service delivery which affects them.
>
> (SEU, 2000).

The creation of new structures to ensure new and improved arrangements for children's and young people's issues across Government was one of the PAT's key proposals. The report paints a gloomy picture of how government policies have failed to respond effectively to the social exclusion of a significant minority of the youth population brought about by broader economic and social changes. Besides the failure to consult young people and involve them in the design and delivery of services, the report highlights:

- Critical gaps in individual services.
- Lack of targeting of scarce resources to the most deprived sectors of the community.
- The fragmentation of policymaking and service delivery at both national and local levels.

At the heart of government? A childrens and young person's unit

In the summer of 2000, the Prime Minister appointed for the first time, a Minister for Young People and a dedicated Cabinet Committee for Children and Young People. The Children and Young Person's Unit (CYPU) a 'visible symbol of this government's continued commitment to improving the life chances of our children and young people' was established in November 2000. The role of the CYPU was to provide a focal point for ensuring that policies across government are implemented in accordance with their vision statement:

> We want to see the elimination of child poverty, child deprivation and youth social exclusion. We want to see excellent joined-up services, at both local and national level, with the interests of children and young people right at their heart. We want to hear the voices of young people, influencing and shaping local services; contributing to their local communities; feeling heard; feeling valued; being treated as responsible citizens. We want our children to be safe, healthy, confident and fully equipped to deal with the future challenges of this century.
>
> (CYPU, 2001).

The Government's strategy was set out in *Tomorrows Future* (CYPU, 2001). The strategy emphasised that every young person deserves the best possible start in life and the opportunity to achieve their full potential. The task of Government is to make this possible.

The Core Principles

A visible commitment is made to involving children and young people, underpinned by appropriate resources to build a capacity to implement policies of participation.

Children and young people's involvement is valued.

Children and young people have equal opportunity to get involved.

Policies and standards for the participation of children and young people are provided, evaluated and continuously improved.

(CYPU, 2001).

The mechanism for translating policy intentions into actions that generate change in the sphere of young people's participation appeared shortly afterwards. *Learning to Listen* (CYPU, 2001a) articulated the core principles for children and young people's participation in the planning, delivery and evaluation of government policies and services. The Minister for Children affirmed that the result of effective participation should be better policies and services:

> Getting this right should also help us to achieve our key ambitions for children and young people: preventing and tackling social exclusion of the significant minority of children and young people, who are experiencing poverty and disadvantage; and making sure that every young person benefits fully from the services designed to help them.
>
> (CYPU, 2001a).

Changing cultures?

Government recognised the importance of investing additional resources in promoting policy within a clear and explicit recognition that 'this is about a change of culture as much as a question of new resources.'

Learning to Listen (CYPU, 2001a) provides an important landmark in government commitment to young people's participation. The core principles:

- Provide a common framework within which government departments can develop tailored policies.
- Provide a set of standards against which progress of, for example individual government departments, can be judged.
- Build on existing work in both government departments and local authorities.
- Reflect Article 12 of the UNC.

The benefits of an increase in participation are seen as directly contributing to wider social policy objectives such as promoting citizenship and social inclusion as well as offering direct benefits to young people, through better services and opportunities for personal and social education and development. The policy is designed to go beyond the obvious service provision departments. The Department of Health is well advanced in promoting the participation of young people who are looked after by the state through the 'Quality Protects' programme. The Department for Education and Skills (DfES) has responsibility for the Connexions strategy that is detailed in the following chapter. Departments of the state as diverse as the Ministry of Defence and the Home Office as well as the Treasury were expected to produce action plans and set timetables for the implementation of the principles in *Learning to Listen*.

The Department of Health, (DoH), which at the time had responsibility for social as well as health care, published its action plan *Listening Hearing and Responding* in June 2002. The 'Vision' of the plan indicated the

extensive nature of the intended changes that the Department is committed to. It goes beyond a commitment to service-user centred developments in acknowledging that '*its about a cultural change in the way in which we think about children and young people*'. It recognises, for example, that the heath care needs of children are different from adults, and that 'making change for children in the health service is much more than just the medical care of sick children'. There is also a commitment to:

- Involving children and young people in the development and implementation of the projects set out in the action plan.
- Embedding participation into the activities of all the agencies and organisations, which deliver DoH policies and services.

This provides one example of government intention to lead from the front and by example. The notion of 'embedding participation' provides a sense of commitment that addresses previous concerns about the extent for example to which young people's participation is seen as optional. The policy frameworks articulated in *Learning to Listen* are being translated into action by departments such as the DoH. At the time of writing there is evidence available that the action plans are being implemented. A new report (DfES, 2003) details the progress being made in different government departments. There are obvious examples such as the CYPU's consultation with young people on the European Commission's Youth White Paper and the Department of Health funding a

major voluntary organisation to involve young people in developing policy on teenage pregnancy. Other examples include consultation with children and young people:

- *. . . in the development of effective and informative leaflets about The Children and Family Court Advisory and Support Service (Department for Constitutional Affairs).*
- *. . . on the review of the Rural White Paper to help determine cross-governmental priorities like housing, transport and local services in rural areas.* (Department for Environment, Food and Rural Areas).

(DfES, 2003).

A government-sponsored research Project *Building a Culture of Participation* is due for publication in December 2003. The outcomes of independent evaluations such as the CYPU-commissioned study of the working of the UK Youth Parliament should provide evidence of the impact of policies designed to increase participation by young people.

Engaging young people at a local level

Local authorities have responsibility for a wide range of young people's concerns and interests such as education and leisure, and it is worth emphasising that concerns about young people's participation and the state of the democratic process did not start with the New Labour government. A commitment to promoting young people's participation in the UK Youth Service, for example, has a long history going back to the *Albermarle Report* (1960) and reflected in the subsequent *Thompson Report* (1982). Baker (1996), reflecting on the history and tradition of young people's participation in the youth service, suggests that participation has emerged as an underlying principle on which youth work curricula are founded. He maintains that:

> *Young people are consistently portrayed in policy documents and curriculum state- ments as partners in the service and not*

simply as consumers, whose active participation in the process of youth work is essential, rather than just desirable to its success.

(Baker, 1996).

Baker concludes, however, that there is limited hard evidence of participatory practice in youth services. The available evidence indicates that 'this method is the exception rather than the rule' (OFSTED, 1994). In spite of initiatives on participation by national organizations such as the National Advisory Council for the Youth Service (NACYS), which maintained that power sharing between adults and young people is a vital issue for all youth organisations, participation appears to have remained an 'optional extra' (NACYS, 1988, in Baker, 1996).

Evidence of young people's participation across the United Kingdom was highlighted in a comprehensive survey carried out by the Local Government Information Unit (LGIU), the National Children's Bureau and the Children's Rights Office (Willow, 1997). The report made the case for participation politically, legally and socially. It also provided evidence of 'what works' and 'how to do it', both factors that are seen as inhibiting adults from promoting young people's participation. The report concluded that:

- Children and young people want to be listened to and involved.
- There was a great deal already happening to incorporate children and young people's voices in local government policy-making and service delivery. The report included examples of new initiatives in local authorities that demonstrated the range of potential activities for extending young people's involvement in local issues.
- There was a growing demand among local authority staff and politically elected members for more information about how to set up, activities which increase children and young people's participation.

At last it seems the case for children and young people's participation is being under-

stood and accepted within local authorities. The remaining challenge is how to transfer fine ambitions into material changes for children and young people.

(Willow, 1997).

The increased emphasis on participation has been seen as one means of overcoming not only political apathy but also for providing greater opportunities for social justice for young people. Willow (2002) sees legislation as important in bringing about change. Domestic legislation such as the Children Act 1989, and the Children's Rights Convention, with its global commitment to human rights, provides the universal framework. This legal foundation was further strengthened in Britain by the incorporation of the European Convention on Human Rights into the Human Rights Act 1998 that was implemented in October 2000.

Willow sees some progress being made with young people's participation 'in a range of decision-making processes but emphasises the importance of 'the vision and political will of many politicians, especially at local level'.

The challenge at the beginning of a new millennium is that new ideas, approaches and solutions are required to confront social and political problems facing society and 'these can only emerge through positive dialogue and partnerships between young and old'.

(Willow, 1997).

However major questions remain about the extent to which the new opportunities for young people to participate are able to compensate for the 'crisis in the legitimacy of political authority' (Cutler and Frost, 2001).

It seems that fewer young people (and adults) are taking up the opportunities offered for participation through existing channels, such as voting. More importantly in relation to the government's agenda for social justice and inclusion those who often have the closest relationship to services from the state are those least inclined to take part in the decisions that are being made on their behalf. Voting rates for instance, are much lower in poor communities, among most ethnic minorities and among first time and young voters' (Cutler and Frost, 2001). Others identify unemployed young people, members of ethnic minorities and low educational achievers as among those more likely than others to be uninterested in politics (Banks and Ullah, 1987, cited in Molloy et al., 2002). Cutler and Frost (2001) conclude that the single most important reason why young people fail to register to vote is that they do not see any direct link between Government institutions and their own lives.

The Electoral Commission, an independent body established by parliament to 'ensure public confidence and participation in the democratic process within the United Kingdom' (Electoral Commission, 2003) is currently carrying out a review of the voting age in a consultation entitled *How old is old enough?* Moreover, the issue of whether the voting age should be lowered, for example to 16 years, was debated at fringe meetings at each of the three major party political conferences in September 2003, indicating cross-party political concern for this issue.

Cutler and Frost (2001) emphasise that real participation by young people should involve more than the occasional opportunity to vote:

> *Participative democracy demands much more frequent and wide ranging opportunities to be involved in the public decisions which are affecting our lives and the community. This is especially relevant to young people under the age of 18 who do not in any case have the right to vote.*

However, the evidence suggests that young people are more likely to be involved in single issue politics, participating in ad hoc groups which focus on environmental issues, the defence of human rights and an 'identity politics' concerned with issues of gender, race and sexuality (Molloy et al., 2002: p22).

Irrespective of their interest in politics, young people engage in 'political' activities like signing petitions or attending demonstrations (White et al., 2000). This was illustrated recently by spontaneous anti-war protests in which thousands of pupils walked out of classes to protest about the war in Iraq. This example provides contemporary evidence of young people's involvement in forms of politics that mirror protests of earlier generations against nuclear weapons, apartheid and the Vietnam War (Wainwright, 2003).

Edwards (2001) suggests that political decision-making is seen as 'a different and distant world' and therefore it is difficult for young people to see their rights and responsibilities within the system (p.6). She uses terms such as 'disconnection' and 'disengagement' to describe a situation in which young people are both 'jaded' and 'see their interests standing in opposition to rather than in tandem with the goals of both central and local government'.

However, in spite of this sense of distance from politics her research indicates that young people are interested in a range of political issues. More recent research, using a larger sample (Combe, 2002) affirmed that young people have a genuine enthusiasm for participation, particularly at a local level (JRF, 2002).

Cutler and Frost (2001) emphasise that young people's participation is an evolving process and that we will constantly have to seek out evidence of progress in spite of what they maintain is 'a recently much improved status quo'. This evidence may be located in the dynamic changes taking place in democratic representation for other sectors of the population. Devolution in Scotland and Wales, as well as more recent debates on Regional Assemblies are likely to have a profound impact on the opportunities for meaningful participation available to young people.

However, there is little incentive for young people to take an interest in local government politics unless their participation influences decision-making on local issues. Combe (2002) found that involving young people often requires different approaches to those traditionally used to engage other sections of the population. This confirms the assertion by Molloy et al. (2002) that existing methods of participation in local government are perceived by young people to be ineffective as they are unlikely to have an impact or effect change in local decision-making. They also maintain that a balance needs to be established between empowering and engaging young people without pressuring them to become involved:

> *Young people seem keen to ensure that there are appropriate mechanisms for their involvement but decisions about participation will be balanced alongside their other interests, activities and commitments.*
>
> (Molloy et al., 2002).

Consequently young people's active involvement cannot be prescribed. General disillusionment and feelings of powerlessness and exclusion from political processes must be balanced by a degree of faith in the efficacy of democratic processes and an acceptance of these as a way of effecting change.

One major obstacle to increasing young people's participation is that politicians are generally viewed as being inaccessible and unrepresentative of young people (Molloy et al., 2002). A partnership project between the Local Government Association (LGA) and the National Youth Agency (NYA) (Wade et al., 2001) establishes a set of standards for the active involvement of young people in democracy. These standards which are seen as 'not the end of a process but the beginning of one' (Beecham (Chair of the LGA), 2001) include an imperative of accountability by local authorities to young people and a commitment to staff and member recruitment, which aims 'to build the attitudes, qualities and skills required to involve young people' (Wade et al., 2001).

Drawing conclusions?

Celebrating what he sees as the success story of the UK Youth Parliament, Hayter (2003) maintains that the:

> *... youth participation movement has flowered in recent years with young people starting to make their voices heard and to influence decision making.*

The Children's Rights Alliance for England (CRAE) affirmed that the appointment of a Minister for Children and Young People and the establishment of the Children and Young People's Unit were 'huge developments' for children in England (2003). The outstanding issue of an Independent Children's Rights Commissioner, which has been the subject of a concerted campaign for over 10 years (see, for example, Rosenbaum and Newell, 1991) and was more recently urged on the government by the Committee on the Rights of the Child, is closer to resolution. A key proposal of *Every Child Matters*, the most recent government policy on the future of services for children and young people in England (DfES, 2003a) is the appointment of an Independent Children's Rights Commissioner. This office will have similar functions to the Children's Ombudsman Services (see Flekkoy and Kaufman, 1997) that are now a common feature in most European Union countries. The Independent Children's Rights Commissioner will champion children by holding government to account and galvanising political, public and professional support for ensuring that effective mechanisms are in place to deal with children's concerns and complaints (CRAE, 2003).

In assessing developments over the period since the advent of 'New Labour' this chapter has demonstrated that there have been significant changes in political and cultural climates that have enabled participation to become more embedded in policy. Whether this progress is sufficiently well established to maintain that there has been a clear and cohesive shift towards participation remains a matter of conjecture and requires that further evidence be built up over time. Government has created structures that appear to be overtly and uncompromisingly committed to the development of youth participation. Initiatives like Best Value and the Neighbourhood Renewal Strategy as well as programmes targeted at young people such as Connexions and Quality Protects specifically require the active involvement of young people. In these ways, government is contributing to the innovative work on children's rights carried out by Save the Children (Cuninghame, 1999) the Children's Society (Willow, 2002) and the other aforementioned voluntary organisations that have established the foundations of participatory structures and practices with young people. But it remains a question of whether young people's participation is essentially 'local, scattered, ad hoc, fragile and experimental' (Prout in Willow, 2002).

We continue to need to be reminded by commentators such as Hayter that these processes are only starting to become a reality. They are at the beginning rather than reaching any stage of maturity and therefore they remain essentially fragile. There are concerns about the representative nature of activities that promote participation and there is little evidence that more marginal, alienated and socially excluded groups of young people are engaging in the new developments. Government policy has at least created a national framework and a set of expectations that youth participation should become the norm at local level. There is a growing literature available that demonstrates what is possible and promotes best practice, but there is no cause for complacency because:

> . . . *If youth participation is exposed as mere lip service, it will end in disillusionment for the young people, who give up their time to participate politically.*
>
> (Hayter, 2003).

This concern is echoed in a government publication (DfES, 2003) which acknowledges that while there is plenty of participation activity, youth involvement in government risks being seen as 'tokenistic' (Hart, 1992) unless young people are given real influence. The need for change to take place within senior management, front line staff and organisation policy in government departments, is recognised. One way of making progress towards the necessary change would be the incorporation of the CRC in its entirety into domestic legislation (Payne, 2003). In itself, it does not guarantee the kind of organisational and cultural changes that Geddes and Rust (2000) suggest are required to transcend the limits of current initiatives. In order to ensure that government policy does not dissolve into rhetoric it remains essential that young people are actual – as opposed to virtual – partners in change. This will require the debate to move beyond the present emphasis on process, to discover the material realities in terms of outcomes for young people across the age range, and from different social and ethnic groups. Evidence will be required that demonstrates a change in power relationships between adults and young people, because as Arnstein (1969) observes:

> . . . *participation without redistribution of power is an empty and frustrating process for the powerless.*
>
> (cited in Oliver, 2002).

References

Albemarle Report (1960) *Youth Service in England and Wales.* London. HMSO.

Arnstein, S. (1969) The Ladder of Citizen Participation in the USA. *Jnl of American Institute of Planners.* July.

Baker, J. (1996) *The Fourth Partner: Participant or Consumer?* Leicester. The Youth Work Press.

Banks, M. and Ullah, P. (1987) Political Attitudes and Voting Among Unemployed and Employed Youth. *Jnl of Adolescence.* 10: 201–16.

Children and Young Persons Unit (2001) *Tomorrow's Future. Building a Strategy for Children and Young People.* CYPU.

Children and Young Persons Unit (2001a) *Learning to Listen: Core Principles for Children and Young People's Participation in the Planning, Delivery and Evaluation of Government Policies and Services.* CYPU.

Children's Rights Alliance for England (2003) The Case for a Children's Rights Commissioner for England. CRAE.

Combe, V. (2002) *Up for it: Getting Young People Involved in Local Government.* Leicester. NYA.

Crimmens, D. (2003) Children's Rights and Residential Care in England: Principles and Practices. *European Journal of Social Education.* 4: 15–29.

Cuninghame, C. (1999) *Realising Children's Rights. Policy, Practice and Save the Children's Work in England.* London. Save the Children.

Cutler, D. and Frost, R. (2001) *Taking the Initiative: Promoting Young People's Involvement in Public Decision-making in the UK.* London. Carnegie Young People Initiative.

DfES (2003) *Learning to Listen Report.* London, DfES.

DfES (2003a) *Every Child Matters.* London, DfES.

DoH (2002) *Listening, Hearing and Responding. Department of Health Action Plan: Core Principles for the Involvement of Children and Young People.* London, DoH.

Edwards, L. (2001) *Politics not Parties. Young People and Political Engagement. Findings from a Series of Discussion Groups with Young People.* London, IPPR.

Electoral Commission (2003) *Debating the Age of Participation.* News release accessed 15th Oct. www.electoralcommission.org.uk.

Flekkoy, M. and Kaufman, N. (1997) *The Participation Rights of the Child. Rights and Responsibilities in Family and Society.* London. Jessica Kingsley.

Geddes, M. and Rust, M. (2000) Catching Them Young. Local Initiatives to Involve Young People in Local Government and Local Democracy. *Youth & Policy.* 69: 42–61.

Hart, R. (1992) *Children's Participation: From Tokenism to Citizenship.* Innocenti Essays no. 4. Florence, Unicef.

Hayter, S. (2003) Young People Will Not Tolerate Tokenism. *Young People Now.* 30 Jul–5 Aug.

Joseph Rowntree Foundation (2000) Young People's Boredom With Politics 'Should not be Confused with Apathy. Press release, 15 May. York, JRF.

Joseph Rowntree Foundation (2002) *Involving Young People in Local Authority Decision-making.* York, JRF.

Molloy, D., White, C. and Hosfield, N. (2002) *Understanding Youth Participation in Local Government. A Qualitative Study.* London. National Centre for Social Research.

NACYS (1988) *Participation: Part A: Making Promises Real.*

OFSTED (1994) *Access and Opportunity.*

Oliver, B. (2002) Links in the Chain. An Analysis of the Participatory Methodology Being Used to Develop the Role of Connexions Personal Advisors. *Youth & Policy.* 76: 29–38.

Payne, L. (2003) So how are we doing? A review of the Concluding Observations of the U N Committee on the Rights of the Child: United Kingdom. *Children & Society.* 17: 71–4.

Rosenbaum, M. and Newell, P. (1991) *Taking Children Seriously. A Proposal for a Children's Rights Commissioner.* London, Calouste Gulbenkian Foundation.

Social Exclusion Unit (1999) *Bridging the Gap: New Opportunities for 16–18 Year Olds not in Education, Employment or Training.* Cm 4405.

Social Exclusion Unit (2000) *Report of the Policy Action Team 12, Young People.* London. TSO.

Thompson Report (1982) Experience and Participation. Report of the Review Group on the Youth Service in England and Wales. London. HMSO.

Wade, H., Lawton, A. and Stevenson, M. (2001) *'Hear by Right' Setting Standards for the Active Involvement of Young People in Democracy.* London. LGA/NYA.

Wainwright, M. (2003) Thousands of Pupils in Nationwide Protest. *The Guardian*. 6th March.

White, C., Bruce, S. and Ritchie, J. (2000) Young People's Politics: Political Interest and Engagement Among 14–24 Year-olds. in JRF (2000). op cit.

Willow, C. (1997) *Hear! Hear! Promoting Children and Young People's Participation in Local Government*. London, Local Government Information Unit.

Willow, C. (2002) *Participation in Practice. Children and Young People as Partners in Change*. London, The Children's Society.

CHAPTER 4

Connexions: An Example of the Evolution of Young People's Participation in England

David Crimmens

This chapter will evaluate the evolution of young people's participation in the development of the Connexions Service, which is a new state strategy for managing young people's transition from childhood to adulthood, focussing on issues of education, employment and training. It has been selected to illustrate the realities of young people's participation because government sees the explicit commitment to participation as fundamental to the development of this youth programme. It therefore provides an example of the extent to which the commitment to youth participation by the New Labour government, analysed in the previous chapter, is being realised in practice. In doing this the chapter will focus upon the development of participatory structures and practices in one particular regional Connexions Partnership.

Connexions: a service for all young people?

At the launch of the Connexions Service in February 2000 the Prime Minister and seven Cabinet Ministers formally committed themselves to giving every young person the 'best start in life'. The Connexions Strategy is designed to achieve the 'social inclusion' of young people, by enabling them to remain in and gain maximum benefit from learning, employment, education or training in order that they might successfully enter and remain in the labour force. Connexions aims to:

> . . . *energise young people to have a greater belief in themselves, raise their aspirations*

> *and actively participate in their own learning and personal development.*
>
> (DfES 2002a).

At the centre of the Connexions Strategy is the Connexions Service, a support service for all young people in England aged 13–19 years.

Key features of the Service are:

- *A network of new social professionals known as 'Personal Advisors' (PAs).*
- *A commitment to working in partnership across existing agency boundaries to ensure that the needs of young people are met.*
- *Modernising services and improving access – bringing together a range of services that young people want to use in places and at times that are convenient to them.*
- *Involving and consulting young people in the design and delivery of the Connexions Service and using their views to influence the provision of other services such as education and health.*
>
> (ibid).

The Connexions Service is intended to be universal and available to all young people in the age group when they need support. However there is a recognition that particular groups of young people, such as teenage parents and young people leaving public care, identified through the work of the Social Exclusion Unit (in for example PAT 12, 2000) and other agencies, are likely to face multiple barriers to learning and will therefore need to be provided with more intensive support by PAs. The priority therefore appears to be the nine per cent of young people in the age range who are not in education, employment or training, and a further 20–25 per cent who experience significant obstacles or setbacks (DfEE, 2000). These young people, who are not in education employment or training, are conventionally described by the acronym NEETs. Connexions therefore constitutes a key element of the government's youth strategy: 'providing a ladder out of social exclusion and breaking the cycle of non-participation and underachievement' (DfEE, 2000).

Consultation is not enough!

The commitment to involving and consulting young people in the design and delivery of the Connexions Service appears to go beyond what is commonly understood by these terms. From the launch of the strategy document committing Connexions to provide 'The best start in life for every young person' (DfEE, 2000) the government committed itself to finding ways '. . . for young people to be directly involved at all levels of policy development, in developing and delivering the Service locally and in ensuring that the service continues to meet their needs' (para 8.1). In the same paragraph government committed itself to including young people in the governance of the new service. It is this commitment which marks a radical departure from the previous rhetoric about young people's participation because it:

> . . . translates as giving young people the power to direct the service.
>
> (DfES, 2002).

Connexions can therefore be seen as a benchmark against which the development of young people's participation can be measured. This apparent shift in the balance of power between adult service-*providers* and child and adolescent service-*users* has no historical precedent. As the government notes, young people:

> . . . need to be involved as more than just service users or providers of the occasional piece of feedback.
>
> (CSNU, 2002).

Youth governance

The *Connexions: Best Start in Life for Every Young Person* (DfEE, 2000) links the building of '*vibrant communities*' with young people's participation in education, training and employment as part of a strategy 'to enable young people to play a full and active role in their local communities'. This commitment is also connected to the needs of individuals and the economy: 'by raising participation and attainment we raise individual earnings and boost economic performance' (para 3.9). Connexions aims to offer a comprehensive and coherent support service for all young people. The overall strategy is about connecting young people with learning opportunities to enable them to participate more effectively in the labour market. It might therefore be more appropriately titled: 'Best Start in Working Life . . .'.

The strategy clearly fits within the policy frameworks identified in the previous chapter. These frameworks link the achievement of policy goals of social inclusion and social justice with the needs of individual young people and their families living in thriving communities. The strategy is designed to simultaneously contribute to individual and collective well-being while promoting the needs for economic growth. The interests of the Connexions Service and the 'community' are seen as synonymous. A link is assumed between young people's positive experiences of involvement in Connexions leading them to become more involved in their local community, for example through voluntary work or, eventually, by taking a more active part in the democratic process.

Grandiose though this may sound, the official documents appear determined to avoid 'tokenism':

> *Meaningful involvement does not mean tokenism. There is little merit in a young person sitting at a boardroom table feeling totally out of place and afraid to contribute to the meeting for fear of 'sounding stupid'.*
>
> (CSNU, 2002).

Connexions commissioned the National Youth Agency to develop *Key Principles of Good Practice in the Active Involvement of Young People* (Wade et al., 2001) and published guides for both managers and practitioners, drawing on evidence of best practice nationally, to produce a framework for enabling Connexions Partnerships to develop local strategies for youth participation (DfES, 2001). Connexions publications abound with examples of where young people are actively involved in:

• governance
• the planning and design of services
• improving quality

These provide contemporary examples of involvement at every level of the development of Connexions including:

• Recruitment of staff, from chief executives to personal advisors.
• Developing web sites to communicate with their peers.
• Developing facilities for delivering services including redesigning premises.
• Promoting the service.

It would appear that no expense has been spared in promoting and marketing the strategy to young people, and other interested adults, through a national website and a quarterly glossy publication, as well as lauding the achievements of Connexions in every official publication. However Connexions has sometimes failed to reach its key target population, the so-called NEETs, yet this reality has done little to temper excessive official optimism. This raises an important question about whether being seen to be *promoting* participation rather than participation *per se* is the priority at governmental level.

A more realistic picture of developments can be gained from looking more closely at what is happening on the ground. In the local partnership under consideration here, significant progress has been made in a relatively short time, but there is a recognition of the difficulties involved in, for example, connecting with the most socially estranged, hard to reach, young people.

A local Connexions Partnership

Connexions Partnerships are regional bodies responsible for the implementation of the Connexions strategy. Membership of the Partnership Board includes senior managers from education and social services departments, local authority politicians, directors of careers services and learning skills councils, employers and senior representatives from health services, police, probation, youth justice, the voluntary sector, further education colleges and other training providers, all working together as partners to achieve the objectives of the local Connexions Strategy. The Partnership Board employs a Chief Executive with strategic and operational responsibility for developing Connexions within their region.

Local Management Committees (LMCs) have devolved responsibility for the organisation and delivery of accessible local services. The Humber sub-region Partnership Board has four LMCs developing Connexions in a medium sized city (Hull), two large towns, (Grimsby and Scunthorpe) and a largely rural area covered by the East Riding of Yorkshire County Council. LMCs have limited funds to spend on augmenting existing services or plugging gaps in provision. Their membership includes managers and staff from agencies and organisations represented on the Partnership Board.

Each local management committee is committed to developing a sub-group to focus specifically on ensuring that the voice and influence of young people is at the core of all local activities. These subgroups are made of a broad range of organisations working together to enable young people to have a direct influence over the development of the Connexions strategy in their local area. Their activities feed back directly into the decision-making processes of the LMC, providing one avenue for young people to be involved in decision-making structures. An early reflection of the commitment of the Connexions Partnership to youth participation was the appointment of a full-time worker and the allocation of a sizeable budget to develop the participation strategy in the region.

Before looking at the implementation of a local strategy, it is worth looking at a theory of youth engagement that has guided the local partnership in developing its strategy.

A framework for youth participation

Simpson (2002) develops a model for youth engagement with the emphasis on process rather than outcomes. This model while critically reflecting on previous linear models and drawing on best practice in facilitating youth participation, is being developed specifically for Connexions Partnerships in the North of England. Simpson sees developing participation as a learning process for adults as well as for children and young people. This learning process is represented as a series of cycles in a wave formation, which repeats itself over time. The waves include periods of positive activity but importantly the model recognises that progress will be subject to difficulties and challenges, including periods for rebuilding and re-learning as well as periods of inactivity.

> *The model affirms all the stages as positive, recognising that there will be periods of difficulty, but that these are positive and lead to important points of learning. It encourages questioning and challenge as healthy components of the learning process.*
> (Simpson, 2002).

Simpson identifies the following factors which taken together provide a framework for building youth participation:

● **Establish an effective culture** that sees children and young people as individuals with rights and responsibilities rather than as 'passive customers of a service', that 'recognises the strength in ensuring

diversity', through establishing practices which are anti-oppressive, and recognises the barriers to young people's inclusion particularly for those groups and individuals who are most disenfranchised.

● **Ensure appropriate practice** that enables children and young people as well as adults to own and feel fully included in participation processes by recognising and attempting to minimise existing power relationships.

● **Link with other activities** and build on existing structures and initiatives that involve young people, by seeing them as opportunities to build up the confidence and capacity of children and young people.

● **Develop a differentiated range of activity**, to increase the numbers of young people involved in participatory processes, develop representational 'mandates' and target under-represented groups.

● **Develop depth and range in involvement** to confront the tendency for existing structures to reflect patterns of adult activity. Simpson recognises the tension between imperatives to develop participation and questions of representation:

> *. . . existing processes and structures quickly leave small groups expressing opinions on the experiences of others. This situation often leads to the patronising of the few and the exclusion of the many.*

● **Existing structures** like youth councils, joint activities with adults, and conventional approaches to soliciting young people's views through consumer feedback are all *positive activities* 'when included as part of a wider whole, but potentially negative if delivered in isolation'.

● **Evidence** of the range of young people's engagement in participatory activities needs to be gathered and disseminated as a contribution to promoting young people's participation and to demonstrate 'what works'!

The imperative on which the strategy for youth participation is built is a culture that is based on a universal commitment to inter-agency partnership, in which all agencies subscribing or contracting into the strategy agree to work together.

Developing a structure for facilitating youth participation

The Partnership is committed to the involvement of young people in the design, delivery and evaluation of the strategy within the region. An action plan, known as the 'Business Plan' defines the specific objectives of the local partnerships and the intended activities for the following year. Young people are actively involved in the process of developing the plan. It is important to acknowledge the tensions in this process. The Government requires that detailed targets are specified in the Business Plan, while the young people's participation must emphasise the processes at this stage in the evolution of the strategy. There is a recognition that the 'menu of opportunity' for participation needs to be wide and not necessarily replicating existing adult structures.

Gathering information from young people as stakeholders in the Connexions Strategy

In July 2002 the Connexions Partnership used a variety of methods to survey young stakeholders:

- A self-completion questionnaire was distributed to schools, colleges and other training places for young people across the region. This was complemented in a series of focus group discussions in schools across the region (SMSR, 2002).
- Local young people were involved with 'Viewpoint', an organisation developing interactive consultation questionnaires using computers, in developing a local consultation that was used at nine sites including schools, colleges and youth

centres across the region (Viewpoint, 2002).

The information gathered from the survey provided the Connexions Partnership with important information about young people's perception of the evolving Connexions Strategy: for example 60 per cent of the young people completing the self-completion questionnaire had not heard of Connexions nine months after the strategy was officially launched in the region. The Connexions Partnership recognises that consultations of this nature do not constitute active involvement of young people in the Strategy, but it did provide a useful starting point for building foundations by working with existing constituencies of young people.

Key elements of young people's participation in the development of the Connexions Strategy to date include involvement in:

- The recruitment and selection of staff. Young people were involved in the appointment of the senior managers, as well as personal advisors.
- The business planning process.
- The quality assurance of service delivery.
- The development of a youth charter.
- The design, delivery and evaluation of Connexions 'access points', i.e. street level agencies where young people can go for help.

The process of developing the Youth Charter provides an example of how principles are implemented in practice. How do initiatives get started? What are the processes for developing participation in local programmes? Connexions Humber is committed to building on existing initiatives in the region, recognising some of the positive work already going on in youth organizations like youth councils. A group of young people were recruited through almost ad hoc channels to start the process of developing the young people's involvement in the new strategy. A group of 28 young people and youth workers committed to participation went away for a residential weekend to explore how the process could be developed. The residential provided the impetus for the young people to keep meeting, and over a period of months they engaged in a range of activities and discussions. One outcome of the process was the production of the Youth Charter. The young people also engaged with the adult workers in the key questions about how young people were going to get involved in developing Connexions.

Young people met with the Chief Executive of the Partnership to discuss how strategies and structures for involvement could be developed. There was a suggestion that a Shadow Connexions Partnership Board comprised of young people could feed into the Partnership Board. It was recognised that there was a need to try things out and that existing adult structures were not necessarily appropriate for engaging with young people. There was also an acknowledgment that not all adult members of the Partnership Board were equally committed to the idea of young people's involvement. There was a need to break down barriers between the adults and the young people. A series of social events including a barbecue hosted by the young people, and an evening of ten-pin bowling, helped to break the ice and get adults and young people talking and getting to know each other.

The residential and regular meetings provided a structure for the young people to engage in training and develop their skills in participation. The social activities provided excitement and challenge as well as creating opportunities for the young people to learn about engagement. They also provided a way of maintaining young people's interest in the issues. The structure needed to be essentially loose to enable young people to move in and out of the activities as they chose while maintaining a core of commitment, which enabled particular activities to be progressed. The social activities are an acknowledgment and recognition of the value of young people's

involvement and as such, provide an important reward structure. In addition young people's learning through their involvement is formally accredited and they can contribute towards future academic and professional qualifications.

Mistakes have been made and hopefully learnt from such as inviting a group of young people to attend a meeting of one of the LMCs, without briefing the adult members of the committee beforehand. This episode highlighted the crucial importance of a willingness on the part of adults to embrace change. Adults need to recognise the ways in which imbalances of power between themselves and young people has traditionally undermined young people's participation. Adults need to be committed to developing a dialogue with young people, which renegotiates the nature of the relationships between themselves and young people. It is therefore equally important that adults are prepared to acknowledge their own needs to learn about how to effectively engage with young people and that this learning includes training in the skills of working alongside young people.

There is clear evidence of commitment by the Connexions Partnership to young people's participation but questions remain about the extent to which this has reached a stage of maturity in which young people's views and opinions are influencing the fundamental content and structures of the Connexions Strategy. Young people are meeting together discussing important young people issues, but are they able to do more than influence the efficiency and effectiveness of delivery of services that remain essentially determined by adults? Is the expertise of these young people about themselves, and their peers and what they want and need, being harnessed to fulfil an adult-determined agenda? To what extent is power sharing between young people and adults beginning to emerge in ways that would indicate involvement in the governance of the Connexions Strategy?

Inter-agency working and youth participation

The key principle underpinning Connexions at both local and national levels is partnership working based on 'joined-up' policy and practice. The Partnership Board and local management committees represent the structures that are designed to facilitate partnership working across all the agencies involved in delivering Connexions. Coles (2000) provides a range of examples of young people actively influencing decision-making in the youth welfare systems. However he concludes that it is premature to evaluate the outcomes of joined up practices and cautions that:

> ... *often different professional groups have their own agenda, working practices and protocols and priorities for action.*
> (Coles, 2000).

Therefore how will Connexions forge connections between agencies that currently find difficulty in working together? Britton et al. (2002) remind us that the creation of multi-agency partnerships does nothing in itself to address the disparities of power between agencies and can undermine effective collaborative working, the keystone of Connexions. Crawford, (1998) evaluating earlier experiences of partnership working in Community Safety Programmes, cautions against 'partnership speak'. He advocates the necessity of separating rhetoric from reality in acknowledging the problems with widely endorsed multi-agency partnerships. He suggests that there is a tendency to ignore conflicts over ideology, purpose and interests and differential power relationships, and questions the relevance of partnerships for front line workers.

More recent research (Crimmens et al., 2004) looking at the potential contribution of detached and outreach youth work to the evolution of Connexions, records the realities of partnership working. The evidence suggests that the professional practitioners who are or who are likely to become personal advisors, namely youth workers and careers advisors, are struggling to find common ground in providing services for young people. The research identified examples of highly effective collaboration at local level. However there were significant indications that partnership working was being undermined by existing professional cultures and a fear that a bureaucratised practice based more on concerns about the achievement of specified outcomes in relation to placing young people in existing education, employment and training opportunities would be at the expense of developing a truly young person-centred approach, which is a key principle of Connexions.

New Labour approaches to welfare have been claimed to encourage diversity at local level, and the autonomy of the local organisation to respond to the unique situations in each partnership area are emphasised in a range of Connexions publications. Yet local autonomy relies heavily on a culture of trust between the government and the partnerships, that is at odds with prescribed plans and targets (Coles, 2000). The emphasis on tracking and the sharing of data can be perceived as a benign attempt to ensure that particularly young people who are members of traditionally socially-excluded groups do not slip through the narrower mesh of the new welfare safety net. However these centrally determined mechanisms can also be seen as systems of surveillance. Garrett (2002) echoes Coles' concerns about the ways in which technological advances can lead to what he terms 'new regimes of virtual control' in warning against the tendency for advice to blur into compulsion.

Hendrik (2003) picks up this notion of surveillance as a policy imperative in describing the 'panopticism' of New Labour's social policy towards young people. He identifies a contradiction between commitments to social inclusion and the 'getting tough' stance adopted towards youth crime and all types of anti-social behaviour by young people, evident in the title *No more excuses* (Home

Office, 1997) a formative policy paper by the new government. He suggests that policy under new Labour is all about the responsibilities of young offenders within an agenda which has no place for considerations of the rights and liberties of young people, Hendrik evaluates the assertion that the New Labour government has emphasised the importance of children and childhood to an extent 'undreamt of by previous administrations' but concludes that the project is less about self-determination for young people and more about investments in young people as a source of scarce resources in future labour markets.

Colley and Hodkinson (2001) question the analysis of the problem in *Bridging the Gap* (SEU, 1999) that locates the causes of non-participation in education, employment and training primarily within individual young people and their personal deficits. Consequently, the strongly individualistic policy solution that emerges from *Bridging the Gap* as Connexions, fails to acknowledge deep-rooted, structural factors in society, such as class, race and gender, all of which may profoundly affect young people's life chances.

While acknowledging that real progress has been made in the area of children's rights, Hendrik maintains that it is too early to evaluate the outcomes of the government's investment in youth participation. But his analysis emphasises the extent to which a commitment to surveillance and control is likely to subordinate any real changes in power in the relationships between adults and young people promised by the rhetoric of the youth participation agenda. Historically certain groups of young people have always been perceived as potential threats to the social order (see for example Cohen,1972 and Hall et al., 1978). The so-called NEETs are the real target of Connexions and the basis on which its success or otherwise will be evaluated.

Many of these young people are the same population that continue to be subject to overt systems of surveillance and control

under the youth crime and anti-social behaviour agendas.

One size fits all?

There is clear evidence of central government's commitment to develop youth participation. Indeed, there has seldom been a better opportunity to implement fully the expectations of Article 12 of the CRC and to demonstrate a progressive national commitment to enfranchising young people. Government has invested heavily in developing an enabling framework. If government guidance alone could produce the kind of cultural change required to structurally change the relationships between young people and adults in contemporary society, then that change would be imminent. Good practice guides on governance for example (CSNU, 2002) are supplemented by guidance on how to establish reward and incentive systems for young people's involvement (CSNU, 2002a). However policy frameworks and guidance are not sufficient to ensure the evolution of youth participation and many obstructions and constraints remain.

Coles (2000) identifies the fact that existing conventional means of involving young people are often restricted to the voices of young people who are privileged and articulate, and excludes the most disadvantaged. Johnson et al. (2000) question whether Connexions will be any more successful in engaging disengaged young people and highlight the contradictory role of the young-person-centred advocate who is simultaneously attempting to fit young people into existing education, employment and training opportunities. In a similar vein Britton et al. (2002) question the assumption that all young people who may be reached by the new service will wish to be re-engaged in mainstream society by routes defined by the government.

What is not clear is what stance will be taken towards those young people who

choose for reasons to be perfectly rational to them not to be helped by Connexions and seek other . . . means for survival.
(Britton et al., 2002).

Wellard (2003) goes a step further in questioning the extent to which:

. . . an essentially reconstituted career ser- vice, with its focus on one-to-one advice and guidance, is able to provide the kind of interventions needed to re-engage disaffected young people.
(Wellard, 2003).

The keystone of Connexions may therefore be the extent to which Personal Advisors are partisan and able to work with young people on their terms. Colley and Hodkinson (2001) suggest that the idea of one PA dealing with all a young person's needs and problems is attractive but only if that young person feels that the PA is on their side. They conclude that if the PAs are seen as policing rather than helping, their influence upon some young people is likely to be extremely limited.

Will these young people be enabled to voice their views and opinions that may include opting out of the 'New Jerusalem'? If asked, many of the young people who constitute the priority group for Connexions may, like Garrett (2002), question the assumption of a linear transition from school to employment, and the predetermined nature of the support which Connexions offers. Young people may agree with commentators like Britton et al. (2002), Johnson et al. (2000) and Colley and Hodkinson (2001) that the timescales for supporting young people up to their 19th birthday are not realistic and that support structures like Connexions need to be available to some young people well into their formal adulthood. However Colley and Hodkinson offer a warning that both the young people and the services set up to help them are likely to be held responsible for any failure to meet the required targets. Young people who fail to take advantage of the service set up to help them are, like

previous generations of drop outs, likely to be ignored by Connexions *once they move beyond the pale of approved support* (Colley and Hodkinson, 2001) The price of their non-conformity will affirm their zero status and is likely to lead to them being subjected to increasing levels of surveillance and control.

Acknowledgements

A particular thanks to Steve Kay, Youth Participation Manager, Humberside Connexions who has shared his experiences of developing youth Governance over the past two years, and to George Simpson who provides inspiration in turning ideas into professional practices in the evolution of youth participation.

References

Britton, L., Chatnick, B., Coles, B., Craig, G., Hylton, C. and Mumtaz, S. with Burrows, R. and Convery, P. (2002) *Missing ConneXions: The Career Dynamics and Welfare Needs of Black and Minority Ethnic Young People at the Margins.* Bristol: The Policy Press.

Cohen, S. (1972) *Folk Devils and Moral Panics: The Creation of the Mods and Rockers.* London: MacGibbon and Kee.

Coles, B. (2000) *Joined-up Youth Research, Policy and Practice.* Leicester: Youth Work Press.

Colley, H. and Hodkinson, P. (2001) Problems with *Bridging the Gap*: The Reversal of Structure and Agency in Addressing Social Exclusion. *Critical Social Policy.* 21: 3.

Connexions Service National Unit (2002) *Good Practice Guide on Involving Young People in the Governance of Connexions as Decision-makers.* CSNU.

Connexions Service National Unit (2002a) *Encouraging and Recognising Young People's Active Involvement in Connexions. A Guide to Providing Incentives and Rewards for Young People Involved in Shaping Connexions.* CSNU.

Crawford, A. (1998) Delivering Multi-Agency Partnerships in Community Safety. In Marlow, A. and Pitts, J. (Eds.) *Planning Safer Communities*. Lyme Regis: Russell House Publishing.

Crimmens, D., Factor, F., Jeffs, T., Pitts, J., Pugh, C., Spence, J. and Turner, P. (forthcoming) *Being There: The Contribution of Street-Based Youth Work to the Involvement of Socially Excluded Young People in Relevant and Accessible Education, Training and Employment*. York: Joseph Rowntree Foundation.

Department of Education and Employment (2000) *Connexions: The Best Start in Life for Every young Person*. London: DfEE.

Department for Education and Skills (2001) *The Active Involvement of Young People in the Connexions Service: Managers Guide and Practitioners Guide*. London: DfES.

Department for Education and Skills (2002) *Good Practice Guide on Involving Young People in the Governance of Connexions as Decision-Makers*. London: DfES.

Department for Education and Skills (2002a) Connexions Annual Report 2001–02. London: DfES.

Garrett, P.M. (2002) Encounters in the New Welfare Domains of the Third Way: Social Work, The Connexions Agency and Personal Advisors. *Critical Social Policy*. 22: 4.

Hall, S., Gritcher, C., Jefferson, T., Clarke, J. and Roberts, B. (1978) *Policing the Crisis. Mugging, the State and Law and Order*. London: Macmillan.

Hendrik, H. (2003) *Child Welfare. Historical Dimensions, Contemporary Debate*. Bristol: Policy Press.

Johnson, L., MacDonald, R., Mason, P., Ridley, L. and Webster, C. (2000) *Snakes and Ladders: Young People, Transitions and Social Exclusion*. Bristol: Policy Press.

Simpson, G. (2002) *Involving Young People*. A discussion paper for Connexions South Yorkshire.

Social and Market Strategic Research (2002) *Connexions Humber Stakeholder Survey: Final Report*. Kingston on Hull.

Social Exclusion Unit (1999) *Bridging the Gap: New Opportunities for 16–18 Year Olds*. London: HMSO.

Social Exclusion Unit (2000) PAT 12, HMSO.

Viewpoint (2002) *Connexions Humber*. The Viewpoint Organisation Ltd.

Wade, H., Lawton, A. and Stevenson, M. (2001) *Hear by Right. Setting Standards for the Active Involvement of Young People in Democracy*. London: Local Government Association.

Wellard, S. (2003) Faulty Connexions. *Zero2nineteen*. August.

CHAPTER 5

Children's Rights in Ireland: Participation in Policy Development

Nóirín Hayes

Introduction

A National Children's Strategy was published in Ireland in 2000. The Strategy articulates a vision of an Ireland 'where children are respected as young citizens with a valued contribution to make and a voice of their own; where all children are cherished and supported by family and the wider society; where they enjoy a fulfilling childhood and realise their potential' (Ireland, 2000). This chapter reviews the growth of interest in children's rights in Ireland and reflects on how the ratification of the UN Convention on the Rights of the Child has impacted on policy and practice. Taking Article 12 in particular, it reviews the consultation process with children that informed the development of the National Children's Strategy.

The National Children's Strategy

The Strategy is an ambitious ten-year plan with six operational principles which emerged from consultation and which reflect the UN Convention on the Rights of the Child. All actions to be taken within the context of the Strategy will be:

- *Child Centred – the best interests of the child shall be a primary consideration and children's wishes and feelings should be given due regard.*
- *Family Oriented – the family generally affords the best environment for raising children and external intervention should be to support and empower families within the community.*
- *Equitable – all children should have equality of opportunity in relation to access to,*

participation in and deriving benefit from the services delivered; and should have the necessary levels of quality support to achieve this. A key priority in promoting a more equitable society for children is to target investment at those most at risk.
- *Inclusive – the diversity of children's experiences, cultures and lifestyles must be recognised and given expression.*
- *Action Oriented – service delivery needs to be clearly focused on achieving specified results to agreed standards in a targeted and cost-effective manner.*
- *Integrated – measures should be taken in partnership, within and between relevant players be it the State, the voluntary or community sector and families. Services for children should be delivered in a co-ordinated, coherent and effective manner through integrated needs analysis, policy planning and service delivery.*
                                        (Ireland, 2000).

Furthermore, the Strategy has identified three National Goals for children. These are:

- *Goal 1 – Children will have a voice in matters which affect them and their views will be given due weight in accordance with their age and maturity.*
- *Goal 2 – Children's lives will be better understood; their lives will benefit from evaluation, research and information on their needs, rights and the effectiveness of services.*
- *Goal 3 – Children will receive quality support and services to promote all aspects of their development.*
                                        (Ireland, 2000)

These principles and goals are laudable and well intentioned. However, there are some inconsistencies within the strategy document itself. For instance, the principle that all actions will be 'integrated' does not name children as relevant players despite the prominence of the concept of the 'voice of the child' within the strategy at Goal 1. A question emerges, as to what extent the strategy reflects the spirit of the UN Convention on the Rights of the Child within the goal of giving children a voice in matters that affect them, and affords that voice due weight?

Childhood, and Children's Rights, and Ireland

Contemporary Irish childhood is under review. Recent factors – both national and international – have created a situation where children have begun to emerge as an identifiable social group deserving of specific consideration. Children represent almost one third of the population of Ireland. They are often represented as the future of the country, but they depend on the present time for the experiences and opportunities that will enhance their own future. Children are considered to be a dependent and vulnerable social group who are often spoken on behalf of, but who rarely have an opportunity to speak for themselves (Hayes, 2002). It is the very nature of childhood that is seen as warranting cherishing, protection and support, that deprives children of the means to assert their rights. Children are not a politically powerful group and do not have a clear and specific voice. Sustaining and improving the quality of life for all Irish children is not an easy task. While estimates vary, it is conservative to suggest that 25 per cent of Irish children live in poverty (Nolan, 2000). There has been a visible increase in the number of homeless children in Irish cities and towns and there is a high level of illiteracy and non-attendance at school. Childhood play spaces are scarce and a 1997 study estimated that 46 per cent of local authorities do not, as a matter of policy, provide playground facilities (Webb, 1997).

Many of the social and educational policies pursued by government are intended to improve the economy and the status of Ireland. Such policies can have unintended consequences for children. Anticipating these unintended consequences by considering children more overtly and inclusively in policy-making could create a situation which supports childhood and family life in a more proactive and balanced way. Such a shift in approach to policy development would reflect a different view of childhood, wherein children would be:

- Respected and valued for what they are, rather than what they will become.
- Protected in a way that takes account of their right to participate in decisions affecting them.
- Enabled to become the adults of tomorrow by having their needs and rights met today.

Respecting children as human beings requires that children are not seen as adults in waiting, objects of protection, but as individual subjects and bearers of rights (Tisdall and Pinkerton, 1997; Pinkerton, 2000; Hayes, 2002). The task of supporting families in their child-rearing responsibilities will be enriched by taking into account the needs and rights of children in the present.

For many of the more vulnerable and troubled children in Ireland their needs and rights are articulated by pressure groups speaking on their behalf. For the majority of children, many of the policy issues which impact directly and indirectly on them are driven by the agendas and interests of others. In the main, parents are considered to be the most appropriate and primary voice of children. Children depend on them for the security, experiences and materials necessary for a happy childhood. The result is that unless there are serious problems, or risks of problems, families tend to be left alone to cope with modern parenthood with only limited state support. Statutory responsibility for children's affairs in Ireland is divided across a number of government departments, and these departments have tended to work in isolation from each other. Social policy has developed in reaction to problems and difficulties rather than as part of a wider vision for children and childhood. A consequence of this reactive approach has been the development of isolated and fragmented services in place of integrated and inclusive services for children and their families. Many of the government initiatives aimed at addressing difficulties and problems in childhood are targeted at resolving a particular problem in the short term rather than deriving from a discourse on the rights and needs of children now and into the future.

This problem-based perspective is evident in the fragmented nature of the policy development approach to a number of issues relating to children. The current policy response to developing integrated and sustainable childcare services as a support to parents and their children is of particular relevance here. In the years 1998–99 there were three major government reports addressing this issue published under three different departments. These reports were issued by the Department of Social, Community and Family Affairs (1998), the Department of Justice, Equality and Law Reform (1999) and the Department of Education and Science (1999). The recommendations from each report involve the establishment of different structures within each department to address, in part at least, the same policy issue – that of developing and supporting childcare services for children and their families.

In an effort to improve cross-departmental communication in respect of children and children's services, a Minister of State to the Departments of Health, Education and Justice, with special responsibility for children, was appointed in 1994. While welcomed as a very positive development on behalf of children, this junior ministry has been primarily concerned with the co-ordination of services to vulnerable and troubled children and is not addressing the rights and needs of *all* Irish children. As a result this Minister had, for instance, no role in the development of childcare policy. However, there is an emerging recognition

that the State needs to be more proactive in support of children through a wider range of mechanisms, and the National Children's Strategy is an important stage in developing such a process.

Consultation with and participation of children

Many adults consider children to be immature and incapable of the rational thinking they associate with participative decision-making. Nonetheless, there are several examples of action and projects to include children which are emerging both nationally and internationally. There has also been a recent increase in awareness of the value of consulting children among practitioners, policy makers and researchers in Ireland. Increasingly conferences on children's issues have afforded children an opportunity to contribute, with differing degrees of success, often by way of drama or art. A number of different associations have held forums to access children's views on different issues. These include the Irish Society for the Prevention of Cruelty to Children (ISPCC), which hosts regional Children's Forums annually, and the youth parliament of the National Youth Council of Ireland. In addition a number of local communities and partnerships have specific projects which give voice to children on issues of importance to them, such as play space (Dublin North Inner City) and creativity in the classroom (Dublin Canal Community Partnership). A conference on mechanisms for including children in research was held in Trinity College Dublin in 1999 and the proceedings were published (Hogan and Gilligan, 1999). Because few of the community actions or project experiences have been evaluated it is difficult to assess the degree to which they are effective and the extent to which consultation will lead to active participation of children in policy development and evaluation remains to be seen.

The idea of consulting with children on issues of relevance to them can mean different things to different people. For some it is no more than including them at a 'vox pop' level on topics immediately associated with children such as toys, playgrounds or television. For others the concept is more radical. Freeman (1992), for instance, argues that empowerment of children is not:

> ... *simply a question of redistribution of power. Putting children on to decision-making committees ... only scratches the surface and does little to undermine entrenched processes of domination. More is clearly required – ultimately a re-thinking of the culture of childhood.*

(Freeman, 1992: 32).

To assist the debate on what participation might mean for children and adults, a number of authors have considered what different levels of participation might mean in practice (for example, Arnstein, 1969; Hart, 1992; Franklin, 1997). One of the first and most influential scales on levels of participation in general was developed by Sherry Arnstein in 1969. This was adapted and refined by Roger Hart to assist consideration of children's participation. Acknowledging that simply identifying different levels of participation will not alter the level of participation experienced by children, Hart suggests that it is through education that real participation can begin. He cautions, however, that:

> *There is no nation where the practice of democratic participation in schools has been broadly adopted. The most fundamental reason seems to be that, as the primary socialising instrument of the state, schools are concerned with guaranteeing stability; and this is generally understood to mean preserving the very conservative systems of authority.*

(Hart, 1992: 43).

This could certainly be said of Ireland where there is a centrally devised and monitored national curriculum at both primary and secondary level. In addition the Education Act 1998 is somewhat circumspect with respect to the democratic participation of children in matters affecting them in schools. While allowing for the establishment of student councils at second level – under particular circumstances and with the guidance of the Boards of Management – there is no such reference to student councils at primary level.

There have been some criticisms of Hart's ladder as too cautious, too adult-centric and too concerned with adults' bestowing opportunities on children. John (1996) argues that we need to move away from doing things to and for children towards doing things with them. In their *Manual for Participatory Research with Children* Boyden and Ennew present an adaptation of Hart's ladder by Barbara Franklin (1997: 53). She has moved beyond Hart's ladder to consider a more detailed and interactive approach to conceptualising children's participation. Franklin's adaptation takes into account a wider range of child-adult interactions than Hart and introduces a useful distinction between non-participation and pre-participation. In this adaptation she extends the levels of participation and characterises the most participative level as children in charge – children decide what to do; adults get involved only if children ask for help.

Many authors (Cousins, 1996; Hart, 1997; Franklin, 1997) recognise that children's capacity to participate in decision-making and policy development varies with their level of development. But the opportunity to participate also contributes to children's development. The process of participation is important for children in that it can help them develop listening and negotiation skills, persistence and flexibility. It can enhance their imagination and build up their self-confidence and sense of responsibility. Adults, in partnership with children, can be crucial agents in these developments when sensitive to children's competence and emerging competencies.

Cousins (1996) notes that children believe adults should behave towards them in certain ways; that adults should relate to children positively, be loving towards them, able to talk to children truthfully and find time to listen to children seriously. Adults should be respectful enough to acknowledge that babies and young children are already people, can be trusted to make their own choices and eventually express their own views. And adults should be responsible in the way that they care and provide for children and in the example they give in their own attitudes, choices and use of power (Cousins, 1996: 20).

Participation and the UN Convention

The United Nations Convention on the Rights of the Child (CRC) is a powerful charter for children. It has the potential to influence policy development in a way that makes children more visible. When Ireland ratified the Convention in 1992 it committed itself to taking account of the special rights of children including their right to participate in a democracy in ways that reflect their age and maturity. Of particular importance to Ireland – given the Constitutional primacy of the marital family (Bunreacht nah Eireann, 1937) – is the fact that the Convention affirms the primacy of the family with respect to children and does not propose rights for children at the expense of others. The Convention does, however, aim to enhance the position of children in society by drawing attention to the particular nature of children's rights, and state and societal obligations to children in this regard. A central concern of advocates for children's rights is that the rights given to the family as a unit may lead to tensions where the individual rights of the child are not explicitly taken into account. This can result in children experiencing an indifference to, and lack of respect for, their opinions on issues that directly affect them. While this shortfall becomes more evident as a concern when considering the older child it is, nonetheless, relevant for younger children and reflects an underlying conceptualisation of children as less deserving of consideration than the older members of a family unit. Respecting the

rights of children does not give them rights to make unilateral decisions at odds with those of the family but it does give them a right to be explicitly considered and consulted. An opportunity to facilitate the participation of children in policy making through consultation arose in Ireland with the development and publication of the National Children's Strategy (Ireland, 2000). The impetus for this strategy can be traced back to Ireland's ratification of the CRC.

The Irish government ratified the Convention without reservation. The government marked the occasion by posting a copy of the Convention to each school in the State. In response to this rather modest attempt to raise awareness about the Convention, a small group of people, working with and for the voluntary and community sector, came together in 1993 and formed a working group which later became the Children's Rights Alliance (CRA). The purpose of the Alliance is to raise awareness of the UN Convention on the Rights of the Child and to seek its full implementation in Ireland. In addition the Alliance actively participates in the review process of the implementation of the Convention.

United Nations guidelines note that in the preparation of the National Report for the UN Committee on the Rights of the Child, governments are expected to consult with the non-government sector. As part of this process in 1995 the CRA had a formal meeting, organised by the Irish Department of Foreign Affairs, with representatives from the various governmental drafting the first National Report before it was finalised. Comments were invited from the CRA, which were noted, and the process acknowledged in the final report. Ruxton (1998) highlights a risk for NGOs in this type of consultation because they may be compromised, their views watered down or the consultation ' . . . used to legitimise otherwise ineffective policies' (p.79). He goes on to point out that consultation by the government with the NGO sector does not preclude the sector from submitting an alternative report. This was, in fact, the case in Ireland where the CRA was consulted in the preparation of the National Report and also submitted its own NGO report *Small Voices: Vital Rights* in May 1997 (CRA, 1997). This report informed the UN Committee in advance of the plenary hearing held in January 1998 and the CRA, among other NGO groups, was present at the pre-session and plenary hearings. While the consultation in preparation of the first National Report for Ireland was wide-ranging, it did not include direct consultation with children and young people.

In their Concluding Observations (CRA, 1998) the UN Committee on the Rights of the Child made a number of recommendations to the Irish Government. These included a call for Ireland to adopt a comprehensive National Strategy for Children, incorporating the principles and provisions of the Convention and to systematically promote and facilitate children's participation in decisions and policies affecting them. There can be no doubt that the Convention and the observations of the UN Committee have influenced policy and have acted as a catalyst in policy development for children in Ireland since ratification in 1992. For example, in 1997 the Government, in response to a List of Issues from the UN Committee just prior to the plenary hearing of the UN Committee indicated that there was no immediate intention to draft a National Children's Strategy. However, in October 1998 the Minister for Health and Children announced, in a speech delivered at the annual CRA conference that, in response to the UN Committee recommendations, his department was co-ordinating the production of a National Children's Strategy. An interdepartmental group was established in 1999 and the Strategy was published in November 2000.

The Consultation Process

Planning for consultation

The stated intention underlying development of the National Children's Strategy was that the process was to be as inclusive as possible. This commitment emerged from the work of an inter-departmental group advised by two sub-groups – one representing the NGO sector and the other the research community. A central part in the development of the National Children's Strategy was a wide-ranging consultation process. Invitations for submissions through the national press sought contributions from parents and others who care for and work with children. In addition, a targeted consultation was carried out with children and young people with the assistance of various schools and voluntary organisations throughout the country and with the support of the Children's Rights Alliance and the National Youth Council. Children also wrote to and e-mailed the Minister of State with responsibility for Children to give their suggestions, comments and observations on growing up in Ireland.

The consultation with children took three forms (NCS, 2000a). First, a notice to children and young people was published in a variety of settings including the media and on the schools' web site, 'Scoilnet'. The notice invited children to send their views on the following questions:

- Is Ireland a good place for you to grow up in?
- What's good about it?
- What would make it better?

All submissions received through this process received a personalised reply from the Minister's office.

Second, the Minister of State visited five primary schools and five post-primary schools, where she met with a number of students – up to 60 in certain schools – and discussed a range of issues with them. The visited schools represented most of the different types of school in the country, including primary and secondary schools, *gaelscoileanna* (Irish language schools), special schools, schools in urban and rural Ireland and schools in areas of particular disadvantage.

Third, ten organisations working with children and young people undertook in-depth consultations with children and young people connected with their organisations.[1] In advance of this aspect of the consultation a number of organisations affiliated to the Children's Rights Alliance and the National Youth Council were invited to attend a preparatory workshop hosted by the National Children's Strategy team. The purpose of the workshop was to give the representatives of organisations and consultation facilitators some background information on the National Children's Strategy. The aim was to provide an opportunity for them to share ideas about good ways of consulting with children and young people and to discuss some of the arrangements for the consultations, such as formats of feedback (NCS, 2000a).

Workshop

A report of the workshop, which was held over one day in Dublin Castle, was prepared by the Strategy team and outlined the preparation for and the results of the workshops, which addressed two broad issues:

- Themes for Consideration
- Planning the Consultation (NCS, 2000b).

1. Themes for consideration

The Strategy team identified themes to be considered by the workshop participants. These themes were developed to guide the consultation because it was felt that the issues and views children and young people might wish to raise could be accommodated in the four themes. The themes were:

- **Key trends and developments** – this theme was intended to explore what children and young people saw as the most significant trends and developments to affect their lives and to detail how these trends affect them. The workshop identified a list of trends and developments they considered likely to arise.

- **Childhood** – this theme aimed to explore the personal experiences of children and young people, identifying what is good and not so good about childhood, and also to explore children and young people's sense of personal power and capacity. The workshop participants developed a list of issues for discussion during the consultation process.

- **Priorities for action/visions for the future** – this theme was intended to explore children's and young people's priorities in terms of the actions or supports they require to make their childhood better. It also aimed to find out about their vision of childhood for the future and what they envisaged the Strategy could do to help them realise this vision. The workshop participants noted the 'adult' language of this theme and expressed a concern that it was not appropriate for the immediacy of childhood as experienced by children.

- **Consultation** – this theme aimed to learn what children and young people want to be consulted about, and to find out what they see as the best methods of consulting them. (NCS,2000b).

2. Planning the consultation

The report of discussions at the Dublin Castle workshop reflect an awareness among those present of the special nature of consulting with children and the requirements necessary to achieve this in a way that respects and involves children. The report indicates that adults were expected to maintain a key role in the consultation. This expectation can be seen in the language of a number of statements quoted in the report. For example, 'It was broadly agreed that while it is necessary to provide children and young people with freedom and choice, the provision of a safe and secure environment and defined boundaries are required from adults'. 'There should be a "blank page" approach to the consultation with children and young people. This implies that, while issues may be introduced by the facilitator, the direction of the discussion should come from the participants' (NCS, 2000b).

While the time available to prepare and carry out the consultations was limited (which was a weakness in the process identified by the participating organisations), as an exploratory exercise in consultation it was welcomed. 'The time available precludes a full and exhaustive process of consultation but it was agreed that it will be possible to initiate consultation which will have an important message for the Strategy.' . . . 'It was suggested that a 'cold' consultation, without the provision of some background information, might not yield the best results but that given the limited time available, it might be the only option' (NCS, 2000b).

The workshops identified a number of barriers to the consultation process. These included areas such as:

- Access to the process, and difficulties associated with culture, gender, disability, literacy and marginalised groups.
- Characteristics of the facilitators, such as personal agendas, attitude, confidentiality – degrees of trust, skills to deal positively with information and emotions.
- Methodological issues, such as lack of clarity of objectives, language, methods of recording information, numbers participating, peer pressure – fear that a contribution would not be acceptable to the group, limited time available, user friendliness and pressure to participate.

It was agreed that the results of the consultations, including samples of points presented using different media such as art or stories, would be reported back to the strategy team by the adult facilitators. Different methods of feedback were discussed. In this regard it was noted particularly that care needed to be taken in the interpretation of the results of the consultation. The facilitators must remain aware of their own 'agenda' and also 'aware of the need to differentiate between what the children and young people say, *what they mean and what they feel they should say*' (emphasis added).

Reporting the consultation results

The results of the consultation process with both adults and children were published by the National Children's Strategy, in September 2000. They were published as one publication with three reports – a Children's Report, the Main Report and an Executive Summary (NCS, 2000a).

Submissions from children totalled 2,488. Of these 825 were received through e-mail or letter; 1,063 came through organisations (ten organisations) and 600 came through schools (five Primary and five Secondary schools).

Of the 2,488 submissions received, 873 (35 per cent) came from children under 13 years of age and 1,615 (65 per cent) were from children of 13 years and over. The age range was 3 years through to 19 years. There was a gender difference in the consultation process, with 60 per cent of the respondents' girls and 40 per cent boys. No detail is available on the degree of national distribution or the representation across different socio-economic groups, although it is made clear in the report that every effort was made to be as representative as possible.

The summaries received from the different consultations represent a diversity of issues of interest to children. They include key themes such as Play and Leisure, The Environment, Social Issues, Having a Say, The Right to a Good Life and Expectations for the Strategy. The report on the consultation process is rich in quotes on a wide range of topics and from children of all ages. However, it is not possible to determine how representative of the overall process are the quotes included in the report, because insufficient detail is provided. The process would have been enriched by the development of procedures to allow children to report back directly to the Strategy team and also to have enabled them to review and comment on the reports before they were finalised.

The consultation process undertaken with children and young people by the National Children's Strategy team represents an important preliminary step, at national level, in encouraging children to participate in policy development. The process can best be characterised, however, as pre-participation rather than participation. It is not representative of consultation as described by Franklin (1997) in her expansion of Hart's ladder. The process is better considered as 'tokenism'. In an extensive discussion of different levels of participation, Hart says tokenism is a difficult issue to deal with because it 'is often carried out by adults who are strongly concerned with giving children a voice but have not begun to think carefully about doing so' (1997). This is indeed the case with the consultation process for the National Children's Strategy. The Strategy team, and those advising them, did want to give children a voice, as evidenced by the First Goal of the strategy as it was finally published. However, there were serious time constraints imposed for the publication of the Strategy document, and the organisation necessary for truly consulting with children was simply not available. The Strategy team acknowledged that the process of consulting with children and young people brings new demands to planning and evaluating supports and services for children. They note that a range of mechanisms needs to be developed and put in place to support this new approach (NCS, 2000a).

Impact of consultation with children on the National Children's Strategy

It is impossible to judge the degree to which results of the consultation process impacted on the content of the National Children's Strategy. The Strategy document identifies seven main themes to emerge from the consultation process, one of which is a list of the key issues identified through consultation with children (Ireland, 2000). Interestingly, this list is somewhat more extensive than that given in the consultation report itself (NCS, 2000a).

The Strategy document reiterates the government's commitment to consulting

with children. However, the language used reflects an adult-centred rather than a child-centred perspective. This can be observed where the report outlines what giving children a voice means. The document states that it means, encouraging children to express their views and demonstrating a willingness to take those views seriously, setting out clearly for the child the scope of their participation to avoid misunderstanding; providing children with sufficient information and support to enable them to express informed views; explaining the decisions taken, especially when the views of the child cannot be fully taken into account.

Here one can see adult management of the process dominating the process of child participation. Despite this, the experience of the consultation process itself has informed the measured nature of the objectives regarding the participation of children. In discussing the goal of 'Giving Children a Voice' the Strategy states that

> *Opportunities . . . need to be found to develop children's understanding of civic values in society so that they can act as responsible citizens and contribute fully to their families, schools and local communities. To develop this understanding children need to learn the social and negotiating skills . . . essential to effective participation. This means providing them with practical opportunities to participate and become involved in the operation of local community activities which are provided for them.*
> (NCS, 2000a).

The National Children's Office (NCO) was established in 2001 to implement the strategy. The NCO co-ordinated and hosted the first *Dáil na nÓg*, or Children's Parliament, in September 2001. The Strategy identified this as a key action to meet Goal 1 and also noted the need for careful preparation in this regard. The *Dáil* 'must have clear objectives and . . . arrangements must be put in place to support its operation. These must ensure that representation is genuinely inclusive . . .

Good local networks will need to be established for developing and supporting national representation'.

The *Dáil* was chaired by the Minister for Children and the children attending were aged from 9 to 17 years old. They were selected from those involved in the original Consultation for the Strategy, and there were representatives from each county. The intention is to hold a national *Dáil na nÓg* annually but the exact mechanism for linking the outcomes from the *Dáil na nÓg* with the national *Dáil* and other policymaking groups have yet to be determined. The NCO also hosted the first local *Comhairle na nÓg* in January 2002. The membership of this *Comhairle*, or Forum, was drawn up by the NCO with the assistance of local schools and voluntary organisations who nominated children to attend. This model *Comhairle* was attended by the Chief Executive Officers of various City and County Development Boards. At a local level the City and County Development Boards have been identified as key structures for the implementation and delivery of the Strategy. These bodies comprise representatives from local government, local development agencies, the State sector and the social partners. Their functions include the identification of gaps and overlaps in general service provision and the securing of coherent service delivery arrangements by agencies operating locally. The Boards and their associated sub-structures provide the opportunity for children's views to be included in their considerations. In the long-run the National Children's Strategy envisages the City and County Development Boards as the mechanism for giving children a local voice that feeds into a national voice for children. The NCO will facilitate these groups in identifying suitable methods for including children in policy development. The degree to which the Boards are supported and advised on the techniques for facilitating the participation of children will determine how successful this mechanism will be. The events to date have been evaluated and the

reports will be used to advise future initiatives at local and national level on different mechanisms for the effective participation of children.

Conclusion

The experience of consulting with children and the consultation process itself did inform the measured nature of the recommendations made regarding the participation of children within the National Children's Strategy. Under the heading 'Building Capacity to Support Participation', the Strategy Report (NCS, 2000b) notes that:

> . . . *Providing the more systematic and comprehensive approach required by the Strategy is new and challenging. Approaches appropriate to the Irish context will need to be developed. The first step will be to work out the detail of how such arrangements can be operated . . . There is research available to support the development of best practice in this area.*

> *(NCS, 2000b).*

In addition to the national *Dáil na nÓg* and the local *Comhairle*, the strategy report identifies a number of structural changes at government, national and local level necessary for the effective and inclusive implementation of the Strategy. These include a National Children's Advisory Council where children are represented and the appointment of an Ombudsman for Children one of whose role will be to 'consult with children on issues of importance to them' (Ireland, 2000). The enabling legislation for this office was published in 2002 as the Ombudsman for Children Act (Ireland, 2002).

The publication of the National Children's Strategy and the development of the implementation mechanisms are important statements in favour of Irish children. The strategy has great potential to improve the quality of life of Irish children and enhance Irish society in general. Of particular importance is the commitment to giving children a voice in the development of policy and practice that affects them, directly and indirectly. The consultation process with children which began during the development of the strategy, although exploratory rather than comprehensive, represents an important first step in this process.

Note

1   The ten organisations involved in the consultation process were: Barnardo's; Border Counties Childcare Network; Catholic Youth Council; Development Education for Youth; Girls Brigade; Irish Association of Young People in Care; Irish Society for the Prevention of Cruelty to Children; National Parents Council – Primary; Pavee Point (Traveller issues); South West Inner City Network Limited.

References

Arnstein, S. (1969) A ladder of citizen participation. *Journal of the American Planning Association.* 35: 4, 216–44.

Boyden, J. and Ennew, J. (1997) *Manual for Participatory Research with Children.* Radda Barnen.

Cousins, J. (1996) Empowerment and Autonomy From Babyhood: The Perspective of Early Years Research, in John, M. *Children in Charge: The Child's Right to a Fair Hearing.* London, Jessica Kingsley.

Children's Rights Alliance (1997) *Small Voices: Vital Rights.* Dublin, Children's Rights Alliance.

Children's Rights Alliance (1998) *Children's Rights: Our Responsibility – Concluding Observations of the UN Committee on the Rights of the Child.* Dublin, CRA.

Department of Education and Science (1999) *Ready to Learn: White Paper on Early Childhood Education.* Dublin, Stationery Office.

Department of Justice, Equality and Law Reform (1999) *National Childcare Strategy.* Dublin, Stationery Office.

Department of Social, Community and Family Affairs (1998) *Strengthening Families for Life.* Report of the Commission on the Family, Dublin, Stationery Office.

Franklin, B. (1997) Reworked Ladder of Participation, cited in Boyden, J. and Ennew, op cit. (p.53).

Freeman, M.D.A. (1992) Beyond Conventions: Towards Empowerment, in Fortuyn, M. D. and de Langen, M. (Eds.) *Towards the Realization of Human Rights of Children.* Amsterdam, Defence for the Child International (pp.19–40).

Hayes, N. (2002) *Children's Rights: Whose Right?* A review of child policy development in Ireland, Studies in Public Policy. Dublin, Policy Institute.

Hart, R. (1992) *Children's Participation: From Tokenism to Citizenship.* Innocenti Essays No 4. Florence, UNICEF.

Hart, R. (1997) Children's Participation: The Theory and Practice of Involving Young Citizens in Community Development and Environmental Care. London, Earthscan/ UNICEF.

Hogan, D. and Gilligan, R. (Eds.) (1999) *Researching Children's Experiences: Qualitative Approaches.* Dublin, Children's Research Centre.

Ireland (1937) *Bunreacht nah Eireann.* (The Constitution of Ireland). Dublin, Stationery Office.

Ireland (1998) *The Education Act.* Dublin, Stationery Office.

Ireland (2000) *The National Children's Strategy.* Dublin, Stationery Office.

Ireland (2002) *The Ombudsman for Children Act.* Dublin, Stationery Office.

John, M. (1996) *Children in Charge: The Child's Right to a Fair Hearing.* London, Jessica Kingsley.

National Children's Strategy (2000a) *Report of the Public Consultation.* Dublin, Stationery Office.

National Children's Strategy (2000b) *Strategy Team Report.* NCO, Unpublished Report.

Nolan, B. (2000) *Child Poverty in Ireland.* Dublin, Oak Tree Press in association with Combat Poverty Agency.

Pinkerton, J. (2000) *Children: Young Citizens.* Paper presented to the National Children's Bureau Conference, May 2000.

Ruxton, S. (1998) *Implementing Children's Rights: What can the UK learn from International Experience?* London, Save the Children.

Tisdall, K. and Pinkerton, J. (1997) *Promoting Citizenship? The UN Convention on the Rights of the Child and UK Children's Legislation.* Paper presented at the Social Policy Association Conference, July 1997.

United Nations (1989) *Convention on the Rights of the Child.* UN.

Webb, M. (1997) *Grounds for Play.* Dublin, Dublin Institute of Technology.

CHAPTER 6

Many Roads Converge on the Same Hilltop: Children's Rights in Scotland

Judy Furnivall, Andrew Hosie and Meg Lindsay

Introduction

All children and young people have rights. It can be argued, however, that those living in public care have historically been those most likely to have their rights denied. Ensuring that rights are respected, in deed as well as word, involves attention to minor detail, and the imagination and courage to achieve major change. It can be argued that children and young people who are looked after by local authorities, particularly those living in residential care, are the group which most need those who care for them to demonstrate such attributes concerning rights. Public enquiry after enquiry has demonstrated the vulnerability of this group – separated from families, frightened to speak out about abuse and maltreatment they have experienced, and seldom listened to or believed if they did (Levy and Kahan, 1991; Waterhouse, 2000; Marshall, Jamieson and Finlayson, 1999).

Children and young people who are looked after in residential care have been the focus of much attention in recent years in regard to how best protect their rights. The two major reviews of the safety of children in residential care (Kent, 1997; Utting, 1997), and the inquiry occasioned by the abuse of children in North Wales (Waterhouse, 2000) have stressed the need to develop techniques for protecting these children's rights, particularly the right of protection from abuse. The Children Act 1989 and the Children (Scotland) Act 1995 have both highlighted the rights of these children (among others) to have a strong voice in decisions about their own lives. Developments in children's rights in relation

to this group, therefore, are of especial interest.

Looking at how the rights of children in care have developed in one small country enables comparison of how the issue is seen on a local, national and international basis. This chapter will explore how Scotland has developed ways of protecting the rights of children living in residential care.

Research by Child Line (Morris, 1994) into the telephone calls they received from all over the United Kingdom from children and young people in the care system, revealed that the Scottish group differed from their peers in two distinctive ways – they were more aware of why they were in care, and of what their rights were. The most likely explanation for this discrepancy is two factors which differentiate Scotland from the rest of the United Kingdom (UK). The first is the existence in Scotland of a distinctive system for dealing with child care decision-making – the Children's Hearing system. The second relates to the development over some 25 years of an organisation – 'Who Cares? Scotland' – run by and for children and young people who are looked after by local authorities. In common with other countries, a children's rights movement has also developed over the last decade, but it interacts with both the Children's Hearing system and with Who Cares? Scotland, which gives the opportunity for a more co-ordinated approach.

This chapter will describe the Scottish situation particularly in relation to the development of the Children's Hearing System, Who Cares? Scotland and Children's Rights Officers, and will then look at international research which showed how children in residential care in Scotland viewed the protection of their rights compared to those in Finland, Ireland and Spain.

Scotland

Scotland is a small country with a distinctive approach to child care. It could be argued that this derives from a cultural background in which community and family have historically formed the core of social organisation. The Gaelic word 'clan' means 'children'. The concept of 'clan' reflects the family relationship between the Highland chief and his people, and the significance of community in all social organisations. With the religious reformation and the development of the Presbyterian Church, this localised, community-based approach to the care of people in need and including children, was sustained. Children who could not continue to be supported in their own families were placed in other families in the community, by decision of the Kirk Session (the ruling court of each local church, which was made up of elected members of the local congregation). By the nineteenth century, this meant that 'foster' care rather than residential care had developed in Scotland as the preferred method of supporting children in need.

However, children's rights as an issue of social policy and practice, does not have a long history in Scotland any more than in other parts of the world. The creation of courts to deal with children's issues came into being in the late nineteenth century. The first such court was established in Norway in 1896, followed by Cook County in the USA in 1899, and Scotland in 1932.

The Second World War brought in its wake a desire to establish human rights and the fledgling United Nations devised a Declaration of Human Rights in 1948. This was followed by the European Convention of Human Rights, devised by the Council of Europe and signed by the British Government on 3 September 1953. Despite that progress, it was not until the 1980s with the creation of Who Cares? Scotland, and the development of the 1989 United Nations Convention on the Rights of the Child (CRC) ratified by the UK in 1991, that the whole issue of rights and children moved 'centre stage' in Scotland. For children and young people looked after by care agencies, the issue was advanced by the publication of the 1992 report *Another Kind of Home* (Skinner, 1992). It is interesting to set out the CRC and the Skinner principles together (see table opposite).

The two are not, and were never meant to be, either comparative or in conflict. The Skinner principles are entirely to do with children looked after in public care. But these principles measure well, when set against the CRC. A more complete picture of the rights of children and young people looked after and accommodated in Scotland, requires the addition of the principles on safeguarding from the Kent Report (Kent, 1997), together with the thinking behind *Valuing Diversity* (Chakrabarti, 1998).

The Children's Hearing system

Scotland's distinctive approach to child care has perhaps its most obvious manifestation of recent years in the shape of the Children's Hearing system, introduced in the Social Work (Scotland) Act 1968.

The core principle underpinning the system is 'needs not deeds' – in other words, decisions about children's welfare should be made on the basis of their best interests – their 'needs', and not on what they have done – their 'deeds' (Kilbrandon, 1964). This system replaced the concept of difference between, for example, children who commit offences and those who have been abused. The issue was not what had been done, but whether the child was 'in need of compulsory measures of care'. In viewing all dealings with children and young people in this way, Scotland moved away from the juvenile justice/child care divide which typifies nearly all other countries. Not only was the system revolutionary in philosophy, it was also innovative – indeed years ahead

Convention on the Rights of the Child	Another Kind of Home (Skinner, 1992)
• Protection from discrimination	• Individuality and development
• Protection of privacy	
• Action taken on the best interests of the child	• Child centred collaboration
• Right to freedom of expression and thought	• Rights and responsibilities
• Right to express an opinion	
• Protection of children without families	• Partnership with parents
• Appropriate care for children with special needs	
• Access to health care	• Health
• A decent standard of living	• Good basic care
• Access to education	• Education
• Right to cultural identity	
• Access to play and leisure provision	
• Protection from exploitation	• A feeling of safety
• Protection from torture and deprivation of liberty	
• Protection from abuse and neglect	

of its time – in terms of method. A Children's Hearing has a panel made up of three volunteer representatives of the local community, selected and trained for their role. The panel is guided by another individual, the Reporter, whose role is to oversee the process and advise the Panel on legal and procedural aspects. The Panel Hearing convenes with the child, parents and any other representative they wish to bring, along with the social worker. This whole group sits around a table and together discusses the situation for about forty-five minutes, after which the Panel makes a decision based on the welfare of the child. The Panel then explains this decision to the child and family, allowing them to give their views and advising them of what will happen next. In using this format, and stressing the centrality of the child, as part of their family, in this process, the system foreshadowed by around two decades some of the work currently being developed in the UK on Family Group Conferencing.

Thus, as early as 1968, Scotland had developed a system which ensured that the child's views were recognised as a significant part of the decision-making process about their future, allowing time for a full discussion with parents and child of

the circumstances surrounding the family and child's difficulties, and listening to their perspectives before drawing conclusions. It also attempted to ensure that decisions were made not solely by professionals distant from the actual situation, but by members of the local community. This was in some ways reflective of the cultural approach of the country over the preceding centuries, in involving the community, along with the family, in decision-making about the child's welfare. It was also predictive of the increasing emphasis on the rights of the child, developed in the following decades.

In order to achieve such a centrality of the needs and welfare of the child, a conscious choice was made to compromise some principles, in deference to the welfare of the child. For example, relaxation of the laws of evidence in the acceptance of a lesser standard of proof in care and protection cases, and in the general informality of the Hearing system. Recently, this has caused debate in terms of the European Convention on Human Rights, in respect of Articles 6 (right to a fair trial) and 8 (right to family life). These issues are currently under discussion, and certain modifications will be made to update the system to take account of these issues. However, it appears that radical change to the system will not be necessary because, in essence, it is in harmony with the principles of human rights embodied in the European Convention, given its welfare approach, and the emphasis placed on the importance of hearing the voice of the child and family.

Considering the research by Child Line, noted above (Morris, 1994), it is possible to see why the Children's Hearing system may have resulted in young people looked after by local authorities being more clear about why these decisions have been taken, and what their rights are. By being included in the decision-making process, and having their views sought, in a setting intended to be less threatening than a courtroom, the young people themselves are much more likely to understand what is going on. Almost as significantly, over the 30 years since the implementation of this system, the adults concerned have been forced to recognise that young people have views and should be consulted concerning the decisions being taken about their lives.

As with any system, as the years have passed, much has been learned about how the system works, and most importantly, how it is experienced by those involved, in particular the young people themselves. What has become clear is that young people still find these settings intimidating and as a result have difficulty in becoming genuinely involved in the decision-making process, for all the good intentions of the system and those operating it. This is a significant point. Even if systems and structures are designed to be child-friendly, more work is still necessary to ensure that the young people concerned can really experience them in this way. To be successful, this is best done by working directly with the young people themselves to understand what is causing the difficulty, and what can be done to improve the system, so that it can meet its original aims. One of the ways of enhancing the young people's experience of the Hearing system has been through the development of Children's Rights Officers posts.

Children's Rights Officers

The first council to introduce a Children's Rights Officer (CRO) in Scotland was the then Tayside Regional Council, who appointed a CRO in 1991. This post was originally designed to focus on the needs of young people leaving care in two of the council's residential units. Work centred on ensuring that the young care leavers had access to the welfare benefits to which they were entitled, and on developing a representative role on their behalf, in particular in relation to the Children's Hearings.

The lead set by Tayside was shortly followed by the then Strathclyde Regional Council. In response to the high profile abuse enquiries such as the 'Pindown' report (Levy and Kahan, 1991), Strathclyde's approach to children's rights was intended to be comprehensive with four main strands:

1. Funding was directed to Child Line in order to develop a children's telephone helpline for children in care. This was in recognition of the particular risks faced by these children, and the need to give them ready access to the telephone helpline, given that the main lines were often busy.
2. Funding was directed to the Scottish Child Law Centre, which supplied legal advice and consultation facilities for children and young people, and those working with them.
3. Two posts were funded at Who Cares? Scotland, the young people's organisation.
4. A Children's Rights Officer was appointed.

This latter post had a vast task, given that there was initially only one Officer in an area which stretched from remote islands to inner city areas, and contained nearly half the population of Scotland (2.5 million people), including several of its most deprived areas. The most important statistic at that time was that the number of children physically in the care of the local authority was 2,500. It took the newly appointed officer an entire year to conduct a visit to every child's home; and work with children in foster care was simply not possible. Inevitably, the work was reactive, responding to young people calling on a telephone helpline, and general educative work about children's rights. As many Children's Rights Officers (CROs) have found, in those early days, work was often met with hostility and suspicion by residential workers, and even managers, and moving to a more positive agenda was a key objective.

Both the number and the role of the CROs have altered in the intervening decade. In contrast to the one officer for the whole expanse of Strathclyde Region with its 2,500 children physically 'in care', the now reorganised council of South Lanarkshire has three officers for a 'looked after'[1] population of 250. This increase in ratio of CROs to young people has enabled the work to become less reactive, and more proactive. Workers aim to know all of the young people by name, and are able to anticipate issues and become involved early. There is much less use of the phone as the first point of contact, and the response of the staff to the involvement of the CRO is no longer defensive. As the role of CROs has developed, they have become perceived as helpful, and referrals to the CROs are now often suggested and encouraged by residential workers.

This change and development of the role of CROs has also enabled better interaction in South Lanarkshire Council between the rights of the young people themselves and the improvement of direct practice. This can be seen best in work done recently in South Lanarkshire on the use of physical restraint in children's homes. Recording of the detail of incidents, and the young people's views of them, has enabled a central collation of information, copies of which are sent to the CROs. Thus, with the involvement of the CROs, external managers have become equipped to discuss individual incidents with Children's Homes from an informed perspective, and changes in practice have

resulted, which have been welcomed by all concerned. In this local authority also, four weekly meetings between the CROs and the Director ensure that he is given independent information about the performance of his children's services which includes the young people's perspective. The role of the CRO has expanded in this council from the provision of a reactive advocacy and representation service to full-blown information, representation and education service, which creates conduits for young people's views and experience to be fed directly to managers and policy makers in a consistent fashion.

The representative role has also developed, and this can be seen in connection with the Children's Panel system. CROs now work closely with young people as their Hearings come up, ensuring that reports from the young person are included with those from the social worker and others, and going with the young person and their family to the Hearing, if wished. In this way, the forum offered by the Hearing system can be accessed by young people who are appropriately supported, so that they can ensure that their views are heard, understood, and taken account of in the decisions that will be made about their future. A key element in this development has been the partnership between the Children's Rights service and the young people's organisation, Who Cares? Scotland.

The role of Who Cares? Scotland

One of the key forces behind the advance of the children's rights agenda for children and young people looked after and accommodated has been the emergence and growth over the last two decades of Who Cares? Scotland. Who Cares? Scotland is an independent organisation, managed and staffed largely by young people with experience of the care system. For the first ten years of its life, Who Cares? Scotland operated on a totally voluntary basis, working as a collective advocacy service for young people living in residential care. Assisted by a cohort of adults willing to support but not to control, these young people began to work to influence the structures and power systems of Scottish social work, to ensure that the young people's voice was heard and their perspective taken into account. Initially, the organisation worked with groups of young people, increasing their understanding of their rights, and campaigning for changes in policy and practice to protect these rights. Gradually, their work paid off, and they became more and more influential at all levels in the Scottish child care system. One approach was to 'translate' documents out of official language into language accessible to young people, which then enabled Who Care? Scotland to obtain young people's views about the most complex issues, and feed these responses back into the system at high level. The fact that this work was largely carried out by young people themselves gave the organisation immense credibility with young people in the care system, but also with politicians, policy-makers, and professionals.

The effectiveness of their approach was amply demonstrated in their impact on the Children (Scotland) Act 1995 as it went through the various stages of the legislative process. The development of political impact was seen dramatically in the role Who Cares? Scotland took in the process of the Bill through government in Westminster of what is now the Children Scotland Act 1995. There was much joint work between voluntary agencies, in which Who Cares? Scotland took an active part. When documents appeared relating to the Bills as the process progressed, these were 'translated' by Who Cares? Scotland staff into more accessible language, and consultation processes with young people were set in motion. Thus, Who Cares? Scotland developed its position on the various aspects of the new Act, and lobbied the authorities, by travelling to London to communicate their views to the relevant people.

Since some decentralisation of government functions has been implemented and a Scottish Parliament established, life has become much easier. Now, a trip to Edinburgh can achieve the same or more significant impact than a trip to London. A recent debate in the Scottish Parliament about children in the care system, and in particular about changes to the support available to young people on leaving care, was attended by a large cohort of young people from Who Cares? Scotland, and frequent reference was made to them, and to the importance of listening thoroughly to their views, on the floor of the Chamber. Before the debate, much work had gone into briefing the Members of the Scottish Parliament (MSPs), of the various parties, on the Who Cares? Scotland position on the particular matter under debate. It is worth noting that, in this case, it was the MSPs who sought them out, rather than they who had to find ways to lobby.

Who Cares? Scotland has developed, in size, role and political significance, such that between 1998 and 2001, the number of the staff at Who Cares? Scotland increased from 13 to 28 – a dramatic expansion over a very short period. Twenty-three of these 28 staff are direct workers, visiting residential units on a regular basis, and a majority are young people who have had experience of the care system.

Who Cares? Scotland is funded from a mixture of sources, including central and local government. The recent expansion has resulted largely from the *Children's Safeguards Review* (Kent, 1997), which advised that increased representation for young people was essential if their rights are to be protected while they are living within the care system. One of the ways local authorities have found of doing this has been to fund workers at Who Cares? Scotland who will work with their peers providing advocacy and representation, as well as promoting their rights through education and campaigning. By January 2001, 29 of Scotland's 32 councils were directly funding such posts in Who Cares?

Scotland to provide advocacy and representation to the young people within their care, and certain independent organisations were also part-funding posts to provide the same service to the young people placed with them.

Who Cares? Scotland is managed by a Board of Directors, at least 50 per cent of whom are young people with experience of the care system. A National Forum, which meets twice each year, ensures that the Board reflects the current issues and views of young people, in addition to bi-monthly meetings in local areas and an annual conference. A magazine and a website also contribute to informing young people of their rights and of the role of Who Cares? Scotland. The organisation conducts regular consultations with young people on issues of importance, and the information so generated is fed back to local and national government. Different techniques are used to enable young people's voice to be heard, including those of children younger than 12 years. Experience has shown that the best information and empowerment of young people comes not from using direct discussion-based, committee-type structures. The use of drama, music, and art, alongside the skill of workers experienced in Who Cares? Scotland's philosophies, has resulted over the years in a very powerful lobbying system which has affected policies on major and minor issues.

Who Cares? Scotland is also represented as one of the five managing partners of the Scottish Institute for Residential Child Care. The Institute was established to transform the training and qualifications for residential workers. A Young People's Forum is being developed by an Institute-funded staff member at Who Cares? Scotland to advise on all aspects of the Institute's work, and to ensure that all training materials are designed with the young people's views at their heart. This forum has a regular membership of about twenty young people and is seeking to expand. The young people have considered issues as diverse as legal representation in panels, the right of young

pregnant women to remain in their own children's unit, education, mental health and improving the allowances available to young people. They have been involved in developing a training video for new workers which is now used widely across Scotland. The forum gives the young people the opportunity to raise their own concerns and provides a further mechanism for establishing a coherent national voice for looked after young people that will directly affect the priorities and focus of the new Institute.

It is hardly possible to overestimate the significance of Who Cares? Scotland in protecting and promoting the rights of children and young people living within the care system. That such a powerful and effective advocacy organisation has been able to sustain such a rapid expansion begs questions as to why this has not happened in other countries, particularly those within the United Kingdom and the Republic of Ireland. Certainly, the small size of the country – population five and a half million – has contributed to this, but this is offset to some extent by the difficulties of remoteness of some of the centres of population. Although Scotland has only around one tenth of the population of the United Kingdom, it has almost one third of the land mass. Furthermore, Wales and Northern Ireland are more compact geographically and have smaller populations, yet neither have young people's advocacy organisations which have developed this degree of influence. The same applies to the Republic of Ireland, also a country with a relatively small population.

A key factor that has helped Who Cares? Scotland's development has been the degree of support and commitment it has consistently received from government. The former Scottish Office and the present Scottish Executive have been committed to the development of a powerful young people's organisation, and have shown this commitment by both funding and using Who Cares? Scotland to influence policy development and implementation. Additionally, it might be surmised that the climate created by the Children's Hearing system has allowed the realisation to dawn amongst adults, including social work professionals, which young people are willing and able to become involved in planning their own futures, and that enabling them to do so more easily will be positive for all concerned.

Whatever the reasons, Who Cares? Scotland is almost unique world-wide in terms of its power and effectiveness. It is easy to believe that such a significant organisation, devoted to promoting young people's rights would have increased the young people's understanding of their position and enabled them to become more fully empowered, thus adding another explanation for the Child Line findings (Morris, 1994) noted above. Further evidence in support of the fact that Scottish young people living within the care system have a better understanding of their rights and reasons for being 'in care' was supplied by European research conducted in 1998.

The young people's voice

Internationally there is growing emphasis on ensuring that young people know what to do if their rights are infringed, and an increasingly heated debate about whether or not rights should be balanced against matching responsibilities. But all of this will be affected by how children define the concept of a 'right'. Defining a 'right' is no easy matter. It tends to be dealt with by listing those things which are considered to be 'rights', which is a somewhat circular approach. What is clear is that if adults struggle to understand clearly what it is to have 'rights' – what this actually means – then it is not surprising that children will find it at least as difficult. It is also reasonable to assume that culture may make a difference, not only to what is defined as a 'right', but also to how the concept of 'rights' is defined. Such meanings are important, because they affect how members of staff are to be trained, what issues are regarded as legitimate for complaints about infringement of rights, and so forth.

Consideration of the rights of children has seldom included researching how children themselves understand this concept. *Care to Listen?* showed, albeit on a small scale, some elements of international differences in how children and young people in residential care understood and recognised their rights. It also provided ideas on how the issue of rights is perceived by young people in general, and it allows some partial comparison of children and young people of different nationalities, and who are living within different systems. The table below shows the results given in response to the question 'How well are your opinions listened to?' Clearly, Scottish children were much more confident that this was the case, although of course the sample is small.

An opportunity to look at these issues was provided in 1998, when EUROARRCC (the European Association for Research into Residential Child Care) conducted a major comparative study of residential child care in Finland, Ireland, Scotland and Spain. This involved the creation of a picture of

Table 1. How well are your opinions listened to?

	Finland	Ireland	Scotland	Spain	Total
Very satisfied – listened to all the time	4	3	12	2	21
Satisfied – listened to most of the time	11	3	2	5	21
Neutral – listened to some of the time	2	1	3	7	13
Dissatisfied – not listened to most of the time	1	5	1	1	8
Very dissatisfied – never listened to	1	2	1	2	6

residential child care in the four countries, including history and statistics. Direct information about the young people was obtained via 200 Child Behavioural Checklists (Achenbach, 1991), 78 interviews with the young people (twenty in each country), and individual and group interviews with around 80 managers, policy makers and staff. The resultant report, *Care to Listen? A Report on Residential Child Care in Four European Countries* (EUROARRCC, 1998), ended with recommendations to the European Union for further progress.

The interviews with the young people contained questions relating to rights, and provides an interesting slant on the issues discussed in this chapter. The young people were all living in residential settings, and were aged between 12 and 18 years old. The interviews were conducted using a semi-structured format, with a questionnaire which had been designed in Scotland by a young person who herself had experience of residential care. Questions ranged over the eight quality principles identified in *Another Kind of Home* (Skinner, 1992):

- individuality and development
- rights
- good basic care
- health
- education
- child-centred collaboration
- partnership with parents
- a feeling of safety

The young people's responses concerning rights were particularly interesting. Most of them – 50 out of the 78 interviewed – had access to some document which told them about rights and responsibilities. Most seemed confident that they knew what a 'right' and a 'responsibility' were. Sixty-three (81 per cent) felt that they knew what a right was, and even more – 71 (91 per cent) – that they knew what a responsibility was. However, their definitions varied, and this seemed to be partly a factor of their country, or perhaps of the documents available to them.

The various concepts of 'rights' given by respondents included:

- 'Things you are allowed to do.'
- 'Freedom of speech and thought'.
- 'The ability of a person to do what they want to do and how they want to do it' (Irish girl).
- 'You can say what you want to say. You have a right to an opinion' (Scottish boy).

In general, Finnish and Irish young people described rights in terms of the former, whereas Scottish young people tended to define them in terms of the latter. Spanish young people seemed on the whole less clear: 'Something that belongs to you' (Spanish girl).

'Responsibility' was also interpreted differently by the children from the four countries. Irish young people, in particular, saw responsibility in terms of care for others, whereas Spanish and Finnish young people emphasised the actions one was expected to carry out, and the Scots stressed taking responsibility for one's own actions:

- 'To take care of your little brother, or to keep the house tidy' (Spanish boy).
- 'If I do something wrong, it's my problem' (Irish boy).
- 'What must be done, what I am expected to do' (Finnish boy).
- 'Everything is on your shoulders' (Scottish boy).

These are important findings. If children understand the concept of rights in a particular way, that will define what they regard as an infringement, and determine how they use any system which is devised to protect their rights.

The majority of the young people (42–54 per cent) did not feel their rights were being denied, but a sizeable minority (29–37 per cent) felt otherwise. The reasons given by young people who did feel their rights were being denied were mainly in terms of loss of freedom. If the young people felt their rights were being denied, they stated that they would be most likely to tell residential staff – 49 (63 per cent) of the young people would use this route. The significance of the role of residential staff in both defining and protecting young people's rights is thus seen as crucial. It may be assumed that staff will also tend to define the concept of rights in terms of their cultural background. Therefore, it is important to ensure that staffs are well trained, and enabled to think through the issue.

These findings show that it is important to ensure clarity of thinking about what a 'right' actually is, and to give young people space to explore the concept itself before moving to issues of protection of rights or definitions of the content of rights documents.

Conclusion

The development of the children's rights agenda in any country will depend on a range of factors, including cultural backdrop, governmental commitment, co-operation between existing institutions, and an environment that allows for the development of new organisations. Some of these factors have been present in Scotland, as we have demonstrated above. The Scottish cultural backdrop, which had elements of a community approach, was inherent in 1968 legislation for Children's Hearings. This significant 1968 law forced a concentration on seeing children's needs in a more holistic light, which included a stress on the need to hear the child's view, and to involve them (along with their families and communities) in decision-making about their own futures. Existing institutions, in the shape of local authorities, then took the situation forward through the development of the role of the Children's Rights Officer. Meanwhile, the young people themselves began to obtain and use power to make their own voice heard through a powerful self and collective advocacy organisation – Who Cares? Scotland. This would not have been possible, however, if the adults in government, both national and local, had not generally welcomed and encouraged this development. Hence, research by Child Line and by EUROARRCC demonstrates some small but discernible difference

between the experiences of young people in care in Scotland and those in other countries.

There is much still to be done, and individual children and young people in residential care still find their rights poorly understood and even less recognised by those who care for them. Nonetheless, we are beginning to find ways of genuinely including young people in the power structures within many of the organisations most concerned with their lives.

Taken together, these have contributed towards the development of a climate that has enabled children and young people who live in state care to be centrally involved, not only in protecting and enhancing their own rights to, for example, participate in decision-making which effects them individually, but also in significantly progressing the agenda for many other children and young people in similar circumstances, living in Scotland and elsewhere.

Acknowledgements

Thanks are due to many people for the information contained in this chapter, in particular:

Alison Shearer, Children's Rights Officer, South Lanarkshire Council.

Charlie Mathers, Children's Rights Officer, Dundee Council.

Deirdre Watson and Stephen Paterson, Who Cares? Scotland.

Note

1   The term 'looked after', that is, 'looked after by the local authority', has formally replaced the phrase 'in care' of the local authority, although the terms 'in care' and 'care' continue to be used.

References

Achenbach, T.M. (1991) *Manual for the Child Behaviour Checklist and 1991 Profile.* Burlington, VT, University of Vermont, Department of Psychiatry.

Chakrabarti, M. (1998) *Valuing Diversity: Having Regard to the Racial, Religious, Cultural and Linguistic Needs of Scotland's Children*. Edinburgh, Social Work Services Inspectorate, Stationery Office.

Children (Scotland) Act 1995. Edinburgh, HMSO.

EUROARRCC (1998) *Care to Listen? A Report on Residential Child Care in Four European Countries*. Glasgow, Centre for Residential Child Care.

Kent, R. (1997) *Children's Safeguards Review Edinburgh*. Stationery Office, SWSIS Scottish Office.

Kilbrandon, Lord C.J.D. (1964) *The Kilbrandon Report: Children and Young Persons Scotland*. Edinburgh: HMSO.

Levy, A. and Kahan, B. (1991) *The Pindown Experience and the Protection of Children: Report of the Staffordshire Child Care Enquiry*. Staffordshire, Staffordshire County Council.

Marshall, K., Jamieson, C. and Finlayson, A. (1999) *Edinburgh's Children: The Report of the Edinburgh Inquiry Into Abuse and Protection of Children in Care*. Edinburgh, City of Edinburgh Council.

Morris, S., Wheatley, H. and Lees, B. (Eds.) (1994) *Time to Listen: The Experiences of Children in Residential and Foster Care*. London, Childline.

Skinner, A. (1992) *Another Kind of Home: A Review of Residential Child Care*. Edinburgh, Scottish Office

Social Work (Scotland) Act 1968. Edinburgh, HMSO.

United Nations, Children's Rights Development Unit, UNICEF (1990) *United Nations Convention on the Rights of the Child*. London. United Nations and UNICEF.

Utting, Sir W. (1997) *People Like Us: The Report of the Review of the Safeguards for Children Living Away From Home*. London, Stationery Office.

Waterhouse, R. (2000) *Lost in Care: Report of the Tribunal of Inquiry Into the Abuse of Children in Care in the Former County Council Areas of Gwynedd and Clwyd Since 1974*. London, Stationery Office.

CHAPTER 7

Beyond Rhetoric in the Search for Participation in Youth Work in Wales

Bert Jones

> *. . . to alienate men from their own decision-making is to change them into objects.*
> (Freire, 1972).

In July 1997 the British Government published *A Voice for Wales*, a White Paper that outlined proposals for devolution for Wales. Following the referendum in September 1997, the National Assembly for Wales, now the Welsh Assembly Government (WAG), began to govern Wales. It has limited legal powers but the potential to bring change to the social and educational profile of its population. In services and public provision for young people its influence could be profound. The metamorphosis of youth service practice and provision began to accelerate, to a point where it became distinct from 'the service' in England, and elsewhere in the UK. While services to young people in England moved towards the advocacy model of Connexions, the Wales Youth Agency led the push from youth workers to create a uniquely Welsh model of practice. Within that model, the seeds of a more dynamic approach to the empowerment and participation of young people took root.

A Curriculum Statement for Youth Work was in place from 1995, couched in the rhetoric of its four pillars of *Empowerment, Education, Expression and Participation*. The statement was revised in 2002, retaining its key pillars. At its relaunch in May 2002, the Minister for Life Long Learning in Wales reiterated government commitment to those pillars. A 'New Wales' offered the promise to turn the rhetoric into reality, that young people would become truly 'empowered'. Difficulties in meaningful participation are already emerging however, and sustainability is known to have been a problem in the past.

This chapter will outline the history of youth work in Wales, and especially the debate around participation. Recent developments in youth work, linked to devolution, are examined, especially the Young Voice, Youth Forums and the idea of Youth Charters.

Youth work in Wales

The values of participation, empowerment and democracy are embedded both within the jigsaw of government policies for young people in Wales, and in the responses from those who work with and for them. The rhetoric rings around Wales, encouraging the believers and perhaps persuading the hesitant to implement the ideas in practice, but both are cautious about the reality of education systems in Wales. Half-explained and half-understood concepts have hovered over youth work in Wales since Circular 1486 was issued in November 1939 (see Albemarle, 1960). These concepts take on new meanings as the economic and social landscape changes in Wales.

Added to the opaqueness of these ideas is the diversity of youth organisations that make up the patchwork of provision in Wales. Some emerged from social movements in the 1920s, ready to defend a notion of Welsh culture, others originated in the industrial and social unrest of the emerging twentieth century. Driven by contrasting opinions on the nature and purpose of youth work, youth organisations each developed their own style of relationships with young people. In much of the voluntary sector, the purpose was often clear and articulate. But the maintained or statutory provision responded to government dictate, expressed in terms of education, welfare, moral, spiritual and social education (with a little touch of social control!).

On the whole, the statutory youth service in Wales responded to the policy and developments that emerged from Circular 1486. What happened in the English Youth Service eventually affected Wales. Recommendations that emerged from reports, the administrative systems, programmes, funding ratios and conditions of employment for youth workers, were fundamentally the same. In structural terms, youth services in both the voluntary and the statutory sector were essentially the same in England and Wales. The Albemarle Report (1960) attempted to find a distinction by offering a section on the 'Youth Service in Wales'.

The movement towards an autonomous and discrete Youth Service in Wales developed some impetus in January 1981, when the Secretary of State for Education and Science set up a review of the Youth Service in England (Thompson Report, 1982). In Wales there was little response to the report, although some local authorities implemented some of the recommendations. Only in the area of the endorsement of professional initial training and in-service training did the report impact upon Wales, leading eventually to the establishment of the Education and Standards Panel (ETS) in 1993–5. The report signalled the break away of Wales from youth work policy decisions emanating from the Westminster Government, and from the prescriptions of the National Youth Agency in Leicester, England.

Following the Thompson Report (in November 1982), a Welsh Office conference , reviewed youth work in Wales, focussing on issues including inter-agency training, resource sharing, identification of youth work priorities, and the promotion of active participation of young people in decision-making. Delegates at the conference prioritised a need for a lead to be taken '. . . from a central body which would assist the Youth Service to clarify its educational objectives, rekindle its zeal and improve its image' (Welsh Office, 1983).

In 1985 the Youth Work Partnership for Wales was established and given a mandate to serve as a designated Wales Youth Service. The co-ordination of youth service affairs in Wales took its first hesitant steps, not without the difficulties of facing up to the diverse nature of youth work organisations in Wales, each long entrenched in individual perspectives. The dichotomy between the voluntary sector and the 'maintained youth service' had in-built tensions which often prevented collaborative approaches to developmental youth provision. As Wales moves into a new era of youth work, the tensions still exist. Early experiences with the Partnership laid the foundations for the Wales Youth Agency founded in 1992. Staffing of the new Agency included an identified post servicing the voluntary sector, representing the Council for Wales of Voluntary Youth Service. Differences and tensions between the two sectors have implications for the implementation and practice of the participation and empowerment strategies implicit in the Curriculum Statement for Wales.

Developing participation in Wales

Since the 1944 Education Act, the Youth Service in Wales reacted to the policies emanating from Westminster, and reports initiated by the National Youth Agency. Most often changes went unquestioned. After the Milson/Fairbairn report (1969), the Youth Service in Wales fell into line by becoming a 'Youth and Community Service'. But, as elsewhere, youth work in Wales paid only passing attention to the ideas and values woven into the pages of Circular 1486 (1939), the Albemarle Report (1960), the Milson/Fairbairn Report (1969), and the Thompson Report (1982).

Even the specifically Welsh commissioned reports on Youth Service provision in Wales, (DES, 1984) and the Coopers and Lybrand Deloitte Report (1992) were given only passing reference. Both reports made strong recommendations for the active participation of young people in decision-making, replicating a recommendation from the Thompson Report (1982) that young people should have the 'final say' in running organisations that were essentially theirs. The Coopers and Lybrand Deloitte Report claimed that '. . . at the heart of our approach is a county forum, with a balanced representation from the maintained and voluntary sector – to define the framework for youth provision (and participation) in each county' (Paragraph 10). The Report was largely ignored, and in some areas actively disparaged. The rhetoric of 'participation' resonated through so many reports, offering great debate and reasons for training workshops, but in reality evidence from practice was limited.

Youth Councils

The Welsh Office Conference of 1982 emphasised the participation of young people, as a priority practice in youth work. Over forty years earlier, in 1939, Circular 1486 advocated:

> . . . *that in order to ensure that free and direct expression might be given to the views of youth, it might be desirable for some representation on the 'proposed' Local Youth Committees to be given to young people of both sexes, not necessarily connected with any particular youth organisation.*

This view was re-emphasised in a 1943 White Paper *Education Reconstruction*, which made particular reference to youth parliaments and youth councils so that 'young workers' point of view can be expressed and passed up to the Authorities'. In the period 1946–49 over 240 Youth Councils were identified across the UK. In Wales responses came mainly from the

Voluntary Sector, in particular the Welsh Association of Youth Clubs (WAYC). Even in 1936 the WAYC strongly encouraged the establishment of 'Youth Committees' (Frost, 1984), and encouraged by this lead, there were twelve operative Youth Councils in Wales in 1949. A feature of their activities was an involvement in community service and projects involving a high degree of meaningful decision-making. It was apparent that experience in these councils contributed to the enhancement of self-confidence among young people: 'many members eventually undertook training to become professionally qualified youth workers' (Frost, 1984).

But these initiatives fell victim to the problem of sustainability, experienced by many youth workers in attempts to set up committees of young people. The expansion of Youth Councils in the late 1940s soon declined, 'few survived for long!' (Davies, 1999). Only three Youth Councils in Wales survived from the late 1940s: Newport Young People's Council, Guides Cymru llais y Ddraig, and the WAYC Members Council (DES, 1984). The 1984 report rather pessimistically came to the conclusion that 'the worth of member's committees must be doubted'.

The New Wales and participation

Interest in participation and empowerment gathered pace in the first years of the new administration in Wales. For some, the catalyst lay in the revelations from the North Wales Child Abuse Trials in the 1990s (see Waterhouse, 2000), which raised concerns about the vulnerability of young people at risk and their inability to find opportunities to 'be heard'. Such concerns were expressed in the context of the United Nations Convention on the Rights of the Child, particularly Article 12. Recent papers in Wales on participation and empowerment make key reference to Article 12. Treseder (1997) suggests that Article 12 is the 'most significant and far-reaching principle' for young people to express opinions and to be part of the decision-making process. In Treseder's view the emphasis of participation should be on young people most at risk within families and communities, and whose lives have been most damaged in terms of personal and social growth. This approach contributed to the appointment of a Childrens' Commissioner for Wales in 2002, characterised by the well-publicised involvement of young people in the appointing process.

A political initiative

The political intervention encouraging participatory democracy in work with young people gathered momentum in 1998 when Peter Hain, Welsh Office Minister, brought together a group of youth workers for consultation. A main focus was a proposal for increasing the active participation of young people in 'the political life of Wales'. Proposals arising from the seminar included a call to establish a 'youth parliament' in Wales, and for the adoption of a Charter for Young People. Despite opposition from the political hierarchy towards a 'parliament', the seeds were sewn for an embryonic 'Council of Young People for Wales'. In 2000, the commitment shown by Hain became embedded in the political framework of Wales, with a pledge by the then First Secretary, Alun Michael, that the new government would address the real current needs of young people and listen to their views.

Llais Ifranc – Young Voice

Outcomes from Hains' initiative became part of the work-programme of the Wales Youth Agency, under the direction of Wayne David, some-time member of the European Parliament. He found influential support within the Welsh Assembly Government for the establishment of a representative body of young people, to be called Llais Ifanc or

Young Voice. From January to July 2000 the foundation was laid, and constitutional links negotiated with national and regional government in Wales. The inaugural Conference of Young Voice or Llais Ifanc took place on 7th July 2000, the grounding for a future where young people would be part of democratic decision-making. However, it was not until January 2002 that a formal recognition of Young Voice's place in the system was publicly announced:

> ... the Assembly proposes to support the development of a representative body for the whole of Wales, entitled Llais Ifanc or Young Voice, made up of representatives from local children and young people Forums, and National and local peer-led groups.
> (WAG, 2002).

Youth Policy

Responsibility for youth policy in Wales is shared across two civil service Divisions, with different Ministers, so there is potential for some confusion in terms of clarification of aims, objectives and purpose. The two Divisions are 'Life Long Learning/Youth Policy' and 'Children and Families'. They have separate areas of responsibility, sometimes overlapping, but kept distinct by discrete objectives. The latter division has concern for children at risk within a social work context. The target groups are different from a traditional youth work profile of working with the disaffected, homeless and those alienated from society.

The Youth Policy Unit of the Welsh Assembly Government makes a financial contribution to this participation initiative, but has limited say in its development. The Children and Families Division of the Welsh Assembly Government has administrative and developmental responsibilities for Llais Ifanc or Young Voice. Most declarations on young people and decision-making emanate from this Division. *Moving Forward* (WAG, 2002) expresses the importance of 'developing the participation of young people across Wales'. The paper commends the Assembly for 'establishing (Young Voice) a clear, productive and sustainable dialogue with the young people of Wales.'

In explaining their vision for Llais Ifanc or Young Voice, the Assembly refers to the aim of broadening citizenship and participation objectives through the strengthening of local youth councils and school-based councils. This vision could embrace the majority of the 338,000 young people aged 13–19 years in Wales, who come within the target group for voluntary and statutory youth services. Young people in care have specific needs requiring a discrete approach, wherein Article 12 is important and the need to 'be heard' is a significant issue.

In June 2002 the Llais Ifanc or Young Voice was faced with a problem over its 'name', and became 'Funky Dragon' (another organisation in England had registered as 'Young Voice'), developing the 'Funky Dragon' web site (www.funkydragon.co.uk). Funky Dragon appears to identify young people only from established Youth Forums, and so its growth is linked to those initiatives. By March 2003 the Wales Youth Agency had registered 171 individuals or youth groups prepared to develop Youth Forums. The total number of young people involved in Youth Forums is vague, but the vision of WAG is to create School Councils in every school in Wales.

These organisations need to be inclusive of all young people of Wales, so that access to national representative groups such as the UK Youth Parliament is open to all and not just to nominated delegates. The embryonic period of 'Funky Dragon' should develop a structure that requires affiliation before an individual can bid for delegate status to the UK Youth Parliament. The spirit of democracy must allow others to be part of any decision-making that affects the life of young people in Wales: otherwise surely Funky Dragon will itself receive challenges from a new generation of politically aware young people.

Extending entitlement – responsibilities for local government

An Advisory Group appointed by the Assembly was commissioned to produce a study to provide evidence and recommendations to support provision for young people that would:

- *Enthuse young people to seize opportunity for learning.*
- *Ensure that all services on offer to young people are of high quality.*
- *Promote equal opportunities.*

(WAG, 2000).

The final report (WAG, 2000) has had a profound influence on the Youth Service in Wales, and is considered as the 'blueprint' for future provision offered through voluntary youth organisations and local government. Publication in July 2000 was followed by a series of National and Regional Conferences, a consultation exercise, and the appointment of a lead officer in the Youth Policy Division to implement the recommendations across Wales.

A dominant theme of the Report was capacity building of young people, so that they can develop independence, make choices and share in the democratic process. The Report recommended that local authorities set up Youth Fora to enable young people to 'develop their decision-making skills, articulate their views and present them effectively to others' and called upon Local Authorities in Wales to:

> . . . set up partnerships (consisting of all local organisations working with young people) to be responsible for reviewing and developing services for the entire cohort of young people in their area. Young people should contribute to the design of the strategy and to monitor its effectiveness.
>
> (WAG, 2000).

The ideology of young people's involvement in strategic decision-making was built into the report's methodology. Efforts were made to include opinions from 'a representative sample of young people drawn from a range of social backgrounds and physical locations across Wales', through focus groups of young people led by a youth worker. However, the report admits to a 'limited number of responses received', and advises that 'caution must be exercised in drawing conclusions about the views of young people in Wales generally.'

Seventeen Focus Groups were assembled, which represented a variety of youth work:

- Seven from youth organisations that dealt with young people within social work provision.
- Three from 'referral units', that identified negative school or work-related behaviour problems.
- Two from ethnic minority backgrounds.
- One comprised 'A-level students'.
- One was identified as 'a welsh-speaking group'.
- Three were not categorised.

Since over 60 per cent of the sample were 'referred' or within the social work target area, it would seem to be a contradiction to claim that: 'as wide a cross section of children as possible should have the opportunity to contribute' (WAG, 2001).

The Entitlement Report (WAG, 2000) led to three important developments:

- The Chief Executive of each Local Authority in Wales to be responsible for setting up 'local youth partnerships' and to encourage the formation of Youth Forums. A directive to be supported by appropriate funding.
- The appointment of a Youth Forum Development Officer at The Wales Youth Agency.
- Re-organisation of the Youth Policy Division within the Welsh Assembly Government and the appointment of a Senior Civil Servant/Officer with the responsibility of implementing the recommendations of the Entitlement Report.

In addition, each of the 22 unitary authorities of Wales were required to establish Young People's Partnerships (YPPs). The YPPs were to comprise a range of professional and interested workers-with-young-people to co-ordinate quality services for young people in their area. By the end of 2002 most Partnerships were in place. The Chief Executives of Unitary Authorities had responsibilty for the YPPs, but with control varying across professional groupings from social workers to careers officers. Holmes (2003) expressed concern that local authority youth service was not guaranteed representation, and only in three YPPs were corporate managers for youth service included. The marginalisation of youth services, was made more evident in a consultative document in October 2002 (WAG, 2002a) advocating the establishment of '14–19' Networks in each Unitary Authority as part of The Life Long Learning agenda. Conflict with the Young People's Partnerships seems inevitable, and the lack of a collective voice for youth workers in Wales exacerbates the promotion of participation and the empowerment of young people.

Youth Forums

By July 2002 all local authorities in Wales had set up 'Youth Forum', some run by voluntary organisations, others within social services, and the majority by the local authority youth service. One forum, the Vale of Glamorgan, has registered as a charity. Other all-Wales Youth Forums include the Boys and Girls Club of Wales, Lesbian and Gay/Bi-sexual Forum, Royal Society for the Protection of Birds, St John's Ambulance, Raleigh International, Scouts, the Urdd Gobiath Cymru, Wales Council for the Blind, and the Development of Rural Youth Work. The pace of development has been rapid, raising questions about the rigour of the planning, the quality of standards and format of practice. Many new appointments of 'Forum Workers' have been made, mostly of unqualified individuals, with little induction or preparatory training.

The potential of the Fora is so important that careful planning and training should have been a prerequisite in establishing the network. The implications for existing youth work provision are profound, where the practice of 'participation' should be inherent in daily work with young people. However, perspectives on progress towards the active involvement of young people in decision-making, are mixed. These are early days for the 'New Youth Forum' initiatives but the Welsh Assembly Government has promised a 'monitoring of outcomes' to interpret young people's participation in education, training and employment (WAG, 2002b). The Institute for Public Policy Research (Combe, 2002) in examining the growth of 'youth involvement work' in England laments the lack of evaluation. With this point in mind the National Youth Agency of England published a set of standards to measure progress in youth involvement (Wade et al., 2001). In Wales the research has not yet been completed, though a commitment has been made by the Youth Policy Unit to make data available by March 2004. Support networks have been set up at Regional and National levels by Youth Forum Workers under the leadership for the Wales Youth Agency.

Youth Charters

The idea of a 'Youth Charter' is not new. In January 1977 youth workers, policy makers, administrators and others gathered in London to produce 'Youth Charter towards 2000'. The aim was to ensure a charter with an 'extensive partnership with young people in the youth service' (Davies, 1999). The highlight was when a young man jumped onto the stage, took hold of the microphone and berated the audience for their failure to formally invite any young people to the conference. Despite active lobbying of Parliament in 1979, '. . . The Charter initiative all but disappeared within a few days' (Davies, 1999).

Charters for young people in Wales are developing. For example, in The Vale of Glamorgan, demands include political rights for young people, equal pay for equal work, minimum wage levels for young people, benefit rights, free education and comprehensive health care. These demands for 'political rights' reflect the earlier proposals for young people to be 'politically educated' in Milsom/Fairbairn (1969).

Political participation

Participation and empowerment of young people in Wales took on a new hope when Lembit Optik, Liberal Democrat MP for Mid Wales, proposed that 'the policy of the Liberal Democratic Party is that we lower the age of voting to 16' a declaration repeated by the New Labour Party of the Welsh Assembly Government in July 2002. Optik suggested that a 'process of social engineering' would achieve this. Thus, the implementation of meaningful power in decision-making among young people, for long inhibited by the reluctance of face-to-face youth workers to struggle against complex restraints, might eventually result from direct government policy and require action from local government authorities in Wales.

A more cynical view might suggest these initiatives were blatantly political, a tactic to engage young people in the electoral process following concern that, according to a Mori research exercise, only 39 per cent of the 18–24 year old group voted at the previous election (May 1999). An alternative view might hold that the interest in peer-led education in the early 1990s, and the setting up of Youth Link Wales, an organisation to promote peer-led activities, caught the interest of the policy makers.

Barriers and constraints to participation

A growing impetus towards participatory approaches with young people in Wales requires consideration of barriers and constraints to success. Problems identified in England include:

- Disengagement of young people.
- Glorified focus groups with no real decision making.
- Adult 'distrust' towards young people.
- Short lived enthusiastic groups (sustainability).
- Too much emphasis on schools, and a failure to reach the 'unattached'.
- Adults reluctant to give up power.
- Challenging the status quo.

(Klaushofer, 2002).

These problems are familiar to the history of youth participation and power sharing in Wales. The inspection of the Youth Service in Wales in 1984 emphasised that 'deep seated problems must be recognised before real progress can be made' (DES, 1984). Retaining the interest of young people in the process of decision-making is recognised as a problem. A survey of youth workers conducted by the National Youth Agency recorded views that young people were:

- 'not interested'
- 'not capable of taking the responsibility'
- 'not to be trusted'

The lack of sustained interest by young people might be claimed as a result of negative experiences arising from tokenism (Arnstein, 1969). Most young people have limited experience of being consulted and heard. Giving young people real experiences in decision-making, with real outcomes, might redress these barriers. But given deep-seated problems within the total educational experiences of young people, youth workers find it difficult to be optimistic about possibilities for participation and empowerment in their work with young people. Rhetoric needs to be understood against the realities that impinge upon the life experiences of young people at school, at work and within the wider community network of traditional social and legal constraints.

> ... youth workers when faced with the challenges of participation and empowerment develop a glazed look and feel overwhelmed by the task. What is particularly

> damaging in this respect is that managers within the service may have to collude in acknowledging a credibility gap between the rhetoric and practice, which creates a situation where the stated objectives of the service are 'understood' to be ideals, but which will only apply intermittently in actual practice. This helps no one.

(Baker, 1996).

The reluctance or uncertainty of youth workers to engage in meaningful participation and empowerment practices was recognised in an earlier survey, in that 'power-sharing models of practice do not permeate practice to the extent popularily imagined' (DES, 1984). There is evidence that some organisations express a commitment to participation that, in practice, would not pass close scrutiny. The survey records the practice of Youth Centre Committees as being constrained and controlled by youth workers, with no member's committees having the 'final say' in decision-making, a model of 'tokenism' not unfamiliar within youth work practice in Wales.

In the 1980s and early 1990s participation and empowerment in terms of the Thompson Reports' recommendations that 'young people should be running organisations which are claimed to be theirs' was driven by an enthusiastic minority in Wales. For example, a small cohort of youth workers set up the South Glamorgan Participation Association. Their frustration in turning the rhetoric to reality is explicit in the Association's Newsletter in January 1987:

> ... opportunities for this kind of participation [i.e. full part in decision making and organising activities] are limited by youth workers who consciously or unconsciously, are reluctant to entrust them with powers which might be abused or misunderstood. Any delegation of responsibility and decision-making means a reduction of control and the risk of things going wrong ... perhaps badly wrong. The youth workers' constant dilemma is to judge the extent to

which power can pass to the members with-out inviting unacceptable risks. The youth worker must be aware of the tension between the need to ensure that the conduct of the youth club and its members is acceptable to the management, be it the LEA or a Volunt-ary Organisation, to parents and the com-munity at large.

(Jones, 1987).

Progressive approaches to educating young people have always attracted hostility. Attempts to make people conscious (Freire, 1972) of their rights and freedoms have been interpreted as systems-disturbing. Contemporary anecdotal evidence from young people and youth workers clearly reflects the denial of rights for young people, where their subordination is expressed in the structural ethos of the youth organisation, or the school. A youth organisation of the Rhondda Valley, funded by the Children and Youth partnership, an initiative of the Welsh Assembly Government, actively discourages 'troublesome' young people coming onto their premises; even the youth worker assigned to the group feels uncomfortable in using the facility. In 1998, a group of young members of the WAYC, average age 17 years, complained that their youth worker had purchased a computer for their club, but had decided to keep it at home because it would be damaged at the club. The matter was pursued through various channels, until finally the adult Management Committee of the club supported the leader. At a large comprehensive school, toilets are locked for most of the day for fear of damage and graffiti, and a school locker system was abandoned for the same reasons; prospective parents are on record in deciding to send their children to other schools because of these circumstances. Encouraged by the call for the empowerment of young people, pupils in a number of Welsh Schools in Wales staged demonstrations against the Iraq War. For their efforts, many were excluded from their school.

Yet the caution of the youth workers can be appreciated, because some constraints are hard to challenge: 'it is difficult to establish representative democracy in youth *organisations*' (DES, 1987). Davies (1999), comments that 'it is difficult to see how it could be made to work' when considering the constraints of 'school regimes' and imposed rules of conduct applied to formal education, reiterating a point made by Milsom/Fairbairn (1969). School regimes are significant because the majority of young people who engage with the Youth Service in Wales are still at school and under 14 years of age. In 1984 it was noted that the majority of members of one of the largest Voluntary Youth Organisations in Wales were based in primary schools' (DES, 1984).

At this time, there were limited examples of real participation in Wales, with some exceptions, including the Young Farmers Organisation where membership was participative at all levels of activity. It was suggested that the young farmers were able to give control to members because they, like other voluntary organisations, were unencumbered by the controls imposed by local government administration. A research project funded by the WAYC in 1992 offered yet another pessimistic outlook on democratic participation in youth clubs. The research gathered data from 83 youth work-units across Wales representing the opinions of over 400 young people. From the range of experiences available in youth clubs, being involved in 'a youth centre committee' was the most unpopular. Less than 10 per cent registered any interest in taking responsibility for planning or organisation in the 'club'. The failure to implement the practice of participation and empowerment may result partly from the veto imposed by responsible 'officers', described as 'the usual kind of adult suspects' (Davies, 1999).

Current participation issues in Wales

It is impossible to ascribe a simple cause to these historical failures to enable young people to participate. Any explanation is complicated by the diversity of 'youth organisations' in Wales, and the far-ranging differentials in 'age-groupings' that constitute declared membership. The very concept of 'membership' is questionable, because of the way data is collected. There are approximately 338,000 young people in Wales aged 13–19 years (WAG, 2002c), and it is suggested that '90 per cent of young people come into contact with the statutory or voluntary youth service'. This claim is not without its critics, since on the ground evidence and small scale research (Jones, 2000) suggests that it is a minority of young people who use youth provision, of whom most are still at school, aged 11–13 years, with young females being very much in the minority.

Treseder offers two comments on the participation and empowerment debate:

1. *Colleagues must first agree on aims, objectives and expected outcomes, and everyone must understand how far children will be involved in decision-making.*
2. *For children and young people to take advantage of participation there must also be some motivation and where necessary training for young people to make the best use of their powers.*

(Treseder, 1997).

The philosophy that underpins the first point is what persuades the believers to achieve enfranchisement for young people. In reality there needs to be a major paradigm shift in the minds of youth workers. For Leigh and Stuart (1985) enfranchisement is the gaining of legal rights and the responsibilities these entail, both enshrined in the concept of personal power. These are perhaps difficult concepts for youth workers to utilise given their role as an employee, with a mandate to fulfil particular expectations. For the Inspectorate, aims, objectives and outcomes from effective youth work are issues of 'quality':

> ... *quality in youth work can be measured by participants showing an increased ability*

to make choices and influence events in their own lives.

(OFSTED, 1996).

A subsequent report by the Inspectorate reinforced the importance of motivation and training, in that 'young people are insufficiently prepared for or involved in the planning of projects and activities in the running of centres' (OFSTED, 1999). The training of young people, and the move towards some model of participation and empowerment, can only be achieved by a change in the mindset of those 'who deliver and manage youth work. It may well be a difficult process to take young people from their conditioned position of 'objects reacting to the world' to 'subjects acting responsibly to the world' (Freire, 1972).

The constraints, therefore, include well-entrenched youth workers, themselves conditioned by long established systems.

Problems of meaning and intent

The tensions underlying a common understanding of the meaning of the term participation, were evident at a conference convened by the Welsh Assembly Government in October 2000. John Rose, Deputy Chief Executive of the Wales Youth Agency, commented that the process of turning rhetoric into reality is a real one for the politicians of Wales' (WAG, 2000a) while at the same conference, Andrew Davies Assembly Member (AM), Business Secretary for the Welsh Assembly Government, advocated that developing individual capacity is at the heart of what Youth Service is about. These two statements reflect the tension between the Government's interpretation of developing individual capacity, and those who challenge that interpretation and its implication for youth work practice. Andrew Davies' interpretation of participation may well be that of increasing participation in training and higher education, particularly for the least advantaged socio-economic groups in

Wales. The political will of the Welsh Assembly Government to encourage participation may well have the intention to frame it within the National Qualifications Framework. Proposals in November 2002 to encourage young people to design their own individual learning pathways and to evaluate the appointment of Learning Coaches, suggests a new kind of tokenism.

The Welsh Assembly Government youth work policy is enshrined in a commitment to the Life Long Learning Strategy expressed in a plethora of statement papers produced within the first two years of devolution. The strength of intent was noted by Andrew Davies: 'effective youth work within the social and economic aspects of the Better Wales Agenda, can be measured in terms of employability, citizenship, crime reduction and improved social behaviour' (WAG, 2000a). In response, John Rose suggested that youth work must be seen as a bridge between the aspirations of policy makers (within the Welsh Assembly Government) and those of young people.

In Northern Ireland, by comparison, implementation of participation is debated in different terms:

> *Responsibility for the participation of young people in the Youth Service in both of general attendance and in 'shaping, managing and delivering of the Youth Service' is not simply the responsibility of workers at unit or club level. It rests equally with the legislators and policy makers to create frameworks and structures that are conductive to involvement and participation. Management at all levels within agencies and organisations are responsible to funders and to the public. We must ensure procedures, operational and strategic decisions, and policies are implemented, but move from* **rhetoric** *towards good practice and recognise accountability to young people is of equal importance.*

> (NIEB, 2000).

There is a need to recognise the inevitability of a more direct government intervention, and an effort to ensure that participation and empowerment does not sink in the rhetoric. Rose's comments perhaps serve as a reminder that the traditional ethos of work with young people has always been 'needs-led', and that personal development is a priority for individuals growing up in a social environment which undermines self-esteem, confidence, self-worth and opportunities. A balance between values-determined youth work and an imposed policy framework should always inform the practitioner in the way the professional task is approached.

The tensions between the expectations of Government policy for young people in Wales, and the traditional responses by youth workers to young people in communities faced with a raft of problems have been well documented (Rose, 1997). Rose suggests that policy often gives little consideration to the lives of young people, and that other agendas are of more importance. Jeffs and Smith (1999) make similar claims, wherein youth workers need to respond to 'unrestrained state interference in youth work'. Funding from the state guarantees a contract culture with prescribed outcomes, a phenomenon no less evident in Wales. The Youth Policy Unit of the Welsh Assembly Government requires the 22 Unitary Authorities of Wales to fulfil declared youth work outcomes. Some youth workers are frustrated and confused, 'unclear about the process being undertaken and their role within a changing scene' (Rose, 1997). Given that participation is essentially about power, the imposition of these expectations from the Welsh Assembly Government may well transform into raising the consciousness of young people and youth workers, and in time lead to meaningful power in the political processes and a citizenship for young people. For youth workers this would mean a rise in the level of critical consciousness in assuming the emancipation of young people.

Activities of Youth Forums in Wales appear to be in low key, including campaigns to energise provision for skateboard facilities, or the organisation of events such as discotheques. There are some examples of issue-based work. A Breaking Barriers Conference in July 2000 organised by Llais Ifanc or Young Voice opened a debate on the Issue of Public Transport, but responses were limited and the campaign not sustained.

'Issues' expressed by young people in Wales are suppressed by Welsh Assembly Government's policies advocating work-based skills, entrepreneurship, citizenship and the Youth Work Curriculum statement for Wales. The entitlement document, the guiding statement for working with young people in Wales, expresses concern at 'the unmet needs of young people', but then arrives at the view that 'young people seem unable to articulate their unmet needs'. In its first three months on-line (October–December 2002), the Funky Dragon web site (www.funkydragon.com) confined its 'issue searching' to 'what do you think of your local park?' 'How do you rate your local youth club?', with only limited contributions to the web-site.

There are efforts to develop issues and the participation of young people; examples of good practice are:

- Theatr Fforum Cymru in West Wales who explore social issues through socio-interactive drama.
- The Welsh Association of Youth Club's ongoing training for Good Parenting and Health and Dieting.

But these stand in contrast to initiatives elsewhere. The proposed Youth Senate for Birmingham (with a 13–35 age group), will focus their business on multi-ethnicity problems in the city. Another youth engagement project in Liverpool is tackling housing problems as part of a community regeneration strategy.

Conclusion

The movement in Wales towards 'participation and empowerment' as a youth work methodology is still, generally, in the realm of rhetoric. Conceptually its roots lie somewhere in the tangle of concerns around the well-being of young people and children at risk, and the demands of a Welsh Assembly determined to create a 'Better Wales'.

Social issues are important aspects of the lives of young people, and the raising of their consciousness needs to be fundamental in the approach of forum and youth workers. If the strategy of the 'forum' development in Wales is to educate young people in decision-making and political processes before moving onto crucial issues, then this should be recognised in training and the evaluation process. The Vale of Glamorgan Youth Forum Charter suggests the adoption of more challenging social issues entering into more provocative political debates, which would require careful planning and strategies.

Rhetoric promoting the involvement of young people in strategic decision-making permeates all contemporary documents originating in the Welsh Assembly Government. But implementation of ideas is still bedevilled by familiar barriers, recognised by many who work closely with young people. The history of youth service in Wales has many examples of youth councils, committees and peer-led initiatives that have withered on the vine. Other barriers include the reluctance of youth groups to engage in decision-making as a direct result of conditioned learning, a lack of experience of the process often frustrated by efforts of tokenism that reinforce a lack of interest. Living and growing up in communities that have a collective consciousness of dependency does not help. The attitude of some authority figures in both the schools and the informal world of youth work, still inhibit the progress of young peoples' involvement in meaningful decision-making.

Despite the cynicism in rehearsing the barriers, the landscape of youth work in Wales gives some hope. There have been several initiatives in a short period, not yet evaluated. Building on the rhetoric of the Welsh Government, there is a need for a commitment from all those who work with young people which will ensure that the values of traditional youth work underpin the declared policy intentions of government.

> ... (young) *people become better citizens if they first become aware of all our potentials as individuals before they descend to the compromises and practical acquiescences of political life.*
>
> (Russell, 1932).

Most of all, commitment requires a paradigm shift in the minds of all involved adults in the way they perceive young people:

> ... *a profound rebirth,* [and] *those who undergo it must take on a new form of existence.*
>
> (Freire, 1972).

References

Albemarle Report (1960) *Youth Service in England and Wales.* London: HMSO.

Arnstein, S. (1969) A Ladder of Citizen Participation. *Journal of the American Instititue of Planners.* 35: 4, 216–24.

Banks, S. (1997) *Ethical Issues in Youth Work.* London: Routledge.

Baker, J. (1996) *The Fourth Partner: Participant or Consumer?* Leicester: The Youth Work Press.

Combe, V. (2002) *Up for it. Getting Young People Involved in Local Government.* Leicester: NYA.

Coopers and Lybrand Deloitte Report (1994) *Youth Service in Wales: Management Issues for the 1990s.*

Davies, B. (1999) *From Voluntaryism to Welfare State. History of Youth Work in England. Vol. 1 1939–79.* Leicester: Youth Work Press.

Davies, E. (1988) *Participation.* WAYC.

DES (1987) *Education Observed 6: Effective Youth Work.* London: HMSO.

DES (1984) *Education Survey 13 Youth Service Provision in Wales.* Cardiff: HMSO.

Freire, P. (1972) *Pedagogy of the Oppressed.* London: Penguin.

Frost, D. (1984) *50 Years Service.* Welsh Association of Youth Clubs.

Gordon, S. (1984) *Balancing Acts: How to Encourage Youth Participation.* Leicester: National Youth Agency.

Holmes, J. (2003) *The Role of the Youth Service in Young People's Partnerships.* WAY.

Jeffs, T. and Smith, M. (1999) *Resourcing Youth Work: Dirty Hands and Tainted Money,* in Banks S. op.cit.

Jones, B. (2000) *Review of the Youth and Community Service of Monmouthshire County Council.* Welsh Association of Youth.

Jones (1987) Newsletter. S. Glamorgan Participation Association.

Klaushofer, A. (2002) Vote Early. *The Guardian.* 28th August.

Leigh, M. and Smart, A. (1985) *Interpretations: The Emerging Crisis in Social Education.* Leicester: National Youth Agency.

Milson/Fairbairn (1969) *Youth and Community Work in the 70s.* London: HMSO.

Northern Irish Education Board (2000) *Youth Service Policy Review.* May.

OFSTED (1997) *Standards and Quality of Youth Work in Local Authorities in Wales.*

OFSTED (1996) Framework for the Inspection of Local Authority Maintained Further Education.

Russell, B. (1932) *Education and the Social Order.* London: Allen and Unwin.

Rose, J. (1997) *An Examination of the Relationship Between Youth Work Policy of a Local Education Authority and the Management and Delivery of Youth Work Provision.* University of Wales, Cardiff. Unpublished M.Phil thesis.

Thompson Report (1982) *Experience and Participation. Report of the Review Group on the Youth Service in England.* London: HMSO.

Treseder, P. (1997) *Empowering Children and Young People.* London: Save the Children.

Wade, H., Lawton, A. and Stevenson, M. (2001) *Hear by Right: Setting Standards for the Active Involvement of Young People in Democracy.* London: LGA/NYA.

Waterhouse, R. (2000) Lost in Care: Report of the Tribunal of Inquiry into the Abuse of Children in Care in the Former County Council Areas of Gwynedd and Clwyd Since 1974. London: HMSO.

Welsh Assembly Government (1999) *Learning is for Everyone. The Best for Lifelong Learning.*

Welsh Assembly Government (2000) *Extending Entitlement: Supporting Young People in Wales. Policy Unit Report.*

Welsh Assembly Government (2000a) *Securing the Future. Social Policy and the Re-emerging Youth Service in Wales.* Conference Report.

Welsh Assembly Government (2000b) *Better Wales Report.*

Welsh Assembly Government (2001) *Extending Entitlement: Consultation Document, Draft Direction and Guidance.*

Welsh Assembly Government (2002) *Moving Forward. Listening to Children and Young People in Wales.*

Welsh Assembly Government (2002a) *Learning Country: Learning Pathways, 14–19.*

Welsh Assembly Government (2002b) *Future Support for Participation in Wales.* Discussion Paper.

Welsh Assembly Government (2002c) *Total Population by Ages 2000.* Digest of Welsh Local Area Statistics.

Welsh Office (1983) *Youth Service in Wales.* Cardiff. HMSO.

Welsh Youth Association (2002) *'New' Youth Work Curriculum Statement for Wales.*

CHAPTER 8

The Relevance of a Children's Policy and the Participation of Young People in Decision Making in Germany

Thomas Swiderek

Introduction

Since the inception of the UN Convention on the Rights of the Child in 1989, a remarkable infrastructure of politics for children has developed in Germany. In many cities children's offices were established and so-called children's representatives were appointed at municipal as well as at local level. At national level, a non-partisan (cross-bench), children's committee has been in existence since 1988. This committee has the task of representing children's interests in the Bundestag, the lower house of the German Parliament.

Besides these representative forms of children's policy, various models for indirect and direct participation by children into decision-making have come into being, and are still developing. At the moment, parliaments for children or young people, children's offices, lawyers for children, forum discussions, 'round tables', 'office-hours at the mayor', and case-orientated participation in projects are the most common attempts in the field of adult-child co-determination. The professed aim of all these different forms of children's policy is to represent and to reinforce the rights of children, to create opportunities for participation, and to act as a lobby for children.

That these strivings of politicians are considered serious and important can be seen partly in the rights, special authority and areas of competence that are conceded to these groups representing children's interests. According to the jurisprudence academic Bernd Jean d'Heur (1993):

What is relevant here is: the more precisely these [permissions to act and competencies] are written down in a legally binding form, in legal documents and laws, the sooner we can trust in the idea of children's welfare not remaining a subject of Sunday speeches, but instead finding a non-spectacular entry into everyday political debate.

(p.250)

What does the claim for more participation by young people in decision-making denote? At best, it leads to more co-determination. The precondition is the awareness of possible ways to participate together with the ability to act in a participatory manner. The different forms of children's policy and the participation of young people in decision-making together arouse and intensify the ability to put 'democracy learning' into practice.

Current discussion about participation and children's policy emphasises the connection to democratisation, every-day democracy and democracy-learning. For supporters of this point of view, children's policy appears to be more than the commitment to a child-friendly Germany. They see children's policy in a much wider context:

We don't have to deal with disillusionment with politics among the young generation, yet. There is, however, the danger of a chain reaction: the current disillusionment with political parties has already changed into disillusionment with the politics of the state. This political apathy can easily result in disillusionment with the state if it continues for a long period of time. The disillusionment with the state can possibly turn into disillusionment with democracy and is finally identical with disillusionment with life on a massive scale – the end of any sensible, i.e. political overcoming of a crisis.

(Hurrelmann, quoted in Hager, 1995).

Until now, the theory of participation in the field of social education, which is especially geared to the problems in the social sector, has remained underdeveloped. This theoretical lack of clarity is, for example, revealed in publications which deal with participation of young people in decision-making in the context of children's policy and in socio-educational theory. In these, many aims are mentioned but preconditions or requirements, which would facilitate a realisation of those aims, are hardly listed. This criticism mainly holds for the 'practical' publications on the different forms of children's policy at the level of local government politics. In spite of legitimate guidelines, children's policy, and participation of young people in decision-making often moves in a speculative space and treads on politically insecure territory (see Sünker/Swiderek, 1998).

In this context, there is the problem of a 'political stage-management', that offers such things as parliaments for children or young people, and 'office-hours at the mayor'. Also the question of the political relevance and competence of children's representatives – especially at a state or county level but also in local governments – being used as a 'mere alibi' should not be neglected. Today the general discussion about children's policy, children's rights and the participation of young people in decision-making remains preoccupied with the question of the status of childhood in our society.

Two different points of view are of prime importance. First, the imagery and definition of childhood is as a transitional stage in deficit in the process of growing up. This stage, which is conveyed through the traditional usage of the terms 'protection' and 'care', can result in a rejection of all further discussions about the rights of children (see Sünker, 1993). Second, there is the position which does not reject the integration of children in pluralistic forms of family life. This position also uses the fragility of the status of children in their families and in society as a whole, especially as a result of socio-political changes and their consequences for the lives of children, as an opportunity to emphasise the connection between children's rights, and human and civil rights in the welfare state. It does so by referring to the UN Convention on the Rights of the Child, (see Sünker, 1989; Verhellen, 1992; Detrick, 1992), and by underlining the position of children as independent human beings in socio-political processes. In doing so, the supporters of this position try to demonstrate the importance of the participation of children and young people in decision-making to democracy-learning as a way of life (see Zeiher, 1996; Lange, 1995; Elder, Modell and Parke, 1993; Sünker, 1993).

Participation as the aim of children's policy in the context of socio-political inter-relations

Participation, especially since the end of the 1960s, has had a determining influence on public as well as scientific discussion about democracy and politics; it is regarded as 'the axial principle' of post-industrial, liberal democracies (Kasse, 1983). The Federal Supreme Court, for example, emphasised in a decision of general principle:

Each individual should be involved in decisions concerning the community to a maximum extent. The state has to pave the way for him to do so.

(BVerfGE 5, 85: 204).

Other statements also stress the important role of the involvement of the individual member of society. For example, 'Der Deutsche Verein für öffentliche und private Fürsorge' (the German association for public and private welfare) in its handbook on the local planning of the social system, states that:

> *Active participation in political and societal decisions is a necessary precondition for the realisation of a democratic community organisation. Involvement (participation), in this context, is to be understood both as a means to introduce and to carry through one's interests, as well as a purpose in the sense of man's self-realisation through involvement.*
>
> (Deutscher Verein, 1986).

Participation in the sense of political involvement is to be understood as:

> *the course of events through which the members of a society convey their wishes and ideas to political institutions. Different approaches in the theory of democracy regard participation either as the realisation of democracy itself (co-determination, emancipation), or they look upon too much participation as a threat to the stability of a political system.*
>
> (Fuchs et al., 1988).

Adorno summarised these approaches by formulating:

> *A democracy, which should not only function but at the same time work according to its concept, demands mature and responsible people. Democracy put into practice can only be imagined as a society of responsible people.*
>
> (Adorno, 1970).

It follows that all three concepts (participation, emancipation, responsibility) relate to democracy and are therefore political concepts. Furthermore, they have an educational implication, i.e. participation, emancipation and also responsibility are basic educational aims of our society. They can be found in almost all objectives of educational institutions and also in the wording of the Child and Youth Services Act (section 1, KJHG). In the understanding of children's policy and of participatory models in particular, these concepts,

together with the aims derived from them, are the main focus of interest. The concept of participation is closely connected with our social system and can be regarded as behavioural and organisational principles for the processes of opinion-forming and decision-making in democratic societies. Does this, however, at the same time mean that participation can therefore be evaluated as a basic concept for democratic societies and the actual living together of people?

In social reality, a representative democracy such as the one in the FRG does not exclude participation; but it *is* mostly regulated on an abstract level; and it is not regarded as the necessary precondition for the functioning of the political system. Participation (in this context) serves more or less as a means of legitimisation, i.e. the realisation of this aim should help to see the actual degree (of liberation) of a democratic society. In the realisation or carrying out of participation, however, a different regard and evaluation of participation becomes obvious, particularly if one looks at the different fields of interest from the point of view of the decision-makers on the one hand and of those who are affected by these decisions on the other (see Busse/Nelles, 1978; Ortmann, 1983).

The legal basis for children's policy in Germany

Children's political and participatory actions in Germany are based on the Kinder- und Jugendhhilfegesetz (KJHG), the Child and Youth Services Act, that came into force on 1st January 1991. The claim of youth services to act as a lobby for children is formulated in the first section of the KJHG. It states that:

> *Each young person has a right to be supported in their development and to be brought up as a self-responsible sociable personality.*

Furthermore, youth services are to work towards putting into practice the right to 'positive living conditions for young people and their families and the preservation and development of a child- and family-friendly environment' (see section 1, 3: 4 KJHG) – which takes youth services beyond the narrower scope of conventional youth service tasks. In terms of broad policy the youth service is also to influence other areas of politics in order to allow for positive living conditions and a child-friendly environment.

Section 8, in conjunction with sections 1, 5 and 9 of the KJHG, can be viewed as the 'basic standards' for the participatory rights of children. In section 8, 1, it is declared that:

> Children . . . are to participate according to their stage of development in all decisions of public youth service that concern them. They are to be informed in a suitable manner of their rights with regard to administrative proceedings as well as proceedings before courts dealing with matters of guardianship and administrative courts.

Thus, children are recognised as individual personalities in their own right with their own desires, needs and interests. In this respect the KJHG clearly corresponds to Article 12 of the UN Convention on Children's Rights. Accordingly the decision-making organs of a state must:

> in official processes that concern a person under 18, allow the person, as far as they are able to reach such an opinion, to voice their own opinion . . . and to take this opinion into account in an appropriate manner relating to the person's age and maturity.
>
> (Schormann, 1994).

Such participation is also to occur in cases of decisions concerning assistance in upbringing (section 36, 1 KJHG):

> When an assistance in upbringing outside the family is necessary the persons listed in section 1 [the child or the young person,] are to participate in the choice of the institution or foster placement.
>
> (36, 1).

For the planning of youth assistance (section 80, KJHG) the legislators have formulated that the requirement has to be established:

> by considering the desires, needs and interests of the young people
>
> (80, 1: 2 KJHG).

The public bodies responsible for youth assistance are asked to devise appropriate methods in order to allow those whom it concerns to participate (see Gernert, 1993).

Given this background and context, the following questions can be raised:

- If and how far the practised child-political means of participation suit these needs?
- What models are most suitable in reality?
- What preconditions are necessary in order to achieve a relevant measure of participation in terms of *learning democracy as a form of living*?

An account of local forms of children's policy

The first local forms of child-political representative bodies in Germany were founded following the International Year of the Child in 1979. At the same time 'Till Eulenspiegel', a non-governmental organisation of the Arbeiterwohlfahrt (Labourer Welfare) in Düsseldorf, became active as a 'children's lawyer' (see AWO, 1994). Apart from this institutionalised and locally political representation of children's rights, other organisations such as Deutsches Kinderhilfswerk (German Children's Aid) or Kinderschutzbund (Society for the Protection of Children) had even earlier advocated for children at both case-to-case and state-wide levels. However, the actual development of local children's policies began in connection with the reform of the Jugendwohlfahrtsgesetz (Child Welfare Act) (particularly in the 1980s), the ratification of the UN Convention on the Rights of the Child (1989) and the coming into force of the new Kinder-und Jugendhhilfegesetz (KJHG) – Children and Youth Services Act.[1]

Since the late 1980s the number of operational areas and forms of child-political action grew continuously. In 1994 one could find in Germany more than 80 different institutions representative of child interests (see Arnold/Wüstendörfer, 1994). Since then there has been an enormous increase in activities related to the participation of children. Today in almost every large city in Germany there is at least one institution of child interest. Parliaments for children and other multiple forms of political participation of children exist in many cities and counties. Two-thirds of these institutions are assigned to public bodies. However, these multifaceted forms and models of participation are not necessarily a confirmation of effective power nor of the quality of children's participation. On the contrary, this situation especially requires critical regard, so that the dynamics of participation do not become absorbed within the normal standard of bureaucracy.

So far no unified structure exists for the different models. On the one hand this is due to the insecure establishment of many institutions within the framework of the existing youth services. On the other hand many forms are not clear-cut. Most of the institutions representing the interests of children operate on different levels and their fields of work and sets of tasks overlap. The systematic listing presented here aims at structuring the different forms according to their primary goals.

Generally, children's political activities can be divided into three groups, At the infrastructure level these are the children's offices, children's representatives, children's lawyers and the office for children's interests ('policies for children'). Further possibilities are provided by children's parliaments and meetings ('policies with children') and open forums, such as round-tables or office-hours at the mayor. Also, activities taking place on special days should be mentioned, such as the World Children's Day, where child-friendly actions, and hence public relations or advocacy work for children, are performed. Such projects take place in nearly all bigger cities and communities.

Administrative or governmental forms

The main characteristic of the models concerning the administrative or governmental enforcement of children's rights is representation. The declared goal is to 'pay more attention to children's spheres of life in politics, administration and in the public, and to enhance the prevailing conditions of their lives' (Blanke, 1993). Representative bodies view themselves as voices speaking on behalf of the children and confronting the interests of the adults. The representation of interests is performed in different ways and from different positions.

Probably the most comprehensive and concise form of institutionalised representation of children's interests at a local level is the 'Amt für Kinderinteressen' (Department for Children's Interests) of the city of Cologne. This department has been working since 1991 and has two main foci: the 'Interessensvertretung und Planung' (representation of interests and planning) (this includes the planning of youth services) and the focus on the task 'Freizaeit und Spielpädagogik' (leisure and play). At the organisational level the department is subordinate to the Department for Children, Youth and Family and thus is equal to the youth services.

A further type of institutionalised representation of children's interests is the Children's Office. The employees of the Children's Office (Children's Commissioners) are either assigned to the head of the relevant department of social affairs or to the mayor (as in Essen, Freiburg or Weimar), or they are subordinate to the youth welfare department or its head (as in Frankfurt or Karlsruhe).

The Children's Offices are co-ordinating and operating locations within community administrations. It is their task to introduce the interests of children into the planning process of community projects across all departments. This mode of operation clarifies the cross-sectional character of children's policy. Any planning such as transport, housing, recreation areas, school building, school reconstruction, or youth services are to be tested in advance, for child-friendliness by the Children's Office and suggestions for changes are to be considered. Moreover, reports for the youth services are written, even though the offices are not granted any power with regard to making decisions:

> *This mere right to suggest, renders clear that each Children's Office holds a special position. On the one hand they are assigned to an office higher than the youth welfare, such as the head of the department of youth or social affairs. On the other hand part of their capacities remains assigned to youth welfare as far as content and organisations are concerned.*
>
> (see AWO, 1994).

The different assignment to departments mentioned earlier also influences a direct focus on tasks. While the Children's Commissioners of the Children's Offices 'who hold a staff position within a higher office . . . are mostly engaged at an infrastructure level and less in direct work on individual cases or with children' (AWO, 1993), a far broader scope of work and work on individual cases can be seen in Children's Offices formally tied to the youth welfare or the department of youth.

The main tasks for Children's Offices can be summarised as:

- Provision of facilities for children according to their needs.
- Broadening inner-city playing facilities.
- Influencing the housing conditions of children and families.
- Planning transport according to children's needs.
- Designing reports on children.
- Providing official bodies that children, parents and institutions can turn to ('spokespersons for children').
- Providing a public ground for children.

A more direct contact with children is held by the commissioners acting as 'Children's

Lawyers'. The literature and my own research point out that this form of representing children's interests is mostly reserved to non-governmental bodies.

The first such institution was founded in 1979 ('Till Eulenspiegel' in Düsseldorf), and more children's lawyers can be found in Dortmund and Herne. This form of legal representation of interests has a historical origin in the Ombuds(wo)men active since the early 1980s in Norway (see Qvortrup 1993). While in Dortmund and Düsseldorf there is no Children's Office supported by public institutions, the Children's Lawyer in Herne co-operates with a Children's Commissioner employed by the council on behalf of the children. The main difference between Children's Offices and the Children's Lawyers is the more direct contact with the children and their real problems and desires. The term 'Children's Lawyer' is programmatic, in that a mandate is held for children and their interests.

Parliamentary forms

Since the beginning of children's political activities in Germany, it is possible to talk of an 'inflationary expansion' of children's and young people's parliaments which, however, should not always be viewed as a sign of good quality or of a radical or progressive children's policy.

The first youth council meeting was organised in 1985 in the Baden Württemberg town of Weingarten, a small community with approximately 20,000 inhabitants. This form of children's policy, and the participation of children, in general is usually found in small- and medium-sized communities, and the spread of this type of participation clearly shows the difference between rural and urban areas.

These parliaments may be elected by the schools based in the communities, for example, in Weingarten each pupil from the seventh grade onwards is allowed to vote. In other communities, the election of the children's and young people's parliaments resembles the classical parliamentary election, even including the possibility of voting by letter. The level of participation or interest is significantly higher in school elections, where the candidates are better known, and it is possible to introduce this type of participation in local affairs into lessons, and so enlighten the pupils. Generally the children's and young people's parliaments show a range of ages between 12 and 16 years, but in some parliaments even nine- or ten-year-old children take part. The candidates are usually elected for three years, and in some communities a third of the members are exchanged after two years (rotation system). In the 'meeting-free period' the children and young people are divided into four workshops focusing on subjects such as school, protection of the environment, youth club house, youth/ societies, where they prepare topics and suggestions for change that are discussed at the irregular meetings and passed on to those politicians who are present.

Models for these children's political activities can be found in France, Austria and Switzerland. France in particular engages in these forms of political education to provide a location where parliamentary and democratic behaviour can be learned. Currently around 800 children and youth parliaments exist, some of them with a budget of their own of up to 25,000 Euro.

Open forms

In contrast to the parliamentary forms, the more open forms of participation offer all interested children an opportunity that allows them to voice their topics and interests. Forums for children do not consist of elected representatives, but they are open to each interested child. Their type of action resembles the children's parliaments: children, politicians, the initiators and interested adults meet at fixed dates, usually in community rooms (town hall) and discuss their topics in parliamentary style.

The example of the Munich forum for children and youth (see Arbeitskreis Zukunftswerkstätten, 1991) illustrates the objectives and ideas of the concept 'forum for children'. The first forum for children was held in 1990 within the framework of the Munich Workshops on the Future. Since then, interested children aged eight to sixteen have met four times a year in the Great Meeting Hall in Munich town hall. An action group prepares the forum, but nevertheless new additional topics raised by the children who attend the forum are taken up. The forum aims at finding out the views and concerns of children and young people . . . with regard to problems in their direct lives, in order to:

- Raise them for discussion.
- Provide a listening ear to the children and a public ground.
- Make sure that the concerns of the children are taken seriously by the politicians, are entered into the administration and are considered in decisions.

The Forum for Children and Youth considers itself to be a form of practical participation of citizens suitable for children and it aims at becoming a permanent institution in Munich (Arbeitskreis Zukunftswerkstätten, 1991).

The interests and concerns of children and youth expressed in these forums, are very similar to those voiced through the Children's Commissioners (Children's Offices) or in the children's parliaments, for example:

- Destruction of nature and the environment (e.g. the increase of ozone in the summer, car and factory exhausts, avoiding waste).
- The problem of inner city development (mainly more bicycle routes, more recreation areas, public transport).
- Individual topics (such as better housing, playgrounds and play areas).

Topics from school, social and private life are dealt with less often. Here a difference to the 'children's lawyer' becomes evident because he or she is more often consulted on private and personal problems. The Forum for Children and Youth considers itself to be a mediator between children and the administration. The adult supervisors are responsible for moderation, protocol, and formulating applications. The prime objective is to restrict the participation of adults as far as possible and hence to allow the children a greater part in the design and organisation of the forum.

Since 1993 the Munich Children and Youth Forum has been located at a freelance institution, the Culture und Spielraum e. V, and is equipped with one permanent staff member and a budget of its own since March 1994. Separate forums exist for children and youth due to the requests of the children themselves, in order to be more able to meet different interests.

Apart from these forums for children there are other open forms for representing children's interests, such as round tables and office-hours at the mayor. The form of the round table is adopted from the political talks at the Round Table that existed during the process of Reunification: that is, sitting together at the same table, listening to one another and beginning to communicate. The only examples of this form of children's policy I know of can be found in the former GDR (e.g. in Leipzig).

Children, politics and participation in research, science and politics

Within social sciences, research on children is a relatively new field (see Lange, 1995; Honig, 1999). Until the middle of the 1980s 'childhood' was barely perceived as a topic by either pedagogues or sociologists, but in recent years the number of publications has increased rapidly. In his book *Putting a price on children: Contemporary Sociology* Thorne (1985), pointed out that:

> . . . *research on the life and experiences of children, is limited to only a few research areas: family, education (Erziehung) or social psychology of socialization . . . The*

> *sociological theories are mainly adult-orientated and focus therefore on children only with respect to the reproduction of the social order. The theoretical framework of 'Socialisation' and 'Development' – which is coined by an historical, individualistic as well as teleological view – defines children more in respect of their development than to their existence/being. Within this framework other sociological possibilities of access is widely shown.*

(cited in Qvortrup, 1993).

But the situation today has changed crucially, in particular action-oriented as well as theoretical research in the field of childhood.[2]

Since the coming into effect of the KJHG, pedagogical and social action deals with the possibilities of political action by and for children in the realisation of this law, which is explicitly related to ideas about the contemporary situation of the children and change within society (see Wiesner, 1995). The work ranges from legal justification to statements and models of children's participation, in addition to the many successful examples of participation in *Jugendhilfe* and school (see Landesjugendamt Hessen, 1998).

Scientific works also cover a wide range. Research in each case is focused on the particular discipline. But one specific point can be summarised in all of these works: the focus of childhood has changed from an object-orientated to a subject-orientated view. Pedagogues, sociologists, psychologists, social scientists, and the legal profession embed this new view of children and childhood into their work and transfer their demands – which were hitherto related only to the juveniles – to the children.

So far it is difficult to provide a structured overview of the various surveys of aspects of children's lives. To collect the different research results, and to merge them with political demands and national measures, it is necessary to classify the social reporting of recent years. On behalf of the Federal Government, two reports were published in

1998. Although published by the same Ministry (Bundesministerium für Familie, Senioren, Frauen und Jugend), both reports emphasised different perspectives, although both the *Zehnte Kinder-und Jugendbericht* and the expertise of *Kinder und Kindheit in Deutschland*, are to serve as a basis for child politics in Germany.

Only the second report speaks of children as subjects, and using the basis of a 'culture of growing up', formulates the tasks which must be mastered by children, as well as the necessary institutional assistance. It has a preference for a policy for children. Politics for children are understood as comparable with the idea of a social ecology of human development; (following developmental psychology.) The fact that this cannot be attained except by means of the KJHG was clearly exposed by the authors of this report.

Promoting the expertise of children places child politics in the context of a family policy, which is orientated to build developmental social environments for children (Bundesministerium für Familie, Senioren, Frauen und Jugend 1998: 14). The idea of child rights 'as individual rights detached by the family or as rights of children against their parents' (a.a.O.: 67) becomes distanced.

As a basis for national child politics, both reports show clearly the ambiguities and the political explosiveness of conceptual questions with regard to protection and participation in the life of children, and the status declared in the UN Convention on the Rights of the Child (see Neubauer/Sünker, 1993). The participation of children in matters concerning their own affairs, in mainly institutionalised forms, is generally affirmed. However, the framework of a policy for, with and of children as independent, autonomous beings remains disputed. Adjusting the national welfare, protection and education basis of the participation-oriented KJHG remains contentious.

Participation: results and perspectives

Only one country-wide survey, *Beteiligung von Kindern und Jugendlichen in Kommunen* (BMFSFJ 1999) deals with a possible transfer of child politics to society. It examines the participation of children in their community. Considering that, to date, all investigations refer to questions of political orientation, the confidence in political institutions and the political participation of young people in this survey is an improvement.[3] The survey was commissioned by the Bundesministerium für Familie, Senioren, Frauen und Jugend'. It focuses on models of social participation (especially existing models and forms of participation) and their spread, content, participants, and basic organisation. This survey is based on a sample of 1,003 municipalities in Germany by the 'Deutsche Jugendinstitut'. The survey covered municipalities as provider of services. Of the 1,003 municipalities surveyed, only 400 answered (about 40 per cent), and specialists in the responsible institutions were the respondees.

The results show a considerable quantitative and qualitative development of the spread and variety of participation offered. It must be the aim in the future to constantly improve and extend the quality of the already developed structures of participation. In the summer of 1998 for example participation activities took place in 153 cities and municipalities. The participating municipalities usually offered several forms of participation. A priority goal must be to give all children and young people the chance to take part in forms of participation. The participation infrastructure must be developed in the municipalities and in the large cities a blanket coverage of activities offered must be established.

Project-oriented forms of participation (the most frequent category, with 70 per cent), minimise the dangers of possible exclusion in the social and the education strata. Both foreign children and girls generally must be merged more into participation processes, that is, appropriate forms of speech and action must be found. Foreign children take part less in representative than in project-oriented forms. In nearly 50 per cent of the representative and in approximately 33 per cent of the open forms foreign children do not participate. That is, the more the method is related to action and exercise, the more foreign children *do* participate.

The relationship of boys and girls in the different participation forms can be characterised as follows: in approximately 46 per cent of the models mentioned they are represented equally. Tensions need to be recognised in that the number of the girls drops over time. At the beginning of a project often more girls than boys are involved, but this changes in the project phases. Crucial here, among other points, are the methods: the more creative, then the more girls; the more structured a project, then more boys take part. The highest participation quotas are with the project-oriented forms.

Two age groups are addressed as priority: 10–13 years old (81 per cent) and 14–18 years old (86 per cent). Nearly half of the participation offers are addressed to children 6–9 years old (46 per cent), but approximately 12 per cent are under six years old. The distribution shows that the younger children predominantly take part in project-oriented participation forms, while those between 14 and 18 years old take up only a proportion of the 54 per cent here.

Participation of young people in decision-making – the discrepancy between demand and reality

Problems occur when putting the concept of participation into practice. The participation of children frequently serves as an alibi for adults; rituals are copied from adults, and children are used as instruments. Therefore, children's policy must succeed in developing generalised structures, forms and methods that allow for a genuine participation of children without depending on an individual adult.

The following areas of conflict repeatedly occur in the participation of children:

- Dangers and problems nowadays exist at a global level. However, the areas of action in participation are local. This means that frustration is bound to occur every now and again, both with regard to topical decisions and the children themselves.
- The existing political power structures in the communities or administrations are also soon recognised by the children. Thus, it is constantly necessary to fight the feeling of being powerless and of being unable to change anything.
- A further area of strain derives from the 'resigned' adults who hinder hope and innovation.
- The transfer effect constitutes a further conflict. Do adults really reflect exactly what children say and want? Is it not a great temptation to filter the children's wishes and opinions, to explain, to overlook and to channel?
- Moreover lack of time and finance repeatedly hinders the participation of children.

Despite these obstacles it must be possible to demand and promote the continuous participation of children and to test new forms of participation.

Evaluation of municipal-level children's committees and children's meetings

Committees and meetings for children and young people work along similar lines to existing community parliaments, and according to nearly the same structural principles. Committees, meetings, rules, votes and postponements are part of the style of the children's and young people's parliaments, and in some even a 'children's mayor' is elected. Children's parliaments are not a legal community body, and cannot make binding resolutions, but depend on the benevolence of the local politicians. This means that there is:

> *frequently a discrepancy between the formal conditional framework and the real possibility of influence, and compared to the actual possibilities of participation and relevance of the children's applications a stark imbalance can often be perceived.*
>
> (Frädrich, 1995).

How far do children's and youth parliaments really mirror what children actually want in their communities, and their authentic spheres of life? The initiators and politicians predominantly regard this as an opportunity to familiarise children with the parliamentary-democratic rules and conventions, but at the same time children have limited rights to a say or decision. Are children's parliaments a learning ground for political education? If we do not want this opportunity to become a mere 'alibi' the following preconditions and conditions must be met:

- The children's and young people's parliaments should not be dominated by adults and their rules.
- Children and young people must find their own rules and conventions in dealing with one another.
- Children and young people must have the possibility to be able to use their own language among themselves as well as when talking to adults.
- The participants need support from the local administrative and political organs.
- The participants should be able to decide on budgets of their own.

The current experiences suggest that most children's and young people's parliaments are at this time only marginally established in local politics and are more tolerated in mainstream politics than welcomed. The politician discussing children and young people throws a positive light on politicians. In the towns and communities where the children's and young people's parliaments receive a positive judgement from the children involved, this success crucially depends on the interest and engagement of individual local politicians. They decide whether, for instance, children are granted a mandate in the adult committees (Children and Youth Aid Committee) as in the case of the children's youth council in Weingarten (see Frädrich, 1995).

Apart from these institutionalised parliamentary forms (that is, parliaments founded on elections) of participation, there are so-called 'open' types of participation. These can be forums for children or meetings that have not been set up by elections and are therefore open to all interested children.

One advantage of the children's forums and meetings lies in the fact that the children are not limited by the right to participate in elections, but each interested child can take part in the meetings at any time. This method of participation at least partly prevents the otherwise likely outcome that only certain, intellectual children, able to articulate in an appropriate manner, can take part in making decisions. At the same time this positive aspect bears a disadvantage. Due to its random constitution, lack of representative selection according to age, type of school, gender, of the children, raises criticisms that the decisions they make do not reflect the opinions of all the children in Munich. A further advantage to the institutional parliamentary forms is the direct and personal concern of the children. This particularly applies to children's forums held at the level of boroughs where the children live.

Fundamental to the evaluation of the parliamentary as well as the open forms of participation is the question of whether the initiators continually develop of their concepts of participation, and test theories against practice and vice-versa. This includes questions of how to ensure that the decisions made by the children do not get stuck in the slow administrative process, or that the children understand them.

Future perspectives

To summarise, child politics in Germany is still primarily a policy *for* children, even if many projects, which directly concern the living conditions of children, are planned together with children. Much rests in the nature of the project, and there is little embedded into the concept of 'everyday learning of democracy'. Continuity, durability and the development of a participation culture in the municipalities are important. Intensive co-operation with the administration, based on reliable transfer structures (taking rights and requesting rights) is crucial.

When asking the children what they imagine their future to be like and what they would like to change, they mention better playing facilities, fewer cars, different schools with less pressure on success, more protection of the environment and the ability to spend more time with their parents. When asking children who are active in children's parliaments, children's forums and other child-political forms of participation what they currently wish for, these desires directly concern lowering the age limit for taking part in elections and the demand for more say and rights to participate in the broadest sense.

No one particular form of participation exists, and neither is it desirable. The best chance for children's policy and children's participation lies in the decentralisation and diversity of the models.

Young people showed great interest in politics once before, 30 years ago. Participation, emancipation and self-development were the guiding terms at the core of the interest in politics. However, the following years were to prove that the expectations of young people were too great in regard to changes in politics and society by means of participation. In a pluralist democracy there is a process demanding great effort that leads to compromise solutions between groups with different interests. Max Weber defined successful politics as the 'art of what is possible' but

that 'we would not be able to achieve what is possible if people all over the world had not repeatedly reached out for the impossible'. Many young people took sides with the politically impossible without viewing the other side, which Max Weber describes as 'a strong and slow process of drilling hard boards with passion as well as perception' (Ostermann, 1994).

The diverse projects on participation today constitute an effort to integrate children and youth into decisions that concern them, but also to raise their interest in societo-political proceedings. The aspect of waking the children's interest in politics, and channelling it where necessary, by means of children's policy and participation should not be disregarded. The earlier fear of the ruling classes and established citizens towards the politicised youth and students was due to the fact that they saw politics and chances for change only outside the institutions, and believed that society was in danger of losing control of these 'politically-interested' young people.

Many models of participation today are institutionalised 'join-in projects' organised and directed by grown ups. This offers the opportunity to direct the political socialisation of children right from the start through the participation of the children, and to keep it in a comprehensible framework. Therefore, the children's parliaments as a form of political socialisation of young people are highly questionable. Examples show that the children's parliaments often are only suitable for recruiting new party members and thus familiarising them with parliamentary rules at an early stage. This leaves spontaneity, fantasy and creativity behind. Considering the complaints in recent years of the lack of interest young people show in politics and societal events, it is not surprising that more and more of these institutionalised models of participation are founded, even if this is done only half-heartedly. While in France and Italy the children's parliamentarians are partly equipped with budgets of their own and thus able to finance their own projects, the children in Germany always depend on the benevolence of local politicians and adults when it comes to putting their decisions into action.

Moreover, it should not be overlooked that the constitution of the children's parliaments is questionable. Few if any foreign children join in these forms of participation. This is partly due to the clear middle-class orientation of the constitution of children's parliaments. Even here it is necessary to possess an ability to articulate and an appropriate vocabulary in order to be noticed and understood by everybody. This implies that perhaps the 'future parliamentarians and politically correct citizens are trained here', who support the existing political parliamentary institutions without trying to articulate and bring through their interests and needs by moving outside the existing system.

My criticism is not intended as support to the opponents of political forms of children's participation. Child policy and the participation of children is necessary and important. Only the diversity of fast-growing child-political forms of participation renders it necessary to keep in mind the aspects of political interest and power. In addition, the non-institutionalised political participation taking place outside parliaments should not be disregarded. The significance and potential of change born by social movements is crucial for long term, global changes in politics and the change of political standpoints. The question 'is democracy built from top to bottom or from the bottom up' should be answered by: 'democracy and the initiator of change usually come from outside'.

If children's policy and the representation of children's interests is really to enable children to participate, and to lead a self-determined life (and thus to create a substantial democratic political culture), and not only to aim at the support of socialisation processes as control processes (for example, in terms of individualisation), then we must become aware of the discrepancy between *formulating* a claim and *realising* that claim.

Notes

1 The new Kinder – und Jugendhilfegesetz (Children and Youth Services Act) became the legal basis in all of the Federal Republic of Germany on 1.1.1991. It had already been ratified in the territory of the former GDR on 3.10.1990, the day of the German unification.

2 In the 'Sozialwissenschaftliche Literatur Rundschau' (SLR) Lynne Chisholm in her review discussion about new trends in childhood research illustrated the conditions at that time in Germany. She asked in a polemical way whether childhood research must be marked as a 'labyrinth without a way out' or as 'puzzles without connection' (SLR, 1992: H 25).

3 See here for example, Hoffmann-Lange, U. 1995 (Hg.): DJI Jugendsurvey 1 (questioning of 16–29 year olds); the ALLBUS surveys of 1992 and 1994; the youth studies of the IPOS of 1993 and 1995 with 14–27 year olds; the shell surveys regularly accomplished since 1953, the most recent the 13. Survey of 2000.

References

Adorno, T.W. (1970) *Erziehung zur Mündigkeit. Vorträge und Gespräche mit, Helmut Becker. 1959–1969*. Frankfurt.

Alemann von, U. (Hrsg.) (1978) *Partizipation, Demokratisierung, Mitbestimmung. Problemstellung und Literatur in Politik, Wirtschaft, Bildung und Wissenschaft.* Opladen.

Arbeitsgemeinschaft für Jugendhilfe (Hrsg.) (1994) *Wie kommen Kinder zuRecht?* Bonn.

Arbeitskreis Zukunftswerkstätten (Hrsg.) (1991) *München – WerkStadt der Zukunft.* München.

Archard, D. (1993) *Children: Rights and Childhood* London/New York.

Arnold, T. and Wüstendörfer, W. (1994) *Auf der Seite der Kinder -Kinderbeauftragte in Deutschland*. Frankfurt.

Arbeiterwohlfahrt (Hrsg.) (1993) *Till Eulenspiegel der Kinder – und Jugendanwalt. Jahresbericht, 1992*. Düsseldorf.

AWO (Arbeiterwohlfahrt) (Hrsg.) (1994) *Konzeption der Kinder- und Jugendanwältin der AWO in Düsseldorf*. Düsseldorf.

Blanke, H., Hovenga, B. and Wawrziczny, S. (Hrsg.) (1993) *Handbuch Kommunale Kinderpolitik*. Münster.

Bühler-Niederberger, D., Tremp, P. Kinder und gesellschaftliche Ordnung generationale Grundlage moderner Demokratien, in Güthoff, W. and Sünker, H. (Hrsg.) (2001) *Handbuch Kinderrechte. Partizipation, Kinderpolitik, Kinderkultur*. Münster (pp.37–66).

Bundesministerium für Familie, Senioren, Frauen und Jugend (Hrsg.) (1998) *Kinder- und Jugendbericht. Bericht über die Lebenssituation von Kindern und die Leistungen der Kinderhilfen in Deutschland*. Bonn.

Bundesministerium für Familie, Senioren, Frauen und Jugend (Hrsg.) (1998) *Kinder und ihre Kindheit in Deutschland. Eine Politik für Kinder im Kontext von Familienkindheit*. Bonn.

Bundesministerium für Familie, Senioren, Frauen und Gesundheit (Hrsg.) (1999) *Beteiligung von Kindern und Jugendlichen in der Kommune. Ergebnisse einer Bundesweiten Erhebung*. Bonn.

Buse, M. and Nelles, W. (1978) Partizipation woran und wozu? in Alemann, U. (1978) (pp.41–78).

Chisholm, L. (1992) Paradise Lost – Lost Paradise. Ist die deutsche Kindheits- forschung zur Entromantisierung fähig? *Sozialwissenschaftliche Literatur Rundschau*. 14: 1, 98–112.

Detrick, S. (Ed.) (1992) *The United Nations Convention on the Rights of the Child*. Dordrecht.

Deutscher Verein für öffentliche und private Fürsorge (Hrsg.) (1986) *Handbuch der örtlichen Sozialplanung*. Frankfurt.

Elder, G.H., Modell, J. and Parke, R.D. (1993) *Children in Time and Place. Development and Historical Insights*. Cambridge.

European Centre for Social Welfare Policy and Research (Hrsg.) (1994) *Kinder, Kinderrechte und Kinderpolitik*. Wien.

Frädrich, J. (1995) *Kinder bestimmen mit*. München.

Fuchs, W. et al. (Hrsg.) (1988) *Lexikon zur Soziologie*. Frankfurt.

Gernert, W. (1993) Zur Partizipation der Betroffenen in der Jugendhilfe. *Zentralblatt für Jugendrecht*. 80: 116–25.

Güthoff, W. and Sünker, H. (Hrsg.) (2001) *Handbuch Kinderrechte. Partizipation, Kinderpolitik, Kinderkultur*. Münster.

Hager, H. (1995) *Vorwort, in Ministerium für Arbeit, Soziales, Jugend und Gesundheit des Landes*. Schleswig-Holstein (pp.5–8).

Honig, M.S.(1999) *Entwurf einer. Theorie der Kindheit*. Frankfurt a. M.

Honig, M.-S. (2001a) Soziale Frage, Frauenfrage – Kinderfrage? *Sozialwissenschaftliche Literatur Rundschau*. 24: 1, 59–83.

Honig, M. S. Kinderpolitik. In Otto, H.U. and Thiersch, H. (Hrsg.) (2001b) *Handbuch Sozialarbeit/Sozialpädagogik*. 2. völlig überarb. Aufl. Neuwied (pp.936–48).

Jean d'Heur, B. (1993) *Verfassungsrechtliche Schutzgebote zum Wohl des Kindes und staatliche Interventionspflichten aus der Garantienorm des Artikels 6, Abs. 2 GG*. Berlin.

Kasse, M., (1983) Partizipation, in Lippert und Wakenhut (Hrsg.) *Handwörterbuch der Politischen Psychologie*. Opladen.

Lange, A. (1995) Sozialwissenschaftliche Kindheitsforschung. *Sozialwissenschaftliche Literatur Rundschau*. 18: 30.

Lüscher, K. and Lange, A. (1992) Konzeptuelle Grundlagen einer Politik für Kinder: Ansätze und Begründungen aus sozialwissenschaftlicher Sicht *ZSE*. 12: (pp.204–18).

Melzer, W. and Sünker, H. (1989) *Wohl und Wehe der Kinder. Pädagogische Vermittlungen von Kindheitstheorie, Kinderleben und gesellschaftlichen Kindheitsbildern*. Weinheim.

Ministerium für Arbeit, Soziales, Jugend
   und Gesundheit des Landes Schleswig-
   Holstein (Hrsg.) (1995) *Demokratie lernen.*
   Alltagsorientierte Kinderpolitik in Schleswig-
   Holstein, Kiel.
Neubauer, G. and Sünker, H. (Hrsg.) (1993)
   Kindheitspolitik International. Opladen
   (pp.9–24).
Newell, P. (1991) *The UN Convention and*
   Children's Rights in the UK. London.
Ortmann, F. (Hrsg.) (1983) *Bedürfnis und*
   Planung in sozialen Bereichen. Opladen.
Ostermann, . (1994) Die Grundwerte der
   Demokratie werden von der großen
   Mehrheit bejaht. Das Parlament vom. 7: 1,
   11.
Qvortrup, J. (1990) *Childhood as a Social*
   Phenomenon. Eurosocial Wien Report, 36.
Qvortrup, J. (1993) Kind – Kinder –
   Kindheit, in Neubauer and Sünker (Hrsg.)
   Kindheitspolitik International. Opladen
   (pp.9–24).
Schormann, M. (1994) Die Rechte des Kindes
   im Sinne des Artikels 12 des
   Übereinkommens über die Rechte des
   Kindes, in AGJ (Hrsg.) *Wie kommen Kinder*
   zu Recht? Bonn.
Sünker, H. (1989) Pädagogik und Politik für
   Kinder. Gesellschaftliche Entwicklungen
   und Herausforderungen, in: Melzer and
   Sünker (1989).
Sünker, H. (1991) Das Kind als Subjekt?
   Notizen zu Kindheit und Kinderleben
   heute. *Widersprüche.* 11: 38, 7–18.
Sünker, H. (1993) Kindheit zwischen
   Individualisierung und
   Institutionalisierung, in *Zentrum für*
   Kindheits- und Jugendforschung (Hrsg.)
   (1993) (pp.15–31).

Sünker, H. and Swiderek, T. (1998)
   Partizipation, Kinderpolitik und politische
   Kultur, in Hufer, K.-P. and Wellie, B.
   Sozialwissenschaftliche und
   bildungstheoretische Reflexionen. Berlin
   (pp.367–89).
Swiderek, T. (2001) The Partizipation von
   Kindern – ein Beitrag zur
   Demokratisierung der Gesellschaft? in
   Güthoff, W. and Sünker, H. (Hrsg.) (2001)
   Handbuch Kinderrechte, Partizipation
   (pp.114–39).
Therborn, G. (1993) The Politics of
   Childhood: The Rights of Children in
   Modern Times, in Castles (Ed.) *Families of*
   Nations. Aldershot (pp.214–91).
Verhellen, E. (1992) Het
   toezichtsmechanisme in de UNO-
   Conventie inzake de rechten van het kind,
   in *De kant van het kind*, Arnhem.
Verhellen, E. (1993) Children and
   Participation Rights, in Heiliö, P.L.,
   Lauronen, E. and Bardy, M. (Eds.) *Politics*
   of Childhood and Children at Risk. Provision –
   Protection – Participation. Wien.
Wiesner, R. et al. (1995) *SGB VIII. Kinder- und*
   Jugendhilfe. München.
Zeiher, H. (1996) *Kindern eine Stimme geben.*
   Zu einer Neubestimmung der
   Kindheitssoziologie und der Sozialpolitik für
   Kinder. Sozialwissenschaftliche Literatur
   Rundschau. 19: 31–2.
Zentrum für Kindheits- und
   Jugendforschung (Hg.) (1993) *Wandlungen*
   der Kindheit. Opladen.

CHAPTER 9

Young People as Outsiders: The Italian Process of Youth Inclusion

Luca Mori

Introduction

This chapter looks at the implementation in Italy of a Law, number 285/97, generally known as 'Turco's Law', and its relationship to the Convention on the Rights of the Child; it also looks in particular, at issues of children's participation. The first section outlines a brief history of the Italian youth policy in the past twenty-five years; this period of time is selected for discussion because the decentralisation process of welfare policies started in Italy in the mid 1970s. The second section describes the provisions of Turco's Law in more detail, with particular emphasis on participation issues. The third section looks at the planning and implementation process. The fourth section elaborates on future possibilities, in particular two potential scenarios to which the translation of the UN Convention principles into the Italian context might lead, and conceptions of citizenship.

Background

The major concern of the organisations which promoted the 1989 UN Convention, first and foremost UNICEF, was to identify strategies to translate the content of the Convention into concrete actions for children, that is, persons aged 18 years and below. For this purpose the Convention was integrated with the Global Action Plan for Children, a typically programmatic document which was also underwritten by the signatory countries and is the guide for any National Action Plan. Therefore, in signing the Convention, countries took upon themselves two different types of

commitment, one law-making and another involving a review of child policies underlying the laws. The law-making commitment implies bringing national legislation on children and young people into line with the principles stated in the Convention, in addition to a general review of all systems (urban, transportation, social control, etc.) that may influence the life of children. The latter commitment requires the planning and implementing of specific actions for the promotion of children's rights (Aster-X, 1999).

Italy was quite expeditious in complying with the law-making task, and integrated the Convention into its legal system by means of Law No. 176 of 27th May 1991. It took a longer time for the second task to be fulfilled, the greatest effort being to set up and disseminate an attitude toward planning which was then totally absent within Italian social policy. The Law No. 285/1997, *Disposizioni per la promozione di diritti e opportunità per l'infanzia e l'adolescenza* (Provisions for the promotion of the rights of and opportunities for children and adolescents),[1] is probably the main instrument adopted by the Italian government in the attempt to achieve the objective of planning. The law is also known as Turco's Law, after the name of the Minister who promoted the bill, and is referred to as such in this chapter. The implementation process of this law implied a considerable reorganisation of the systems responsible for planning and providing services to children and adolescents. Thus, the content and implementation design of the law, as well as the problems and discussions which emerged and continue to arise concerning the law, are very important elements of the Italian experience and discussed below.

Towards decentralisation and planning: twenty-five years of policies for the young in Italy

The lack of planning in Italy is a deficiency only in the field of social policy. Some instances of planning in other contexts, such as the environmental or the economic sectors, date as far back as the post-war years: for example, the *INA-Casa* plan,[2] the twelve-year agricultural development plan, the motorway system plan, etc. (Siza, 1994). Social planning instruments are absent because of a widespread lack of political and cultural interest in this area, and because there is no framework law on social services, although one has now been awaited for over thirty years (Centro di Documentazione e Analisi per l'Infanzia e l'Adolescenza, 2000). It is not surprising that, until the first half of the 1970s, action for the youth population was the almost exclusive responsibility of central state agencies. A considerable body of *ad-hoc* regulations was produced without any connection to a general framework: for example, measures against youth unemployment, drug abuse, as well as provision for the introduction of social participation in school management (Neresini e Ranci, 1992). Some impulse toward changing this status quo came during the summer of 1975, when the Italian Government issued decrees which allocated many functions to regional and local administrations. Different planning approaches in social service policy for the youth population started gaining some ground alongside these changes in administration. In short, actions were designed in broader terms than in the past. In the late 1970s and early 1980s representations of young people as a problem which was to be confined to deviation, repression, and containment actions, slowly yielded to an idea of childhood and adolescence perceived as discrete life stages with specific needs that institutions must represent and satisfy (Castellani, 1993).

However, this theoretical revolution had to come to terms with a political administrative background that was both still very short of suitable professional resources and, more importantly, lacked an attitude of generalised planning in spite of decentralisation. The initial actions for adolescents taken by local administrations were therefore largely fragmented and experimental exercises. A trend can be identified within child and adolescent policy planning efforts of the early 1980s, towards an integrated social policy through the removal of barriers between various sectors (education, health care, juvenile justice). At that time, planning and action units called 'Progetto Giovani' (literally translated, Youth Project) were started by the administrations of some cities, provinces and regions in the north of Italy. Their efforts were directed to people over 18 years, while neglecting the entire population of children, but a short discussion of the features of these units is useful in describing the unfolding of decentralised social policy in Italy.

Neresini and Ranci (1992) state that these *Progetto Giovani* schemes had a distinctive and fundamental effect: they consolidated the different actions of each local administration into a systematic strategy, as instruments for the satisfaction of young people's need for representation within administrations. Many *Progetto Giovani* schemes created consultations, *forum* or *ad-hoc* commissions through which socially active sections of the local younger population could communicate with the local institutions, and share in the design and evaluation of relevant social policy efforts. However, these were élite instruments, because the vast majority of those involved in such participation schemes were (and are) already members of formal associations (sports, cultural or political groups). Such membership experiences are mostly typical of young people raised in families with high cultural capital, and seem to be alien to girls and boys with a working class family background and who already have a job (see numerous research works conducted in the last twenty years, such as Garelli, 1984; Cavalli and De Lillo, 1988, 1993, 1998; Altieri, 1991, 1997). The most innovative *Progetto Giovani* were those which tried to start a debate on young people's life conditions, involving several institutions at the same time, such as Local Health Trusts, Labour Offices, Juvenile Courts, Provincial Education Offices. Further limitations of this practice of social involvement are explored below.

The Turco's Law treads the path marked out by the *Progetto Giovani* experience, in stipulating that local authorities are responsible for approving community-based, three-year social action plans, relevant budgets, and provision of funding. The law gave emphasis to children's issues in those regions that were already responding with some social planning, and it underlined the need to plan in those regions unused to such planning. This law became a sort of test while Italy was waiting for the social services framework law, that arrived at the turn of the century – Law No. 328, 8th November 2000, *Legge quadro per la realizzazione del sistema integrato di interventi e servizi sociali.*[3]

It is important to highlight the twofold effect, which the Turco's Law is having in Italy. On the one hand, it is true that its objective is limited to the promotion of families and resources that children and adolescents can use to develop their personal identities (Presidenza del Consiglio dei Ministri, 2000). On the other hand, its implementation scheme implies the introduction of social planning tools which, by their very nature, can be generalised and exported into contexts other than childhood and adolescence. The Turco's Law is disseminating throughout the Italian regions a range of policy consultation, planning and management processes that are new to the country.

The provisions in the 'Turco's Law' and their implementation

The Turco's Law No. 285/97 is an uncomplicated piece of legislation: a short text of six pages, divided into thirteen articles. The first article provides for the establishment of the *Fondo Nazionale per l'Infanzia e l'Adolescenza* (National Children's and Adolescent's Fund). The law establishes the purpose of the Fund and how it is to be apportioned. The Fund's objective is to implement national, regional and local action promoting the rights, quality of life, development, self-fulfilment and socialisation of children and young people (Law No. 285/97, Art. 1, § 1).

Article 3 summarises the different types of services and action which can benefit from financial contributions from the National Children's and Adolescent's Fund, and Articles 4 to 7 give a detailed description of all possible action areas. Funding through the Law No. 285/97 is granted to plans for:

1. The implementation of services supporting parent-child relationships and confronting poverty in families, measures to provide alternatives to the admission of minors into educational and care institutions, and also has regard for the life conditions of foreign minors (Art. 4).
2. Innovative developments and experiments with social educational services for young children (Art. 5).
3. The implementation of recreational and educational services for the free time of children, even in the periods of time when school teaching activities are discontinued (Art. 6).
4. The promotion of children's and adolescent's rights, the exercise of fundamental civil rights, the improvement of the fruition of the (urban and natural) environment, the protection and cultivation of gender, cultural and ethnic characteristics with due respect to any diversity (Art. 7).
5. The implementation of services for natural or foster families having one or

more minors with disabilities, in order to improve the quality of the family group as a whole and prevent any marginalisation and institutionalisation (Art. 4).

Social actions are to be implemented through three-year community-based plans. The unfolding of the first round of such social plans under the Law No. 285/97, from 1997 to 2000, produced 6,601 activities which have been collected in the data bank of the *Centro Nazionale di Documentazione e Analisi per l'Infanzia e l'Adolescenza* (National Documentation and Analysis Centre for Childhood and Adolescence). There are a number of points worth considering in the actions taken under the law, such as the role of families, social marginalisation, and especially participation.

Substantial focus in the plans has been given to the role of families, and the interaction between families and social services. In accordance with the UN Convention, both the Law No. 285/97 and the Italian National Children Plan state that families (be they natural or foster families) are the environment best suited to the promotion of rights, quality of life, development, self-fulfilment and socialisation of children and young people (see Art. 1, § 1, Law No. 285/97; Presidenza del Consiglio del Ministry, 2000: 21). Thus, family-related services include both those expressly dedicated to the household, and those targeted at the creation of links between social services and families. From the data bank, the first group, of household services, includes parents support services (356) family mediation services (210) and fostering services (102).[4] The second, linking group of services, includes parent training (167), play centres (218), home care (158), educational day centres (156) and school support (102). Many of these services require the active involvement of fathers and mothers, such as the play centres, which are often managed by parents together with children. Overall, these services aim at facilitating and enhancing the educational

and socialisation functions of families, above and beyond their current situation (Mazzoli, 1999). This means that service planners have paid special attention to difficult family situations, such as single-parent families, families where one or both parents are detained in custody, and immigrant families in particular conditions of cultural and economic deprivation.

A second consideration is the Government's decision to confront social distress and marginalisation through means other than institutionalisation. This is well in accord with the need (also recognised in this law) to promote situations suitable for the development of personal identity while respecting ethnic and cultural diversity. In other words, it seems that the approach of Turco's Law is based on a general concept of respect for children's rights, in line with the UN Convention.

The large number of workshops, socialisation centres and recreational centres[5] for young people throughout Italy suggests that value is attached to 'normality' as the main locus for social action and, accordingly, for the development of one's own identity. The problem with these projects is to maintain their efficacy: any socialisation centre or workshop requires a number of human and material resources, as well as a creative turnover of ideas, all of which are difficult to maintain in the long run. Experience suggests that such projects pass through different stages. For example, an early period when they produce a high environmental impact, as shown by indicators such as attendance, multi-ethnicity, number of activities performed, etc.; after which they become less creative and stagger, eventually losing all the vitality that initially made them so successful (De Ambrogio and Setti Bassanini, 1996).

The emphasis on personal identity promotion and development projects should not be taken to mean that action against overt social marginalisation and deviation was dramatically reduced. Many of these latter activities follow financing tracks, which are separate from those under the

Law No. 285/97, such as funding available under the laws against drug abuse or juvenile crime. But the innovative scope of Law No. 285/97 also had an impact, albeit marginal, on these areas of social marginalisation: a new type of activity in Italy, the 106 street work projects, which are rapidly catching on thanks to Turco's Law.

Participation

The projects concerning children's participation are the most thorny and controversial activities. In this respect Turco's Law is rather ambiguous, since children's participation is given two different definitions which both government and local administrations often confuse, perhaps deliberately. The first definition vaguely refers to a sort of political inclusion[6] of children. Provision is made for funding activities that 'promote the participation of children and young people in the local community, even in the local administrative life' (Law No. 285/97, Art. 7). The second definition is based on the concept of participation as a form of social inclusion. The Law clearly promotes modifications to the urban and natural environments to make them more suited to use by children. The framework, in which both meanings of children's participation are set in this law, is the common requirement for dissemination within the local community and particularly among social service providers and administrators, as provided for in Article 7.

The basic ambiguity emanating from Article 7 reflects the general difficulties that are intrinsic to many theoretical discussions of youth citizenship, in particular the thinking behind youth citizenship in the wake of Marshall, as a stratification of different rights (see discussion below). Such ambiguities have considerably affected the design of specific activities promoting children's participation.

At the moment in Italy there is no specific category of projects focusing on children's participation, apart from the 'childhood and urban space' group, and activities for the dissemination of children's and adolescent's rights. Children's participation projects do exist in several Italian regions, although their content and number vary greatly. Some administrations (but very few), decided to reach out via youth consultations and *fora*. Other administrations developed children's participation activities focussed on specific issues, such as traffic control plans or town plans, but the degree of acceptance of children's suggestions in the decision-making process remains to be seen. Other administrations by-passed the issue of children's and adolescent's *political* inclusion and replaced it with *social* inclusion. Thus, some municipalities began from an educational perspective, such as guided tours to art galleries, museums, other institutions and city parks during school hours. The prevailing idea of children's participation in these administrations had a strong pedagogic connotation, because the understanding of democratic decision-making mechanisms, symbols and transmission is seen as preparatory to the exercise of some real influence on civic life.

These issues were placed on political agendas recently, and as a consequence the dissemination of active participation by children is still rather scarce. My perception is that the Italian regions that are more sensitive to this issue, such as Umbria, Calabria or Emilia-Romagna, are slowly experiencing the development of a hybrid type of children's participation. These regional administrations do not seem to approach the issue by setting up particular activities or specific institutions, such as the well-known mini-parliaments of young people. Rather they involve children in starting from the steps required to set up and manage any activities, which is absolutely necessary if services responding to young people's needs and promoting their rights and opportunities are to be provided. The design and accomplishment of any socialisation centre or play centre, including all management decisions, operating hours, activity content, space organisation and furnishing, as well as action evaluation, may turn into an activity promoting the real participation of children and young people.

Turco's Law deserves appreciation for the attention it pays to ethnic and cultural diversity, a focus which is not always evident in Italy. In this context Law No. 285/97 is performing a pioneering role. Ethnically speaking, the Italian peninsula has been relatively homogeneous for the past century. Previously, it was crossed by massive migration flows, but usually Italy was just the corridor towards northern Europe. For about the past decade Italy has became a destination for many immigrants, especially from North Africa (Morocco, Algeria, Tunisia, Senegal, Mali), the Indian subcontinent and Eastern Europe (mostly Albania). The presence of African and Asiatic families in particular, has meant that many Italian schools have been educating increasing numbers of 'foreign' students, with all the linguistic, learning and integration problems that this implies. To the best of my knowledge, the Law No. 285/97 is the first Italian governmental effort that puts special emphasis on ethnic issues within policy for children and adolescents, indicated in the special consideration given to the conditions of foreign minors and the protection of gender, cultural and ethnic characteristics in Article 3.

The planning process

As mentioned, activities were distributed throughout Italy via a complex planning process organised into different administrative and territorial levels. On closer examination, the process started by the Law No. 285/97 has the appearance of a graduated series of boxes, one inside the other. At a general level there is the Italian Government Action Plan for Children and Adolescents which enunciates the general principles for fostering children's and adolescent's rights nation-wide. The level below covers regional framework legislation: basically, Regional Administration Acts which adapt the principles of the National Plan to the local situation and arrange the regional territory into discrete districts which are to receive allocations from the National Children's Fund. Often such districts coincide with Provincial Administrations or the administrative subdivisions of the Italian National Health Service. The Law No. 285/97 stipulates that such territorial districts are to exclude fifteen large Italian cities for which 30 per cent of the National Fund is reserved. For the purposes of Turco's Law these special-funding cities were considered as separate territorial subdivisions with their own planning arrangements.

Following the territorial subdivision and the allocation of funding, each district drafted Local Action Plans covering a three-year period.[7] Planning was based on common procedural steps, the first of which was the establishment of a *Gruppo Tecnico Territoriale* (GTT, that is, Local Technical Workgroup) responsible for planning in each local district. The most innovative feature was that, for the first time, planning workgroups included representatives of entities relevant for young people: Article 2, § 2 of the Law No. 285/97 stipulates that representatives of Municipal Administrations, Health Trusts, Provincial Educational Offices and Juvenile Justice Offices must be members of these workgroups.

This combination of different experts ensured adequate performance in the second planning step, the analysis of the situation of children and young people in each planning district. In spite of many limitations, the GTTs proved to be appropriate in analysing causal relationships and setting planning objectives. Once the plan was designed, and objectives identified, the planning workgroups began designing individual actions. However, excluding the projects which *inter alia* contemplate street work and the sporadic actions which formed youth consultation mechanisms, the Law No. 285/97 did not cause any real revolutionary breakthrough in youth policy. Its most visible effect can be likened to the principle of communicating vessels: many of the efforts of excellence treasured in any specific planning district extended homogeneously throughout the relevant region, and this happened more or less all over Italy.

The last step of any plan was the initiation of individual projects. Probably, this was the most controversial stage of the entire planning process, and to understand why this was so, it is necessary to allude to the recent development of non-profit-making organisations in Italy. The Italian non-profit world (which in Italy many refer to as 'third sector' to differentiate it from the 'first' and the 'second' sectors, that is, the state and the market, respectively (Donati, 1998; Ascoli and Pasquinelli, 1993; Boccacin, 1993) has undergone a stunning acceleration of its differentiation dynamics and spheres of action. Social work co-operatives and foundations entered among the number of service providers, alongside the typical, traditional activities of volunteer, non-profit organisations. Starting from the mid-1970s, the presence of such service organisations has grown annually, and their roles increased exponentially, so much that many authors maintain that the nature of the Italian welfare state has changed radically and now can be termed *welfare mix* (Melandri, 2000; Frisanco and Ranci, 1999; Stanzani, 1999; Jovine, 1999). This term refers to the diversity of entities and perspectives that nowadays contribute to the definition of welfare requirements and strategies for meeting their needs. In conjunction with the state, which focuses on representation criteria, and the market, which follows the logic of profit, there is now the so-called third sector, a galaxy composed of a plurality of interests and value criteria. It goes without saying that conflict in establishing respective spheres and scope are by no means rare, and Turco's Law was not immune from such controversies.

Third sector exponents have argued against the recent efforts for children's policy made by the Italian State and Regional Administrations. Their arguments centre on the exclusion of social work co-operatives and volunteer organisations from the planning process. Judging from the literature examined, and personal interviews conducted, it seems that the assistance of many such co-operatives and organisations traditionally providing services to minors was asked at the analysis stage, which greatly contributed to the quality of the studies made. But, apparently, requests for such assistance did not occur during the project design stage, when the content of individual activities was decided upon. According to representatives of Italian institutions, the third sector was excluded from the decision-making process, because there are no socially accepted criteria to ascertain the representativeness of any non-profit co-operative or organisation. In short, Regional and Provincial Administrations preferred keeping the action and ideas process within a particular circle of institutions because of the large variety of values and organisational types which characterise the non-profit world, and given the absence of representation criteria to warrant the inclusion of some entities in the decision-making process to the detriment of others.

Future possibilities

Italian institutions made great efforts to fulfil their statutory planning requirements under Turco's Law, especially considering the brand new elements only recently included in the child and adolescent policy and the strict deadlines imposed by government. Therefore, the first three-year planning cycle can be regarded as a test period, and it is extremely difficult to foresee the developments which this piece of legislation may initiate. The institutions concerned with the implementation of the Law No. 285/97 are redefining their required roles, activities, responsibilities and professional profiles, and nobody can confidently predict the outcomes that will emerge from the debate.

However, a consideration of possible

future scenarios may assist in focussing on the issue of the impact of the action planning process on the promotion of children's rights. In particular there is a need to understand if and how action plans can be functional to the conceptual and practical promotion of children's citizenship. Here two possible future scenarios are considered, one rather pessimistic and another decidedly rosier. The first I call the *institutional closure* scenario, and the second the *informed participation* scenario.

Institutional closure

In the institutional closure scenario, the passing of a social services framework law in 2000 could make the planning processes recently established a component of the social policy domain, as is highly desirable. This process could integrate action plans under the Law No. 285/97 with the general social-health care plans. Meanwhile, public administrations could train and employ specific professionals exclusively dedicated to the management and close follow-up of project work for children and adolescents. In consequence, the required planning procedures could become standard routine operations in most regional administrations. The current situation could be analysed through data possessed by the various services and information from evaluation surveys, predominantly therefore through so-called 'experts' monitoring. The content of projects could become consistent among planning districts and regions and, in essence, there could be a highly integrated planning system specifically dedicated to children's policy planning.

At least three elements of this scenario deserve special attention. First, the integration of action plans under the Law No. 285/97 under the umbrella of social-health care planning. Second, the system differentiation processes to which Turco's Law might lead, such as the training and use of professionals explicitly dedicated to child action plans. Third, the possible consequences of local action standardisation,

with the debasement of evaluation processes down to experts monitoring.

If action plans under the Law No. 285/97 were included in regional social-health care plans,[8] they might be part of an extremely general scheme, subject to decision-making structures at the top administrative levels. Such an arrangement might be very effective in ensuring a high degree of consistency in the policy for children and young people. For example, such integrated social-health care planning might prevent the risk of having a two-speed welfare system in Italy, since actions under the Law No. 285/97 enjoy generous financial coverage from the National Children's Fund, whereas other child-related actions receive more fragmentary funding. But in this case, quite probably children's contributions to problem definition and problem-solving strategy design would be completely dispersed in moving direction from bottom-up to the highest levels of the administrative pyramid.

The same point applies in the idea of training and using professionals specialising in Turco's Law. This law encompasses a huge area, its funding spurs a sizeable variety of action projects and, obviously, there are many people involved in action design, provision and evaluation in different capacities. Such a situation may favour what I define as *system differentiation*. Within municipal, provincial or regional administrations, as well as among non-profit organisations, there are already some full-time personnel in charge of following the progress of the Law No. 285/97. On the one hand, some believe that such organisational set-up indicates good efficiency; on the other hand, it might be a factor against the homogeneous dissemination of a culture for children's rights within institutions and non-profit organisations alike. In other words, the very view that special personnel must be available for promoting the rights of children and young people once again means relegating such rights to a specific area, whereas I believe that the promotion of these rights should cut across the several activities which concern children, either directly, or indirectly.

Evaluation processes are potentially a very useful strategy to make children's participation real, but can be easily turned into exercises which go in the opposite direction. This occurs when the focus is almost only on service monitoring by experts, which is what happened during the first three-year planning cycle. The evaluation of projects through standard indicators and survey instruments is very useful to gain insight in variations and discrepancies from expected results. Efficiency and effectiveness indicators make it possible to control financial distributions and, if standardised, to compare similar services provided in different districts. However, what is missing in all this is the voice of children. In the majority of cases, their involvement in the evaluation process is limited to the registration of their attendance at the various services, which of course helps to understand the demand for such services. In summary, if this tendency becomes established, it would distort the very spirit of social action evaluation which in Italy is based on the concept that service recipients enjoy the wider status of *citizens* and *intentional social actors* (Altieri, 1997).

Local action standardisation might, then, become the padlock which definitely closes children's access to, and participation in institutions. Local action standardisation approximately means the fairly homogeneous regional, and in some cases national, dissemination of an action which became well established in one particular district. So far, this effect has spread child and adolescent services almost everywhere in our country, but the perpetuation of an integrated, standardised approach could minimise, if not prevent, any experimentation with new project content. Proven, specific actions would be well disseminated and financed, without paying the smallest attention to children's desires and needs. It is no coincidence that nearly always children's needs have been assessed via the lenses of social services, as noted above.

Informed participation

In this second scenario, the participants to the children and adolescent pact would positively ponder on the implications of attributing the citizen status to minors, the types of rights involved and the concrete exercise and fruition thereof. In addition to this, children's needs would be assessed in detail through practices endorsed by special survey procedures based on ethnographic and ecological approaches on top of statistical ones. Action projects should not be exported from one community to another as a fad (fad being a reasonable doubt, which gains some ground considering the nature of the first three-year plans) but this export should be warranted by the presence of community-specific requirements. This would leave a rather large margin for experimentation and innovation. The integration of action plans under the Law No. 285/97 into regional social-health care planning should be carefully engineered, trying to be always attentive to child-specific needs. In this respect, consideration should be given to financial integration as well, so as to avoid imbalances between the different action areas (parent support, personal identity promotion, social deviation and marginalisation prevention, unemployment, etc.), while keeping action project planners separate.

For all this to be meaningful, children's participation should be stimulated and really accepted, and to do so, two basic, interdependent, conditions need to be satisfied. First, the area of children's rights should acquire a cross-sectoral dimension informing the entire implementation process of the Law No. 285/97. Second, it should be understood that often child and adolescent identity development processes are based on cultural references, which are totally different from those of adults. The first condition was discussed above, and the second is discussed further here.

Most Italian scientific research work on youth deals with the identification of hierarchies in the values of adolescent's 'subcultures'. In essence, the young people interviewed are asked to place typically adult cultural objects, such as politics, democracy, family, social commitment, career, work, etc., into a hierarchical order. Yet the very idea of 'subculture' implies a different order in the issues and practices which are typical of the adult world. In summary, the foremost dilemma that challenges the legitimacy of this concept of youth can be epitomised in two questions. Is it correct to think of the life of adolescents as a set of special lifestyles, behaviours and attitudes which fit in with what the culture of adults regards as structural components of life? And if this were the case, is it really certain that the relational dynamics developing around these components are the fundamental basis for the construction of personal identity among young people?

These are extremely complicated issues which require a very large, in-depth discussion that is not appropriate here. Many British authors have responded to these questions, and certainly the indications coming from their work do not recommend picturing young people's culture as more or less similar to the culture of adults (Blackman and France, 2001). Italian scholars, such as Maria Teresa Torti, Alessandro Dal Lago and Angela Castellani, began by analysing the communication aspects in the world of youth, and came to conclusions which are not far from the results of the British researchers.

Probably, the most useful indications from such type of studies are those which see the informal dimension of socialisation as the most fertile ground for personal and collective identities to blossom. Indeed, many of these authors feel that the communication form and logic regulating informal socialisation cut across – often with a violent impact – the formal dimension of socialisation, such as schools, sports clubs, cultural or religious associations; young people's subcultures still exist and proliferate even within high schools or scout groups.

Conclusions: the Turco's Law and conceptions of children's citizenship

The principal innovations introduced in Italy by the Law No. 285/97 can be condensed into four points:

1. The endowment of a National Children's Fund apportioned by Regional Administrations to their planning districts and, accordingly, the creation of these territorial subdivisions to determine the demand for child and adolescent services. This Fund is the most considerable resource allocation ever available for child social policy, and its development was a new, strong political sign of the importance attached to the issue of children's rights.
2. The integration and centralisation of need assessment and response processes as lead by the GTTs thanks to their analysis and project development functions.[9]
3. Uniform action coverage throughout Italy, since the number of areas without infant services and/or projects for young people is becoming smaller than in the past, although still only 8 per cent of children have access to day nursery services in our country.
4. Introduction of evaluation among the project management processes with the objective of re-designing actions in the course of their deployment, as necessary.

Turco's Law suggests at least two possible future scenarios. Those discussed here, that of institutional closure and informed participation, have very different outcomes for the development of children's participation. The first offers a standardisation and predominance of expert, adult, opinions. The second is based on perceptions of the nature of childhood and young personhood, suggesting a difference from adult hierarchies of categories of social life.

I believe that these latter considerations have some bearing on the theme of children's participation, because they challenge all the strategies which until now were adopted by public administrations to promote forms of active citizenship among boys and girls. In practice, I wonder whether the mechanisms for children's participation suggested so far, such as youth mini-parliaments and consultations, are just examples of how adults try and apply their political participation and decision-making instruments to the world of young people, although such instruments have very little to do with the culture of young people. I feel it necessary to reiterate once more that the pursuit of children's participation should intersect the various action spheres, and, for both the determination of children's requirements and daily service activities, importance should be attached to their informal involvement and meetings, where roles and functions are perceived in a more nuanced, softer way.

Notes

1 In the Italian sociological literature the meaning of the words 'young people' is very general and refers, most of the time, to the young adult population (20–35 years). The Turco's law is addressed to children (0–12 years) and to adolescents (13–18 years), and this is the reason why the expression 'adolescent' is used here.
2 INA-Casa was a post-war housebuilding plan started in 1949 and finished 1963 (Di Biagi, 2001).
3 Literally translated: *framework law for the constitution of an integrated system of social services and social interventions.*
4. In Italy the term 'parents support' indicates several types of actions for easing the material living conditions of families. For example, the free distribution of children's products, special health care provision or 'small gentleman's loans'. (Small gentlemen's loans are small loans, maximum 2,500–3,000 euro, lent without any economic guarantee, relying only on the beneficiaries words.) 'Fostering services'

includes the procedures required to establish whether two spouses are unfit for parenthood and the various steps for the temporary assignment of a minor to a different household. Generally, 'family mediation services' offer psychological support to ease tensions and conflicts within families. In the vast majority of cases, services are directed not only to legally established families, but also to *de facto* families or cohabitations.
5 'Workshop' means a place dedicated to performing specific activities, usually related to music and the arts, such as theatre, sculpture or photography. 'Socialisation centre' indicates a more or less similar service, although it is more focused on the gathering and socialisation of young people. 'Recreational centre' means a place for ludic activities (that is, activities that have something to do with education through recreation, such as games, readings, performances, etc.). Generally, workshops are intended for older young people and, in some cases, people over 18; socialisation centres are more often for young people; recreational centres are typically directed to younger children.
6 The distinction between social inclusion and political inclusion mirrors the difference between a simple participation in societal relationships and real membership in the political community.
7 In the year 2000 the projects started with the 1997 planning came to an end. While I am writing this paper, the 2000–2003 plans have been available for a year, but from what I could read, there are not relevant changes in contents of policies.
8 Given the comparatively short period of time that has passed since the promulgation of the framework law, the direction of this process is not yet clear.
9 The term 'centralisation' might sound a trifle ambiguous; indeed, the GTTs were set up as local, decentralised structures for demand analysis and project development. Nevertheless, I decided to use this word to allude to the fact that the

situation of children is examined through the centralising of analytical resources into a local, decentralised structure.

References

AA VV. (1993) *Ragazzi senza tempo*. Genova: Costa & Nolan.

Altieri, L. (1991) *Tracce di libertà*. Milano: Angeli.

Altieri, L. (1997) (a cura di) *Tempi di adolescenti*. Faenza: Homeless Book.

Ascoli, U. and Pasquinelli, S. (Eds.) (1993) *Il welfare mix: Stato sociale e terzo settore*, Milano: Angeli.

Aster-X (Agenzia di Servizi per il Terzo Settore) (1999) *Primo rapporto sullo stato d'attuazione della L. 285/97*. Roma: Ministero degli Affari Sociali.

Blackman and France (2001) Youth Marginality Under 'Postmodernism', in Stevenson, (Ed.), *Culture and Citizenship*. London: Sage.

Boccaccin, L. (1993) *La sinergia della differenza: un analisi sociologica del terzo settore in Italia*. Milano: Angeli.

Castellani, A. (1993) *Stereotipi incrostati* in AA. VV. (1993) *Ragazzi senza tempo*, Genova: Costa & Nolan.

Cavalli, A. e de Lillo, A. (1988) *Giovani anni 80*. Bologna: Il Mulino.

Cavalli, A. e de Lillo, A. (1993) *Giovani anni 90*. Bologna: Il Mulino.

Cavalli, A. e de Lillo, A. (1998) *Giovani verso il 2000*. Bologna: Il Mulino.

Centro nazionale di documentazione e analisi per l'infanzia e l'adolescenza (2000) Il calamaio e l'arcobaleno: orientamenti per progettare e costruire il piano territoriale della L. 285/97. Firenze: Istituto degli Innocenti.

Dal Lago, A. (1981) *La produzione della devianza*. Milano: Feltrinelli.

Dalla Mura, F. (2000) I servizi sociali in attesa della legge quadro. *Cittadini in Crescita*. 1: 1, 19–29.

De Ambrogio, U. and Setti Bassanini (Eds.) (1996) *Tutela dei cittadini e qualità dei servizi*. Milano: Angeli.

Donati, P. (Ed.) (1998) *Sociologia del terzo settore*. Roma: Carocci.

Donati, P. (Ed.) (1993) *Fondamenti di politica sociale: teorie e modelli*. Roma: NIS.

Donati, P. (Ed.) (1988) *Ripensare il welfare*. Milano: Angeli.

Foucault, M. (1972) *L'ordine del discorso*. Torino: Einaudi.

Frisanco, R. e Ranci, C. (1997) *Le dimensioni della solidarietà: secondo rapporto sul volontariato sociale italiano*. Roma: Fondazione italiana per il Volontariato.

Garelli, F. (1984) *La generazione della vita quotidiana*. Bologna: Il Mulino.

Griffin, C. (1997) *Representation of the Young*, in Roche, J. and Tucker, S. (Eds.) *Youth in Society*. London: Sage.

Hebdige, D. (1979) *Subculture: the Meaning of Style*. London: Routledge.

Hebdige, D. (1988) *Hiding in the Light: On Images and Things.*, London: Routledge.

Jovine, N. (1999) *Il libro del terzo settore: l'universo del non-profit tra impresa e solidarietà sociale*. Roma: Adnkronos Libri.

Kauffman and Pijnenburg (1999) Playing Simultaneous Games of Chess. *Social Work in Europe*.

Melandri, V. (2000) *Il fund raising per le organizzazioni non profit*. Il sole 24 ore, Milano.

Melucci, A. (1982) *L'invenzione del Presente*. Bologna: Il Mulino.

Melucci, A. (1984) *Altri codici: aree di movimento nella metropolis*. Bologna: Il Mulino.

Melucci, A. (1991) *Il gioco dell'io*. Milano: Feltrinelli.

Mori, L. et Galloni, P. (1998) La TRC Chilienne: Une Lecture Critique Sous Deux Prospectives. *L'At Srée Revue de Droit Pénal et des Droits de l'Homme*. 2: 8, 27–34.

Neresini, F. e Ranci, C. (1992) *Disagio giovanile e politica sociale*. Roma: NIS.

Pitch, T. (1982) *La devianza*. Firenze: La Nuova Italia.

Presidenza del Consiglio dei Ministri (2000) *Piano nazionale per l'infanzia*. Roma: Agenzia Poligrafica dello Stato.

Siza, R. (1994) *La programmazione e le relazioni sociali*. Milano: Angeli.

Stanzani, S. (1999) *La specificità relazionale del terzo settore*. Milano: Angeli.

Vallentine, Chelton and Chambers (Eds.) (1998) *Cool Places: an Introduction to Youth and Youth Cultures*. London: Routledge.

Wagner Pacifici R. (2000) *Theorizing the Standoff*. Princeton: Cambridge University Press.

Wagner Pacifici R. (1998) Come teorizzare le contingenze, ovvero l'analisi degli stalli, *Rassegna Italiana di Sociologia*. 4: 387–411.

Wagner Pacifici R. (1988) *The Moror Moraliti Play: Terrorism as a Social Drama*. Chicago: University of Chicago Press.

CHAPTER 10

Young People Active in Youth Research in The Netherlands: An Innovative Approach

Jan Laurens Hazekamp

Introduction

This chapter deals with the involvement of young people in policy-oriented research. In the course of eight years the Alexander Foundation has established an innovative youth research approach in which young people are *promoters of* rather than the *object* of research. In the initial and pioneering period most attention has been given to the development of methods in working with young people. For example, to recruit young people for voluntary research projects, to kindle them with enthusiasm for it, to train and coach them as well as to establish a relationship of real cooperation between young people and the supporting professional researchers. After that period, the role of young people has been extended in such a way for them to take an influencing role on the institutions they have to deal with as well. They function not only as a researcher but also as an inspector or as a consultant.

This chapter looks at the work of the Alexander Foundation and its research, as an example of the participation of young people. First will be provided information about youth participation in the broader context of the development of participatory methods in youth research. Second, the practice of young people involved in research projects will be described, with particular attention paid to projects involving young people in care. Third, an overview will be given as to methods used for young people to be active in policies as an inspector or a consultant.

Youth participation

Since the end of the 1980s, under the influence of the Council of Europe, youth participation has received high priority in Dutch youth policy. Young people need to be able to influence policy in schools, leisure time, urban planning, and social welfare services, at the working place and in local politics. Boys and girls should be more involved in decisions being made about their lives.

In the last decade, the national government enacted laws which oblige schools, welfare institutions and other helping services to organise participation that enables their target groups to have a say in their policies and programmes. These laws are not prescriptive in the detail of how participation has to be realised in the institutions, but only give a frame of reference within which every institution has to work out participation according to their own terms. In Dutch culture the relative autonomy of non-government institutions has to be respected by the central governmental authorities.

The Dutch Ministry of Health, Welfare and Sports has a pivotal role in stimulating youth participation. By means of several large-scale pilot programmes, especially in the field of local youth policy, the issue of youth participation has been put on the political agenda of many local communities.

In 1997 the amended Law on Youth Care was put into operation. In this law the right to complain and the right to have a say in policies was formulated. Youth Care

Institutes are obliged to organise a client council and to develop procedures for the treatment of complaints. Moreover the institutions are permitted to introduce a client trust person. This law has recently been evaluated. The new Law on Youth Care expected to be operational during 2003 will stress the importance of the strengthening of the position of the client in youth care.

Although we live in a solid democratic society, and despite all the initiatives and activities in the field of youth participation, to give a permanent voice to all kinds of young people in policy matters is easier said than done. Usually young people are primarily seen as pupils who have to prepare themselves for an adult future and as 'objects' of services and youth policy. They are hardly being spoken to as young citizens and partners with their own ideas and opinions. There is a clear lack of communication between authorities and professionals on the one hand and young people on the other hand. To enable young people to participate, and to include them in policy making, needs hard work, especially from the side of the adult world.

Adult barriers

The opinions of adults about young people are often one-sided and dominated by the so-called deficiency model. That means that adults are inclined to see young people as having a lack: they *need* education, they *need* help, and they *need* welfare programmes or correction. In this view, the social competence of young people or the potential for it, to be a partner in policy and practice of education, helping services, welfare and correctional programmes, is overlooked. This is the more the case when it concerns young people who do not respond to the average middle-class standards and are hanging around in the streets. They are negatively stereotyped by adults imbued with moral concern. This is why an equal partnership in society between adults and young people is still far from every-day practice.

The most important and necessary condition for stimulating youth participation is starting a learning process from the side of the adults, the adult professions and the adult institutions. To take youth participation seriously – as an educationalist, a teacher, a social worker, a volunteer or as a policy-maker – means to reflect on your own attitudes and the hierarchical culture in your own institution in order to be able find out how to involve young people as real partners in youth policy and practice. Some years ago I accepted this challenge as a professional youth researcher.

Young people and youth research

As a senior lecturer at the Free University in Amsterdam I have been involved in youth research programmes for more than 20 years. I was increasingly concerned by the gap between the stable and ageing world of the Dutch youth researchers and the ever changing and new young generations being researched. On the one side youth researchers continue writing articles, publishing books, attending seminars, formulating and changing theories about young people in present society. On the other side young people are living everyday, and having not the faintest idea about all those articles, books and reports about their lives and the influence these works have on youth policy and practice. The only thing they are allowed to do is to fill in questionnaires, perform as an interviewee or be observed.

This insight troubled me and led me to seek a new path: involving young people themselves in policy-oriented youth research programmes. To facilitate my plans I established the *Alexander Foundation*. The philosophy of this foundation is to empower young people as an active partner in youth research, to give them a chance to influence youth policy and practices themselves. On a voluntary basis young people are involved in the research process: developing questionnaires, carrying out individual and panel interviews amongst peers and with adults, interpreting the results, and presenting the results to the policy makers.

Sharing expertise

Scientifically skilled adult co-workers of the Alexander Foundation share their research and consulting expertise with the every-day life expertise of the young people involved in the projects. In the process of every project a balance has to been found between the input of adult co-workers and the input of the young people. Coaching and training of the boys and girls in research and consulting practice is always necessary and expected by the young people, as well as the writing of the first drafts of questionnaires, analysis and reports.

The degree of participation by young people in policy and practice of our projects depends on the starting situation. For instance, it will be clear that if the board of a youth organisation mandates the Alexander Foundation to support them in their own research (in other words when the young people have the ownership of the research), the balance between the input of young people and the input of co-workers will be different to that in a project in which boys and girls who at the beginning are unknown to each other, and who are invited by the Alexander Foundation to join for a short time in a project. They might not be motivated to spend a lot of time on the project. In this respect strict rules and procedures concerning an adequate balance have not been developed yet and it may be that it will never be possible.

Sharing experiences in the project enables young people to be active in research. They appreciate being taken seriously in the research process, to learn something from each other and to have fun at the same time: also for them to be able as a researcher to talk with their peers about their life issues, and to feel competent to address authorities and organisations and actually involve themselves in decisions being taken about them.

Challenges

To take young people seriously in youth research means that new ways have to be found by professionals to cope with new challenges. Traditional codes have to be re-interpreted. In the case of the Alexander Foundation, as a vanguard of innovative youth research, new standards have to be developed regarding the validity and reliability of the research as well as the quality of the policy consultancy and youth work. At the moment the Alexander Foundation does not fit in the world of science, or in the world of youth policy, nor in the world of youth work. It is a new mix situated on the cross roads, which means intriguing new perspectives for innovation, but at the same time also a confusing and sometimes awkward position towards regular funders and discipline-oriented critics.

A broad scope of themes

The research practice of the Alexander Foundation shows a broad scope of themes. To give an idea some examples are given below, including youth councils (another form of participation), young mothers, migration and residential care. In particular, the evaluation project on residential youth care will be described extensively as the final example.

Evaluation of local youth councils

The Dutch Ministry of Health, Welfare and Sports commissioned the Alexander Foundation to carry out evaluation research on the functioning of the comparatively recent phenomenon of local youth councils in the Netherlands.

The Alexander Foundation recruited a panel of twelve boys and girls varying in ethnic background, educational level and region and with or without a disability. First, this panel discussed its own experiences concerning local youth councils. Second, the members discussed the methods they would use in the research, the planning and time allocated, and how they wanted to be coached and trained. The co-workers of the Alexander Foundation supported these discussions and gave the panel a lot of technical information. Finally, it was decided that the young research panel would divide into two-member teams, and would hold extensive evaluative group interviews with members of local youth councils. Twelve local youth councils were selected for the research.

On the basis of the findings of the research, a multi-coloured poster, which folds like a booklet and contains recommendations formulated by the young researchers themselves, was produced. This poster/booklet is a guide for young people who want to start a local youth council. Thousands of posters have been sent to all kind of institutions in the country and up to now hundreds of research reports have been ordered. (For further information on this project, see The Young Research Company and Stichting Alexander 1998.)

Teenage motherhood researched

Hengelo, a city in the eastern part of the Netherlands, commissioned the Alexander Foundation to do research on the problems and wishes of young mothers. For the research a team of young mothers was recruited with the help of social welfare agencies as intermediaries. Young mothers discussed the topics on which they wanted to interview other young mothers (unknown to them) in Hengelo. They decided to hold individual interviews. At first most of the young interviewers had to cope with feelings of uncertainty. But during the process they gained self-confidence. Moreover, they discovered they were not the only ones with problems, with questions about child raising and especially with financial difficulties.

The results of the research were presented to aldermen, councillors and representatives of local institutions. The local authorities were very impressed by the involvement of young mothers in the research. One of the

political effects has been that the city of Hengelo established an information annex and meeting-centre for young mothers (see Naber and Kayser, 1997).

The Cape Verdian research

This research was the result of cooperation between the Alexander Foundation and the young people's own organisation of Cape Verdian Youth. This organisation saw itself as 'the silent migrants'. They wanted to be able to leave and move on from this position by doing research themselves amongst the young Cape Verdian generation because of concern about their bleak prospects for the future. The local government of Rotterdam commissioned the research project, but it was arranged that the organisation of the Cape Verdian Youth got the ownership of the research, and the Alexander Foundation became the research partner with them.

An interesting learning process started between the Cape Verdian Youth organisation and the Alexander Foundation: how to cooperate with equal competencies and different responsibilities. Themes for questionnaires were discussed, panel meetings were held, interview training was given, and arrangements made for processing and analysing the empirical data. In addition, time schedules were developed and had to be observed.

In an intensive up-and-down process, both partners finally managed to produce a book full of experiences, knowledge and recommendations which was presented to members of the Dutch Parliament. From then on the organisation of Cape Verdian Youth was very actively involved in developing projects for young Cape Verdians on the basis of their research (see Naber and Veldman, 1998).

Evaluation research in a residential setting

Since the end of the 1980s, a long process to raise the quality of policy and practice of youth help began in the youth care sector, including ambulant care, foster care and residential care. Legislators, the Employer's Association and directors of youth care institutions cooperated in the complex process to improve the accessibility of the youth care system, to accomplish more cohesion in the offer of care for young people, and to achieve a more standardised and effective registration in the youth care system.

In this process of renovation of the youth care system attention was also focused on the position of the clients – both young people and parents. The prevailing idea of those wishing to introduce change has been that the position of young people and parents has to be strengthened. If clients are not allowed to have a say in policy and practice of youth care, then the offer of help can never be adequately linked to their way of life.

The traditional offer of youth care was standardised. The problems of clients were diagnosed and interpreted from the view of the specialised institution and the clients had to fit in with the offer of help that was made. There was no question of a dialogue with the clients, and no partnership with the professionals which would give the possibility to adapt the offer to the needs of the clients and to improve the quality of the offer with help of the feedback of clients. In 1996 an investigation among 160 institutions in the youth care system showed that an active input of clients in the policy and practice had not been regulated (Jumelet and Haarsma, 1998).

In recent years legislation was passed to force youth care institutions to take seriously the participation of young people and parents. Laws are now operative on clients having a say in policy matters, and having 'the right to complain'. Institutions are obliged to establish an independent complaints commission as well as to appoint a trusted representative for clients. Moreover, every institution in the youth care system has to start a client council.

Participation of young people in the policy process in residential institutions is not a matter of course. What does it mean if young residential dwellers have a say in matters concerning the conditions of their stay and psycho-social treatment? Will unrest arise if discussions have to be held about any rule? Will group leaders accept teenagers with problematical behaviour as policing partners although they at the same time are involved with them in a helping process?

In order to gain more knowledge about the possibilities and the problems of youth participation in 1997 the Ministry of Health, Welfare and Sport commissioned a pilot project in two residential institutions, respectively De Leo-Stichting in Borculo and De Hoenderloo Groep in Hoenderloo/ Twello. The leading philosophy of this pilot project was that establishing an institutional youth council as a form of client council is meaningless without changing the organisational culture as a whole. Only if the culture of the institution will be open and supportive to deal with a youth council, and the group leaders are willing to cooperate with the teenager clients as partners, is there a chance that young people will gain a real say in policy and practice of the institution.

The pilot project

For these reasons the pilot project aimed at starting an intensive process in which the young residential dwellers as well as the professional adults were involved. Members of the Board, directors, sub-managers, group leaders, along with young people were involved in the preparation of a youth council which would be firmly embedded in the policy culture of the residential institution.

The project consisted of two parts. In the first part – the information phase – information was given to teenage clients about the legislation on youth care, about the significance of having a say in policy matters, and the lawful rights and duties of minors in residential settings. This information was given by teams of young residential dwellers, trained for this purpose as peer educators.

In the second part – the communication phase – so-called 'improvement sessions' were organised between young residential dwellers and the professionals working in the institutions. In these sessions discussions could be held about the problems of living together in a residential setting, the lack of open communication, and the ways in which this could be improved through the establishment of a youth council – whatever form it would take – that would be taken seriously by the adults in the institution. The information phase and the communication phase were executed by JP 2000, Lelystad and Stichting IVIO, Lelystad.

The Alexander Foundation was asked to carry out an evaluation research of the pilot project. In order to disseminate the experiences and insights of the pilot project to other residential institutions.

Young ex-clients as junior researchers

From the beginning three boys and one girl aged 18–19 years, and of different ethnic origin, were involved in the research as junior researchers. They had a broken, low-vocational school career, were unemployed, and three of them had a residential background. They were employed by the Alexander Foundation for half a year by means of the national Jeugd Werk Garantie Plan, which guaranteed unemployed young people a paid job on a temporary basis. Co-workers of Alexander discussed intensively the research plan, and the themes to focus on, with the young researchers as well as the research instruments that would be used. They trained and supported the young researchers during the research process to enable them to take the role of junior researcher.

Evaluation research: zero-measurement

Before the information phase and the communication phase of the pilot project started, a zero-measurement had been made.

Two research instruments were constructed, a questionnaire and panel discussions.

The themes and the structured questions of the questionnaire were drafted by co-workers of the Alexander Foundation and thoroughly discussed with, and amended by, the junior researchers. The topics chosen were: the intake, the treatment plan, the living-group, complaints and wishes, and expectations about having a say in policy matters of the residential institution. In total 275 youngsters (231 boys and 44 girls) completed the questionnaire (91.4 per cent of The Leo Stichting and 84 per cent of The Hoenderloo Group). The respondent group reflected the composition of the total group of clients living in both the institutions.

The junior researchers explained to the respondents the aim of the questionnaire and the way it had to be filled in. They assisted the clients during the process of filling in the questionnaire. Co-workers of the Alexander Foundation made a first draft of the analysis of the results of the questionnaire and discussed these thoroughly with the young researchers.

Panel discussions

Three panels were organised with a selected, heterogeneous group of twelve young residential dwellers in each panel. Co-workers and young researchers together selected the panel members with the help of the questionnaire on which the respondents could make clear if they would be willing to attend a panel meeting.

The first draft of a schedule for the panel meeting was formulated by the adults and afterwards discussed and amended by the junior researchers. The schedule focussed on themes regarding information and experiences of the panel members about their life in the residential setting and the treatment plans, in addition to any critique and wishes they had regarding the possibilities of influencing the policy and practice of the institution. Each panel meeting was facilitated by one co-worker of the Alexander Foundation and two junior researchers. The young researchers were trained and coached to do this job.

Evaluation research: process evaluation

The process of the information phase and the communication phase was evaluated by means of four panel discussions and a questionnaire that had been filled in by all panel members. Each panel had a different target group, which were respectively peer educators, receivers of the information by peer educators, and young residential dwellers who worked together with adults in the meetings of the communication phase. In total 13 girls and 21 boys participated in the panels. The role of the junior researchers as well as the coaching and training in the process evaluation were the same as in the phase of the zero-measurement. In each panel evaluative semi-structured questions were formulated about the different aspects of the pilot project.

Results of the evaluation research

In the zero-measurement phase, the outcomes of the panel discussions and the questionnaire showed that young dwellers of residential institutions have clear ideas about the present policy and practice in those institutions, and that they have outspoken ideas about the improvement of their position as a client.

Information

Young residential dwellers need more and better structured information. The general comment is that the information given at their intake and during their stay is lacking a systematic approach. Many of them ascertained a discrepancy between what had been said and written down about facilities, rules and procedures on the one hand and the reality on the other hand. 'You get a brilliant flyer and than you arrive, you notice it does not fit with reality.'

More than a few were dissatisfied with the information provided during their stay in the residential institution. For example, information about their behaviour had been discussed with their parents and not with them, and the decision about a transfer to another group was made too suddenly. 'They think it is normal; they think it is not necessary to give you a reason. For them it is normal to tell you the evening before, to say that there will be a new intake.' Although most of them received information about the treatment plan, they did not feel they had any influence on it.

Communication structures

From all the communication structures in the residential setting the young dwellers valued the group meetings with the group leaders most. However, they wished to be more involved in the agenda-setting of these meetings. 'When we want to have a meeting, we won't get it, whereas when they [group leaders] want it, then it happens. That is very stupid.' Some of them complained about the culture of only having meetings about problem solving and imposing rules and tasks. Instead they preferred meetings about their ideas and wishes and positive developments. 'If we behave very annoyingly, then we get meetings, but otherwise, no, no meeting. That's due to the leaders.'

Regulations for complaints

Young residential dwellers complained about their lack of knowledge concerning procedures to lodge complaints, and their feeling of being put in a powerless position. They felt rather powerless especially regarding complaints about the relation between them and the group leaders.

> Then you object, say, because you think you are right, and then they start talking about one of your learning goals. And that's very nasty, because then you don't see any way out.

Many remarks of the young people in the panel discussions show that, according to them, the attitude of the group leaders towards them is not respectful nor on an equal level.

> *With us they can say everything, or make stupid jokes, and then they think they are funny with their 'own team'. It can hit you. But if you make a joke about them, they are immediately in a dreadful temper, and then they say 'Yes, you have to go to your room', or 'I don't want to see you, I got sick of you'.*

Most of the young dwellers seemed not to be informed about the regulations for complaints. In most cases it is not a topic discussed during the intake, and only a small percentage of the young people received an information booklet about the regulations.

> *When you [the young researchers] came here, we got booklets from you. We never did see them before, so you can see how it works here with information.*

Having a say

Young residential dwellers hoped for an increase in 'having a say' in the policy and practice of the residential institutions. For instance, many of them were allowed to read reports concerning their treatment plan, but had no say in the decision-making.

> *Before you can say something, they have already decided. They say 'you agree with it?' And you say 'no', and then they start pissing again.*

Young people were discontented not only about their lack of influence on the treatment plans, but also about their influence on the establishment of group rules and the kind of activities they were offered. According to the young dwellers, some of the group leaders are positive about their having a say, but others are more or less against it.

> *I think they think 'it is my work, I will soon be ready and within a few hours I go home', and that is it.*

The panel discussions and the questionnaire showed that the young people involved

wish to have a say in four topics: group rules; rules of the residential institution; activities; and the treatment. Most of them explained it would certainly be an improvement if a youth council would be established.

> *What does it matter if it is in my leisure time, I try to do something with it, then I will put my leisure time in it.*

They realise that it will be a learning process on both sides, that is for the young people as well as the adults. They really wish that adults would take them more seriously than has been the case until now.

Process evaluation

In the process evaluation attention was paid to information sessions given by the peer educators, as well as to the so-called improvement sessions with adults and young people.

Peer education

Peer educators were highly esteemed by the young residential dwellers. The performance of peer educators was more informal, teenagers felt freer, put questions and there was more space for joking.

> *You listen better to those guys, because they are your peers. Older people are more diffi-cult to understand.*

However, some critical remarks were also been heard.

> *But they have to know what they are talking about.*

Peer educators themselves appreciated a supporting adult in the background during their performance. Young residential dwellers indicated the importance of strict selection criteria for peer educators. For example, they should not be younger than the teenagers, should be able to talk in an easy way, and should have lived for quite a long time in a residential setting.

> *Young people living at home do not know much about the institution. Those who live*

here, know how it is, what happens, they are in the middle of it.

Improvement sessions

According to many panel members the meetings between young residential dwellers and professionals had proved that discussion about problems and possible solutions could take place on equal terms.

Everything is written down. What the young people say is written down, what the adults say is written down. Every possible solution is screened for what is the best. After that there will be a vote.

Despite agreements about the equality of all participants not everyone felt safe.

Even if they say 'Yes, it will not be used against you', you are continually paying attention to 'I must not say wrong things'.

Topics were brought by all members. 'Say, for instance, young people do not know the treatment plan. We want to have that information. Then we have to find a solution so that young people do indeed know about the treatment plan.'

Many panel members thought the aim and function of the improvement sessions rather confusing. They would have preferred to start with a youth council and after that, when necessary, organise improvement sessions.

We now have improvement sessions, but not yet a youth council. In this way we won't make any progress.

Presentation of the results

Co-workers of the Alexander Foundation made the first draft of the findings of the research. These findings were broadly discussed with, and amended by, the junior researchers. The final report was presented by the junior researchers, some members of the panels and the co-workers to a large-scale conference that was attended by more than 500 representatives of residential institutions from all over the country.

Opinions of the junior researchers

In an interview the four junior researchers stated that it is much better that young people themselves are active in the preparation and execution of the project, better than 'scholarly old people' (Keesom, 1997). One of the junior researchers said:

The fact that we are also young, is very important, it makes a world of difference with the helping professionals.

He added that the young residential dwellers found their presence okay, and fun.

At first we were afraid that we took away their lunch time, but then they said 'Are you going already?'.

The junior researchers explained that the young residential dwellers received them with open arms. They were glad to talk about their life-situation, the tensions, the rules, and the attitude of the group leaders. They appreciated that the junior researchers had a use of language that was familiar to them, and recognised their problems, because of their own residential past. The most striking fact according to the junior researchers was that the young residential dwellers had a great need for attention and especially for respect.

One of the junior researchers said:

Young people in residential institutions wish to be treated on equal terms, and not be put away like dogs or criminals; that is the basis of all they want.

The only female junior researcher who did not have a residential background was impressed by the contact with the young people in the institutions:

I had a rather negative image of them; those were young people who have done wrong things. I did not know how one-sided this image is, and how young people suffer for that.

The junior researchers made clear that they really do have the feeling that something is changing now in the residential institutions:

This project shows that a lot is wrong in the institutions. Five years ago I could do nothing as a residential dweller, had no influence at all, but now by cooperating in such a project I have. That really is progress!

Effects

For some years youth councils have been developed in many residential institutions, partly as a result of the findings of this pilot project. In practice it became apparent that most youth councils up to now have not had much influence in stimulating the conditions under which young people can have a say in the treatment plans. It still remains a challenge to involve young people as partners before, during and shortly after the helping process. Only if young clients are invited to give feedback on their treatment as a partner can the quality of the institutional helping offer be raised.

Youth inspection teams

The Alexander Foundation developed the method of the youth inspection teams in local youth policy. Young people are recruited to inspect the quality of the provision and activities in a town or village. The young inspectors are trained and supported to select themes, to construct questionnaires, to hold individual interviews, and to hold panel discussions with their peers, to analyse and interpret the results and to present them to the authorities. In practice it proves to be a method which has really established a fruitful dialogue between young people and representatives of youth policy, provision, and activities for young people on an equal level. This method seemed also to be an excellent instrument for youth councils in residential settings. It supplies them with systematic information about the opinions, criticism and wishes of the client population.

The BJ-internaat De Hollandse Rading, an institution for residential youth care, gave the Alexander Foundation the opportunity to implement this method. Four ex-clients were recruited to inspect the quality of the helping process and the conditions under which clients live. The results were presented to the professional staff, the management, and all the young clients in a special meeting. Indeed, this method produced a lot of information for the youth council to make a programme of action. After a year a new youth inspection team can be formed with the task of checking if the programme of action of the youth council was effective, especially to see if the professional staff and the management take the proposals of the clients seriously (see Boschfilm/Alexander, 2002; De Rading/Alexander, 2000; IFCO, 2002; Stampfl and Koekkoek, 1999; Vriens, Haage and Jumelet, 2002).

Youth consulting teams

There are segments of youth care, such as custody, child protection, day-centres, and youth rehabilitation, in which it seems rather difficult to organise forms of youth participation. It makes a difference if you are living 24 hours in an institution or only have temporary contact with it. The need to form a youth council is certainly not strong in those situations because of the lesser involvement in the institution.

Another factor is that professionals and management in these sectors have strong doubts about whether youth participation can be realised at all: the idea is that young clients are not interested in it, and the staff themselves wonder if youth participation will not complicate the helping process in a negative sense. In 2001 the Alexander Foundation was given the opportunity by the National Steering Group for Quality Care to work out a method of youth participation which would suit the shorter-contact segments. The concept of youth consulting teams was the result, and was first practiced in the field of youth rehabilitation and custody. Youth consulting teams make use of the same tools as those of the youth inspection teams: individual interviewing, interviewing panels, analyzing and interpreting, and presenting. However, there is the addition of the consulting function: the members of a youth consulting team, who are ex-clients, consult the professional staff and management about how to improve the quality of the helping institution and how to introduce different forms of youth participation. They exercise a clear intermediate function between the clients and the institution. Besides the youth consulting teams, parent teams (parents of ex-clients) were also introduced. To date two pilots have been completed and the results are promising (see Bruggeman and Jurrius, 2002; Jurrius and Klimmer, 2002).

Perspectives

Until recently, the focus of the innovatory work of the Alexander Foundation has been, primarily directed at methods to give voice and influence to young people themselves – and sometimes to their parents – about life in and concerning adult institutions. Young people doing research themselves, young people as inspectors, and young people as consultants are an example of these activities.

Attention has been recently paid to the development of train-the-trainer programmes in order to transfer the knowledge and skills of the Alexander Foundation to professional staff in youth care, youth work, or voluntary organisations. These trained professionals will form a guarantee that on a large scale young people can be trained and coached by them to raise their voice, to speak up and to influence policy and practice.

At the same time the Alexander Foundation offers training and coaching for practitioners, managers, civil servants and politicians in how to cope with youth participation in their own field (Hazekamp 2002). If they are not prepared to take young people seriously in their views, and to change their attitudes and institutional codes in order to make dialogue on an equal level possible, youth participation will become a spent cartridge.

References

Boschfilm and Alexander (2002) *Het Jongeren Inspectie Team (The Young Inspection Team)*. Video 12 minutes, broadcast by The Box.

Bruggeman, D. and Jurrius, K. (2002) Consulenten Teams Jeugdreclassering; Waar ben ik in terecht gekomen? (Consultant Teams Youth Rehabilitation, in Stichting Alexander. *What did I drop?* Amsterdam.

De Rading and Alexander (2000) *Goed dat wij ook wat te zeggen hebben (Okay, We Also Have a Say)*. Video 20 minutes.

Hazekamp (2002) *Jongeren actief in het Amsterdamse jeugdbeleid; Een uitdaging voor de politiek (Young People Active in the Youth Policy of Amsterdam: A Challenge for Politics)*. Stichting Alexander. Amsterdam.

IFCO (2002) *Youth Inspection Team Foster Care*. Video 20 minutes, English version/ subtitles.

Jumelet, H. and Haarsma, L. (1998) Empowerment in de jeugdzorg: Cliënten als participanten (Empowerment in Youth Care: Clients as Participants), in Royers, (Ed.) *Empowerment; eigenmachtig worden in de hulpverlening*. Utrecht, NIZW.

Jurrius, K. and Klimmer, A. (2002) *Consulenten Teams Gezinsvoogdij Drenthe: 'Want gezinsvoogden zijn ook niet perfect'. (Consultant Teams Family Custody: 'Because a Family Guardian is not Perfect Either')*. Stichting Alexander. Amsterdam.

Keesom, J. (1997) Dat wij ook jongeren zijn, is heel belangrijk; de jonge onderzoekers van Stichting Alexander. (That we also are Young People is very Important: The Junior Researchers of the Alexander Foundation). Vernieuwing. *Tijdschrift voor Onderwijs en Opvoeding*. 58, 3, maart.

Naber, P. and Kayser, T. (1997) *Jong moeder; Nou en?! (Young Mother; so What?!)*. Stichting, Hengelo, Jeugdzorg Twente.

Naber, P. and Veldman, F. (1998) *De stilte voorbij; onderzoek naar de leefwereld en de maatschappelijk positie van Kaapverdiaanse jongeren in Rotterdam en Zaanstad (Past the Silence; Research on the Life-World Societal Position of the Cape Verdian Young People in*

Rotterdam en Zaanstad). Rotterdam, Cape Verdian Interest Organization.

Sinke, P.A.M., Verfaille, S. and Wiebing, R. (1997) *Meetellen is meepraten; opvattingen en ervaringen van jonge internaatbewoners ten aanzien van inspraak. (Opinions and Experiences of Young Residential Dwellers Concerning Having a Say).* Stichting Alexander. Amsterdam.

Stampfl, K.H.E. and. Koekkoek, E.H.J. (1999) *'Goed dat wij ook wat te zeggen hebben'; Jongeren over de kwaliteit van de zorg in De Rading ('Okay, We Also Have a Say'; Young People about the Quality of Care in De Rading).* Stichting Alexander. Amsterdam.

The Young Research Company and Stichting Alexander (1998) *Lokale jongerenraden in Nederland (Local Youth Councils in the Netherlands).* Stichting Alexander. Amsterdam.

Vriens, G., Haage, B. and Jumelet, H. (2002) *'Ik ben geen probleem op pootjes!'; Een participatief onderzoek naar de kwaliteitsbeleving en inspraakmogelijkheden van jongeren in de pleegzorg. ('I am not a Problem on Little Paws!' A Participatory Research on the Experience of Quality in Possibilities for Having a Say of Young People in Foster Care).* Stichting Alexander. Amsterdam.

CHAPTER 11

Participation Rights in Norway

Ingvild Begg

Norway is regarded by many as a country where children are well looked after. It is a country with a high standard of living, and other countries in Europe have referred to Norway and our Office of the Commissioner for Children (hereafter called the Ombudsman) when arguing for how children's rights might be protected. This impression is basically correct, but not without flaws. Consequently it is important not to be too complacent, but to try to address areas where there is still a need for improvement.

This chapter will look at the child's individual right to be heard, with particular concern for the situation of children and young people who, for one reason or another, are in a vulnerable position. The focus will be on the child's participation, both in the sense of being listened to and as a party in the proceedings concerning his or her own case. Second, the use of Children's Councils in the municipalities will be looked at to examine this type of participation in the light of training for democracy, and as a continuum of individual rights.

Article 12 of the United Nations Convention on the Rights of the Child (CRC), together with Norway's two reports to the United Nations and the replies of the UN Committee (UNC) are used as the basis for this chapter. A short summary of the background for, and the safeguarding of, children's right to participation in Norway, will be followed by a closer look at the practice of their right to participation. Comments from the UN Committee will be examined and these will be discussed in the context of relevant research and the representation of children and young people in a number of newspapers.

Sources

Except for some general literature in English, all sources are Norwegian and can be divided into three main categories:

1. Internet searches regarding children, children's rights, UNC and participation. All of these have been specific searches, for instance in newspapers, sites belonging to the Ombudsman, the Ministries, District Councils etc.
2. Interviews with people connected to children's organisations such as Save the Children, the Ombudsman, people involved with Children's Councils etc., and with seven young people between the ages of 12 and 18 years.
3. Relevant books and articles, including 131 newspaper articles or news items.

This chapter offers only a fragment of available information about children's rights in Norway. For example, an internet search on 'children's rights' got nearly 900 hits. There are a considerable number of publications dealing with children's rights and participation. Some of them describe different projects, while others offer advice on how to involve children and young people.

The young people

My young informants were not many, but they were all enthusiastic and willing to discuss a variety of subjects. All of the seven young people (aged 12 to 18 years) are, or have been, members of a Children's Council or other types of Youth Councils. The choice of informants was completely random. I told them that I was interested in their personal views and opinions. I used a few basic questions about their involvement in the councils and their opinion about individual rights for children and young people, but left it very much up to them to speak about the subject in a way they found interesting. The interviews were useful in selecting a focus for my presentation here, and the young people have been an inspiration through their enthusiasm. This consultation was never meant as a systematic gathering of information, and their views will be presented as short comments throughout the article.

Background for children's and young people's participation in Norway

It is claimed that Norway was the first country in the world to adopt a special legal framework for the protection of children (Dahl, 1992). The Act 'Concerning the Treatment of Neglected Children' was passed in 1896 and came into force in 1900. However, this Act did not make any provision for children to be consulted or to be allowed to make any decisions about their own person or their own future.

The first Acts to confer specific rights on the individual child dealt with religious matters (1891 and 1913). At the age of 15, children could decide to leave or enter the church, or to have their bodies cremated at death. In family matters, the Adoption Act of 1917 stated that children over 12 years old had to consent to be adopted (except in certain cases where they were being adopted by foster parents). Ten years later a general clause about the child's right to be consulted in personal matters was included in the Guardianship Act (§ 40).[1]

Since that Act of 1927, only a few legislative changes have been made concerning the individual child's right to be heard in personal matters. The changes have been directed toward increasing the number of laws with specific provision for when a child should be consulted, or when a child has the right to decide in a personal matter.

Also, greater emphasis has been placed on guidelines for interpreting the provisions of the Acts and on defining more areas where the interests of children must be safeguarded.

The Children's Act of 1981[2] has become a cornerstone for the formal description of the progression from participation to self-determination for children. In this process the section about a child's right to be consulted became central, and it was moved from the Guardianship Act to § 31 of the Children's Act. The wording of the section was altered slightly and now states that children above the age of 12 years

> ... *shall be allowed to state his or her opinion before decisions are made on personal matters* ... *Great importance shall be attached to the child's wishes.*

This section must be adhered to both by parents and everybody else involved in decisions regarding a child's 'personal matters'.

As a further emphasis to this rule, the Public Administration Act[3] gives children above the age of 14 years a personal right to receive notification and to express his or her opinion, before a public body makes any decisions regarding them. However, the Child Welfare Act of 1992 appears to be a development in the opposite direction. The right of a child (above the age of 12) to be consulted is limited to situations where the child might be placed in a foster home or institution (§ 6-3). This is a clear restriction or limitation compared to the Children's Act, and the preparatory documents to the Child Welfare Act of 1992 Act, do not allay this impression.

To present an historical review of Norwegian children's participation in a democratic sense is more difficult. The age of majority is 18 years and has been so since 1979 (Andenæs, 1984), but gaining influence and participation is more complicated than simply attaining the age of majority. It involves functional rights such as freedom of speech, access to information, freedom of assembly and freedom of press, among other elements (Flekkøy and Kaufman, 1997). As in other countries, children's participation in Norway is closely linked to changing attitudes to children and to the general development of society.

> *Children have increasingly become independent participants in arenas outside the family ...', and '... increasingly [given] status as an individual conveying opinions*[4]
>   (NOU, 1995).

It is probably fair to say that the first efforts to encourage and enable children to become active partners in the decision-making process were channelled through the schools. It is claimed that '... the interest for school democracy in Norway has fluctuated in three main waves, with approximately twenty years between them' (Hareide, 1972). The first Pupil's Council was introduced in a girl's school in 1919, while the first statutory duty to elect pupil's councils was introduced for the folk high schools in 1949 and for junior and senior secondary schools in 1964 (ibid). Hareide listed five elements, which he considered essential for a school to function as a 'school democracy':

1. As far as possible all members of the school should participate in the running of the school on an equal footing, in accordance with the principle 'one person one vote'.
2. As far as possible the school employs a direct decision-making process (direct democracy).
3. The decisions cover the most important issues concerning the school.
4. The decisions must have real consequences for the school.
5. The school must be able to fight against conditions, which hinder human liberation.

The use of Pupil's Councils continues and pupils now also have representatives in the co-ordinating committees for their schools (The Education Act § 11-1[5]). However, the effort has also gradually been directed towards the involvement of children in the wider society. During the 1970s and 1980s Norway introduced several measures to increase children's influence in matters concerning their own surroundings and their own future. A Child and Youth Council was established in the county of Telemark in 1972 (BFD/KS, 1997), and although the attempts were sporadic, several projects were started in the next ten years. In 1988 the first Children's Council was formed in a small municipality[6] with 2,850 inhabitants (Skimmeli, 2000). Despite considerable pressure from central government only 50 municipalities had established Children's Councils by 1997. However, the numbers increased steadily to 182 municipalities by December 1999. At present 338 municipalities have established Children's Councils and ten out of nineteen counties have established Youth Councils (STI, 2002).

From July 1986 it became a duty for municipalities to appoint a spokesperson for children in planning matters (The Planning and Building Act of 14.06.1985 § 9-1), but this person is described as a public servant or a director of a municipal department. In other words, children will have no say in the matter if this person does not instigate some form of democratic consultation with children affected by any proposed action.

Official bodies safeguarding children's rights

Norway has a population of nearly 4.5 million, of which just over one million are between the ages of 0–17 years. Compared to most other countries in Europe this is a low population and it ought to be relatively easy to monitor and follow up the various provisions for safeguarding the children's interests. In this regard, Norway has chosen to create an extensive network of both public and private bodies, some with statutory responsibilities. It would be impossible to list them all and it could be argued that too many protectors might create a watering down of responsibility. However, it may be asserted that the main statutory responsibility rests with Ministry of Children and Family Affairs and the

Ombudsman, and a short presentation of their roles is given below, in addition to a brief consideration of the role of schools. After the change of government in 1989, government departments were reorganised. The Ministry of Family and Consumer Affairs was created to strengthen work in connection with children, young people, family, equal opportunity, consumer protection and product safety. To further emphasise the importance of child protection, the name was changed to the Ministry of Children and Family Affairs from 1st January 1991. By then the government had withdrawn the bill for a new Social Work Act, and extracted the child care section for the benefit of a new, separate Act on Child Welfare Services. In addition, a major programme directed toward improving child care services was launched. The Ministry co-operates with the Norwegian Association of Local and Regional Authorities (KS) on major projects and programmes concerning children, for instance about Children's Councils. The Ministry is the supreme authority regarding matters concerning children. Both the municipalities and counties report to the Ministry, and the Ministry issues instructions and guidelines.

The Office of the Commissioner for Children (the Ombudsman) is formally placed under the jurisdiction of this Ministry, but is independent, autonomous and non-party-political. The Norwegian Parliament passed the Commissioner for the Children Act in 1981 and with that established the first Ombudsman for Children in the world. In December 1995 the government published a white paper, *The Ombudsman for Children and Childhood in Norway* (NOU, 1995). This report was an evaluation of the Office of the Ombudsman and also an account of different ways of strengthening organisations and projects to protect the interests of children and young people. According to this paper, direct communications from children to the Ombudsman reached a peak in 1992 with 2,145 contacts. In the following couple of years the numbers went down, but the 1997 annual report (on the internet) shows that 96,000 phone calls were made to 'Klar Melding Inn' (Straight to the Point – In) but due to lack of capacity, only 2,470 were registered and documented. In the report from the agency, these calls are divided into four categories:

1. Questions about rights and information.
2. Opinions about the situation for children and young people.
3. Individual personal crisis.
4. 'Telephone-graffiti'.

For the year 2000 the Annual Report states that 23,200 people dialled the number, while 17,000 got through to leave a message. In 2000 there was also a considerable increase in e-mail messages. Even if the calls are not all from children it indicates that the Ombudsman is well known and regarded as important.

Schools also have an important role in safeguarding children's rights, first and foremost through their day-to-day contact with children. A Norwegian child spends about 9,500 hours at school until the age of 16 (GD, 20.05.00[7]) and the schools have a responsibility in teaching children about their rights through guidelines called *Læreplanverket*[8] (KUF, 1996). These guidelines state that children should: '. . . gain an overview about international work for human rights. Find information about . . . the content of UNC' (7th year); and 'Identify and discuss rights and duties for children and young people' (8th year). How the different schools organise these tasks varies considerably, and my young informants do not remember having heard about children's rights at school. In a survey conducted at the end of the twentieth century, 60 per cent of the teachers placed the main responsibility for education in the wider sense of the word on the parents[9] (Nolet, 2000). If this became the prevailing attitude among teachers, information about children's rights and, for example, experience in problem-solving among peers might no longer be regarded as central to school work. However, although representatives for teachers' unions have expressed concern about teachers getting increasing responsibilities for the general education of children (ibid), the above survey does not reflect the official view of the teachers' unions. The school is an arena that is still important for character formation and an arena where the children can test out their rights. It is also a place where the children can get an opportunity to participate and influence their own future.

Participation and self-determination for the individual child in Norway today

In Norway, as in most countries in Europe, there appears to be an increasing trend for young people to make their own decisions in personal affairs, independent of the views of their parents. It has been a development towards a greater emphasis of individual rights and individual worth compared to a more collectivist view of society (Giddens, 1998; Frønes and Brusdal, 2000), which becomes particularly important when examining the social situation of children and young people.

The Children's Act gives the child an unconditional right to be heard after the age of 12 years. Further, the section concerning the right to self-determination states that 'Parents shall steadily extend the child's right to make his or her own decisions as he or she gets older and until he or she comes of age' (§ 33). In other words, a right that probably reflects the state of affairs in most families.

Thus, to the ordinary child or young person growing up in an ordinary family, their legal right to self-determination probably feels of little significance. If parents remain married (or the divorce is conducted without too much conflict), and the relationship between parents and children is reasonable, there is no need for the child to claim a legal right to be consulted or to decide in personal matters. Conflicts occur

in all families to some degree, and at 14–16 years of age it appears that many young people want more freedom. Between 15 and 18 years many young people leave home, some to go to school, a few to set up home with a girl or boyfriend, or for independence. During the last ten years there has been a clear development of young people leaving home earlier (Statistics Norway 2000). This appears to cause few legal problems, despite the fact that the Guardianship Act (GA) does not give young people under the age of 18 any extensive right to look after their own affairs. For instance, a child under 18 years cannot sign a rent agreement for a flat or house (GA § 33b), and although they can administer their own self-earned money from the age of 15, this right can in theory be taken from them under certain conditions (GA § 33). On the other hand it is now accepted that it takes a lot to stop a 15 or 16-year-old doing something they have decided upon and it can even be difficult to prevent a 13-year-old. Parents may 'put their foot down', and say 'no' to moving away from home, mixing with friends who take drugs etc., but in reality there are few effective (and legal) sanctions to back 'dos' and 'don'ts'. As one of my 13-year-old informants said: 'they [her parents] might be right, but I have to be allowed to make my own mistakes'. Five of my seven informants claimed that they had not heard about the Convention on the Rights of the Child (CRC). Three of them did not have any specific knowledge of the Children's Act or about any rights conferred on Norwegian children. When taken into consideration that all my informants were members of different types of Youth Councils with particular emphasis on children's rights, it would seem reasonable to assume that a considerable number of children are not aware of the content of the Children's Act or the CRC. On the other hand, none of them had experienced any problems concerning self-determination, although I did not ask in detail what they were allowed to decide and not allowed to decide. Even if the schools have a responsibility for making the content of the Children Act and the CRC known to the pupils, the task might be more difficult if many children are of the opinion that formal rights are of little significance. But one informant (12 years old) who knew about neither the CRC, nor any rights children had, said she had:

> . . . *learned a lot about children and justice at school, and to say things straight to each other and to be able to cope with things and to talk about things. That's important.*

On the other hand, without knowledge of rights it is difficult to exercise rights, and children have to depend on adults assuming responsibility for informing them in a constructive way.

The children who have to individually claim a legal right to participation are those who get into trouble or come from families in conflict. If the parent's divorce is messy, children have a legal right to be consulted. If the child gets into some kind of trouble they can be a party to their own case from the age of 15 or younger.[10]

In conclusion, it may be claimed that the majority of children and young people do not appear to have significant problems concerning the individual right to self-determination as described in the Children's Act. Their individual right to be heard in matters concerning themselves is likewise well regulated and safeguarded.

Democratic participation and Children's Councils

It is impossible to give a brief account of all the arenas where children may gain influence in the community, but the following guidelines from the Ministry of Children and Family Affairs might serve as an example (see table p.130).

The table is based on the experiences of a project called *Growing up in a municipality*, and is directed toward municipalities. The main purpose is to show that participation and influence by children can take place on different levels, but also to encourage greater

diversity and imagination in the way municipalities listen to children's views or obtain insight into the wishes of children.

Probably one of the most significant efforts in increasing participation for children and young people was the introduction of different types of Children's Councils. The idea behind the Children's Councils is to give children responsibility, and to allow them to raise issues and decide on matters which they regard as important in the local community. They also learn how to reach decisions through discussions with others, and by having to make priorities within limited resources.

The existing Children's Councils operate in different ways, but most consist of children between the ages of 10 to 15. District Councils allocate a sum of money for the running and use of the Children's Councils, and also provide a secretary. Some Children's Councils meet only once a year, others more often. Some of them are more concerned with issues, while others mainly allocate money to causes and events they find worthwhile. Closely related are different forms of Youth Councils, often consisting of representatives from different municipalities. The age range for the Youth Councils is usually wider, and they receive financial backing from the Regional Councils. An example of how a Children's Council works is given below, from Øvre Eiker district.

Øvre Eiker Children's Council

Since 1992 Øvre Eiker district[11] has had a Children's Council which meets once a year. Representatives are chosen from 6th year primary school (12 year olds) and 8th year junior secondary school (14 year olds).

The different School Councils, with representatives from all the classes at a given school, are presented with suggestions about topics from the other pupils in late autumn. They decide which cases they or the school can handle themselves (A-cases), which cases should be decided by the Children's Council (B-cases), and which

Level of participation	Ordinary arenas for participation			
	Municipality	Local community	School/nursery	Leisure arenas
I. Children as informants	'Day of the child'. Children on the agenda	Questionnaires Children observe other children Children's drawings	Questionnaires Talks/Interviews Municipality interviews Project teaching Children observe children Children's drawings Class/school paper	Talk/Interview Children observe other children Children's drawings Children's page in local newspaper Photographing/ video
II. Children as informants in dialogue		Hearings for children and young people Children and young people's gatherings	Comments by class/ pupil's council Map making/area registration Hearings for children and young people	Log books Map making/area registration Children and young people's council
III. Children as participators in the process	'Children and young people's Councils 'I	'Work book' Inspection by c and y planner	Art training which visualises physical surroundings 'Work book' 'Play about millions'	
IV. Children who decide	'Children and young people's council' II	Playground for building	Planning for themselves Design the playground Pupils' enterprises	Try self Children's festival Media activity Self run youth houses

Participation – Methods and Experience: From: BFD/KS – Fra barnetrakk til ungdomsting – Q-0927.

cases ought to go to the Municipal Council for further consideration (C-cases). In January and February the pupils of 6th and 8th years prepare the cases after a member of the local authority has instructed the pupils on how cases to the Council should be prepared.

Each school sends two representatives chosen by and from 6th and 8th years. The case papers are sent to the Municipality, and in March the schools receive the official agenda for the meeting of the Children's Council with all the relevant papers from the different schools. In April the Children's Council first meet to get to know each other, for a 'practice meeting', but with the Mayor in the Chair, as in ordinary council meetings.

A couple of weeks later they meet formally to make decisions.

A few examples of cases from Øvre Eiker Children's Council in 2000:

– Application for a climbing wall at one of the primary schools (C-case).
– Free bus trip to a given place without adults present from a junior secondary (C-case).
– Better showers at one of the schools (C-case).
– Hairdryer in a sports hall (B-case).
– Drums in a primary school (B-case).
– Repairs and improvements to a school canteen (B-case).

When cases are discussed by the Children's

Council, most of them are well prepared with drawings, permissions, and costings as in any other case dealt with by a Municipal Council.

The community worker for Øvre Eiker and other community workers with responsibility for the Children's Council all emphasise the point that to give children real influence takes considerable effort from the responsible adults (personal comment). Children need help both to organise themselves and to express themselves in a way that carries weight. At the same time it is important not to impose adult ideas and adult procedures on children, nor to curb their free expression. One of the youth workers also pointed out that the attitudes of the schools are of great significance since the preparatory work for the Children's Councils is carried out there. Some critics have pointed out that Children's Councils are not conducted on children's terms. Instead, children are praised when they behave like small adults and put in their place when they do not. The question is whether it is to the child's benefit to learn the accepted norms of how adult councils are conducted, or if they should be allowed to find their own way of conducting their participation and decision-making.

My young informants were all positive about the Councils. They had personally learned a lot and they found it interesting to be part of decision-making. However, three of them explicitly mentioned that they were disappointed by the lack of interest from others in their peer group. One of them (18 years old), was fairly pragmatic about this and reckoned that it had to be accepted that not everybody is interested in the same thing. Another (17 years old), said that,

> Only a few show an interest, and only a few make suggestions or raise issues. You don't get representatives from the wider popula-tion in this system either.

He had started to question if this process was the right way to go about getting more people involved. Also, he had noticed that the interest was greatest in primary school.

'His' council met primary school pupils once a year, and found them enthusiastic and creative, 'and then it dies out'. Although most of my informants were slightly reluctant to use the expression 'resourceful' about themselves, they all agreed that it was only the 'resourceful'[12] ones that were involved.

The United Nations Committee on the Rights of the Child and Norway

Norway has so far submitted two periodic reports to the UN Committee, the first in the summer of 1993, and the second dated June 1998 (BFD Q-0827E and Q-0983E). The UN Committee's concluding observations of the initial report (dated 25.04.1994) listed only five principal subjects of concern, none of them dealing specifically with Article 12, but two of them dealing with asylum seekers. However, the committee suggested that ' . . . the State party encourage measures to further involve and facilitate the participation of children in matters affecting them, especially at the local level' (Paragraph 22). Norway's second report added little to the first[13] with regard to Article 12, besides admitting that some concern had been voiced concerning the situation of asylum seekers. However, in September 1999 the Coalition for the Convention on the Rights of the Child[14] submitted a Supplementary report to the UNC concluding that:

> . . . there is much to be achieved before it can be said that children have a real influence on situations which directly affect them.
> (Supplementary Report, 15).

The UN Committee's response (dated 22.05.2000) to the second report appears to be more critical. Twenty-four principal subjects of concern are listed, and among them a slightly more strongly worded comment than before about asylum seekers. Under the heading that includes matters relating to Article 12, the committee expressed the concern that:

... the best interests of the child are not always taken into full consideration ...

(paragraph 22).

In paragraph 24 it expressed the concern

... that in practice children's views are insufficiently heard and taken into consideration', and '... that many children are not aware of their rights ... or of the opportunities which have been created ...

Research and legal theory about children's participation

Research is an important means of establishing both how successful the implementation of CRC has been, and the situation for children in general. Numerous institutions and individuals are involved in research on children and it is not possible to provide a summary of it all. This section focuses on some court cases and a few studies, which illustrate the problems raised.

The individual right to participation appears to be taken care of by the fact that a child has a right to be consulted after the age of 12, and after the age of 15 is a party to his or her own case in child care matters. In 1998 and 1999 there were three High Court (HC) cases about 13- and 14-year-olds wanting to be granted status as a party to their own cases (HC1998/1471, HC1998/1592 and HC1999/490). Although the court did not find in favour of their claims, the cases might be regarded as a safeguard for children's right to participation, by the fact that they were admitted entrance to the High Court. In two of the three cases the High Court emphasised that the purpose of the provision granting children status as party to their own case must be to ensure that their views are properly represented. On the other hand, a later High Court case which dealt with a child's right to be consulted in a question of custody, stated:

It is doubtful if it can be considered a general rule that children above the age of 12 should be allowed to give their opinion in cases

regarding a temporary decision about where the child should reside.

(HC2000/874).

Although this concerned a temporary decision, there is nothing in the Children's Act to invite a narrow interpretation of the right to be heard for a child above the age of 12 years.

In asylum cases the main directive was changed in 2000 to ensure that children are consulted. The change concerns all children regardless of age. There are two exceptions. First, the interview with the child can be dispensed with if 'obviously unnecessary', and second, parents can refuse to allow their children to be consulted (FOR 1990-12-21 nr 1028, § 54).

Children's right to express their view is also emphasised in legal theory regarding children (for example, Smith, 1980; Smith and Lødrup, 1998; Lindboe, 1998; Haugli, 1998). They all comment on the wording in the new Child Welfare Act, which limits the right to be consulted to the situations where children are due to be placed in foster care. Recent research indicates that, despite rules and safeguards, children are not often enough being consulted. In a report on counselling in divorce cases it is stated that the child was consulted in only 2 per cent of the counselling cases (Ekeland and Myklebust, 1997). Likewise only 30 out of a total of 329 children were given the opportunity to talk to the Judge (Forum for CRC, 1999).

In a recent study of emergency cases in the child care services, it was found that 63 per cent out of a total of 153 children above the age of 12 years were quoted as being a source for the information collected, but only 52 per cent had their views noted down. For children who were party to their own case, 60 per cent of a total of 116 were quoted as being a source for some of the information collected, while 50 per cent had their views noted down (Oppedal, 1999). One of the conclusions in Oppedal's study was:

Maybe one of the most discouraging finds is that the child's reactions and the possibility

*for continuity in connection with the inter-
vention and placement is given so little
attention in the documents of the child care
services.*

(330).

In other words, clear rules and directives do
not always produce the sought after effect.
This was also pointed out by the Forum for
CRC and was noted as an area for
improvement by the UN Committee on the
Rights of the Child. In a survey from 1997,
with answers from 1368 child care workers
(approximately two-thirds of the total
number), one of the questions concerned the
basis for decision-making. The view of the
child was regarded as important in 47 per
cent of the cases, not very important in 15
per cent and without significance in 25 per
cent of the cases[15] (Næss et al., 1998). What
emerges is that both in divorce and in child
care cases the most vulnerable children are
also those who will find most hindrance in
expressing their wishes.

Problems

There are two types of problem. First, there
is an external problem in the sense that the
children are not given sufficient opportunity
to present their views and therefore have
very little influence on what happens to him
or her. This is a problem which has been
emphasised both by the UN committee, and
by the government appointed committee
who presented a comprehensive White
Paper about the status of child care in
Norway (NOU, 2000). Second, if it is agreed
that children's participation is important
and a serious attempt is made to increase
their participation and influence, there is still
an internal problem in that many children
do not know how to express themselves. In
other words consideration must be given to
how best to help them to express their
views. Few suggestions have been made
how to address these problems except
through improved training in how to speak
to children (for example, Sandbæk and
Tveiten, 1996).

Improved awareness and improved
training in communication ought to be a step
forward and should increase the individual
child's right to influence matters concerning
their person. Still, this does not fully answer
the question of how to ensure that all
children get the opportunity to be heard and
given the ability to express their views.

*Modern children are expected both to be seen
and heard. Today's 14-year-olds have grown
up in a society which emphasises the development of social competence and self-suffi-
ciency in children. The period of adolescence
commences earlier and lasts longer.*

(Frønes and Brusdal, 2000).

Those bold words are presented in a book
with the subtitle 'Cultural prediction for the
near future'. If these statements are accepted
there should be no need to worry about
participation, but again they basically seem
to be talking about children from secure and
generally well-resourced backgrounds.

One way to approach the problem is to see
the child's right to be heard in individual
matters as just another side of the right to
participation in all matters concerning the
child. 'To deny a person rights is to fail to
recognise his capacity for autonomy'
(Freeman, 1983). In other words children
need to be granted their rights to develop
into individuals with freedom and ability to
take responsibility for the future. The
individual's right to be heard and influence
matters concerning themselves is closely
linked to the idea of democracy, which
among other things is based on the
assumption that people have access to
information and are free to voice their
opinion. It is also dependent on people
being able to and willing to participate in a
democratic process (Flekkøy and Kaufman,
1997; Ezioni, 1995). Participation is a
presupposition for democracy to function
and is also regarded by many as a duty.

In this connection Norway's attempt at
involving children in local decisions is
important.

Result of newspaper search October 1999 to May 2000

Types of cases	News/articles etc	Individual cases	Voice of child	N = 132
Children general	10		2	
Child care services	23	15	(1)	
Child care topics	26			
Family/child	1	1		
Participation	3			
CRC – topics	6			
CRC – general	9		1	
Refugees	6	3		
Crime	12	13		
Drugs	1	3	1	
	97	35	4 (5)	132

'Voice of child' = one boy (16) interviewed about school, 2–3 children collectively talking about a new school system, ( ) = indirectly – a research report from an institution, girl (9) about the right to play, boy (17) about use of drugs.

Newspaper representation of children and young people

In Article 17, 'State Parties recognise the important function performed by the mass media and shall ensure that the child has access to information and material . . .' One of the stated aims to ensure this is to 'Encourage the mass media to disseminate information and material of social and cultural benefit to the child and in accordance with the spirit of article 29;' (Article 17a). Newspapers are part of the mass media and important purveyors of opinions. They have a lot of power and they often focus on individual cases, preferably with some drama involved. 'Social and cultural benefit to the child' is open to wide interpretation, but it seems reasonable also to include listening to children and presenting children's points of view.

On this basis I conducted a small survey of newspaper's concerns about children and young people, particularly their representation in relation to Article 17, and whether they could be seen as advocates for the children's right to be heard. Major national, some regional, and a couple of local newspapers were searched for articles and news about children in general, child

care, and children's rights and especially about the CRC. Over 100 newspaper articles[16] were examined dealing with children in the seven month period from October 1999 to May 2000. However, it is important to point out that the choice of newspapers was fairly incidental, although I made systematic searches in three of the biggest national papers – *Aftenposten*, *Dagbladet* and *Dagsavisen*.

During the period I found one national newspaper which ran several stories about the CRC,[17] but in the few stories dealing with children as asylum seekers, there is no mention of the rights of the children. Of all the articles, 35 deals with individual cases, most of them divided between children committing crimes and cases linked to the Child Care Services. In the child care cases the headings often read something like: 'The Child Care Service grabs children from parents!', or 'Child Care Services never did their job – parents beg for help!' The age of children most often referred to in the first case is 0–10 years, while the second group consists of children between the ages of 13 and 18 years.

The general articles are more varied. They deal with the same basic topics, particularly whether the Child Care Services are helpful, or nasty, or useless, or try their best, and they express concern about the increased violence and more serious crime among young people as young as 13 or 14 years old. A few articles attack private child care institutions and three of the general and one of the individual stories explicitly refer to staff being violent towards children.

There are one or two exceptions. One local paper[18] had two articles about Children's Councils, and one about how pupils can mediate in conflicts between themselves. One of the bigger regional newspapers[19] had several articles about a municipality with visions for schools. The papers keep their main focus on problems connected to such changes, but also present positive sides.

There is one special exception in Norwegian media where children's views are presented. The journalist and author Simon Flem Devold has, since the mid-1980s, had his own page in one national newspaper,[20] where he answers letters mainly from children and young people. On this page he is told about happy and sad occasions – from getting a new boy or girlfriend to thoughts about divorce and to letters from a dying child. Children and young people also present their thoughts and opinions on society and how it ought to be run. Several of these letters and answers are presented in separate articles, and his views on bringing up children have been both commended and criticised over the years. Despite its fame and the fact that the newspaper has good internet coverage the page is not available on the net.[21] It is difficult to assess to what extent these newspapers' presentation is of benefit for children, but it is interesting to note that nearly half the news items were critical assessments and dramatic stories about children as criminals and about the Child Care Services. Very little in the papers seems to be directed at children. The papers write about children, but with the exception of the usual 'Children's Page', 'Music Page' etc., they do not appear to speak to children and young people. Neither do they emphasise the child's angle in cases where that might

be expected. Finally, very few children's voices are to be heard.

Conclusion – children's and young people's perspectives

Children and young people in Norway receive a reasonable amount of attention, both from the various institutions set to safeguard their interests and through the media, here exemplified by articles from some newspapers. To a great extent this attention and effort seems to be motivated by a wish to include children and to increase their opportunities to active participation. However, it is difficult to see how the newspapers' representations can be said to aid children's participation or be a purveyor of children's views.

Maybe children and young people should be allowed to give their perspectives in the matter of participation? A youth conference entitled *Roads to influence* was held in April 2000. More than 200 young people gathered to discuss questions such as, Why do we need influence? How do we get more influence? What kind of issues are young people concerned with? They shared experiences from different types of councils for young people and looked at areas which, in their opinion, need further work. Experiences and recommendations were published on the internet and give an insight into the variety of issues, thoughts and opinions of young people when discussing participation.

Under the heading of 'These areas need further work' the young people list 107 statements or recommendations (BFD, 2000). Some of the statements partly overlap. However, seventeen dealt with the need to involve more children and young people from different parts of the society. For instance:

> *Try to engage young people from different backgrounds, not just the ones that are clever at school.*

Eleven of the statements concern a wish to obtain more real influence. For instance:

> *Politicians are interested in hearing our opinion, but to what extent are we actually listened to?*

If statements expressing the need for better influence in general are added, the total number of statements regarding influence is twenty-seven. The statements indicate that young people are interested in being consulted and in gaining influence in matters concerning themselves. Also, they appear to be concerned about lack of involvement from their peers and particularly the need to involve and include children from different backgrounds.

The conference in itself might be seen as an effort to give young people more real influence by listening to their views and hopefully some of their recommendations will be followed up. The recommendations indicate that the shortcomings already pointed out are also shortcomings the young people are concerned about.

I think it is fair to say that the overall impression of the opportunity for participation and self-determination for Norwegian children is good. Children's rights are well regulated, and there are numerous arenas for participation. Still we have no reason to be self-satisfied. The UNC has rightly criticised Norway for the way asylum-seeking children are treated, and it is still the most vulnerable children who are denied the right to be heard, and only a minority who participate in democratic processes.

Notes

1 Act of 22nd of April 1927 relating to the guardianship of persons who are legally incapable. The child ought to be consulted after the age of 12 and had be consulted after the age of 15.
2 Act of 8th April 1981 no 7 relating to Children and Parents.
3 Act of 10th February 1967 relating to the Public Administration.
4 All quotes from Norwegian sources are translated by me.
5 Act of 17th July 1998 relating to Primary and Secondary Education.
6 Norway has approximately 435 districts in 19 regions. More than half of the districts has less then 5,000 inhabitants.
7 The newspaper *Gudbrandsdalen Dagningen*.
8 Probably somewhat similar to the National Curriculum. Lreplanverket for the 10-year's basic education – subject: Samfunnskunnskap (equivalent of 'PHSE and Citizenship').
9 The survey was part of an evaluation of some specific 'educational material for schools concerning the prevention of criminal behaviour'.
10 The Child Care Act of 17th July 1992 § 6-4.
11 14,700 inhabitants.
12 The expression 'resourceful' is not very precise, but is commonly used. Here it indicates a child or young person who, usually because of background and upbringing, is an average or above average achiever at school, who takes part in different activities and who has a certain amount of confidence both verbally and in their general behaviour.
13 With regards to Article 12, the first report covers more or less the same topics as this article.
14 The Coalition was established in 1993 and comprises 50 non-governmental organisations, institutions of higher education, research institutes and individuals that are interested and involved in the implementation of children's rights in Norway.
15 It must be taken into account that 40 per cent of the approximately 1,000 children involved were less than 7 years old.
16 The majority from the biggest national newspapers, but also a few from local newspapers.
17 *Dagsavisen*, 11 stories in November and December 1999.
18 *Ringsaker Blad*.
19 Stavanger Aftenblad.
20 'På skråss med Simon' in *Aftenposten*.

21 78 articles based on the letters and answers are available for sale at the price of kr 10.00 each, less than £1.00.

References

Andens, J. (1984) *Statsforfatningen i Norge.* Oslo, Tanum.

Barneombudet: http://www.barneombudet.no/trond.htm (31st July 2000)

BFD Home page -http://odin.dep.no/bfd/norsk/dep/om82dep/ (24th July 2000)

BFD *The Rights of the Child.* (Norway's initial report), Circular – Q-0827E

BFD *The Rights of the Child.* (Norway's second report), Circular – Q-0983E

BFD *Veier til innflytelse. Erfaringer og tips fra konferanse for ungdom.* (15th September 2000)

BFD/KS (1997) *Fra barnetråkk til ungdomsting.* Circular – Q-0927

CRC/C/15/Add.126 (2000) *Concluding Observations of the Committee on the Rights of the Child: Norway.* Unedited version, June.

Dahl, T.S. (1992). *Barnevern og samfunnsvern.* Oslo, Pax Forlag.

Ekeland, T-J. and Myklebust, V. (1997) *Foreldremekling: brukarperspektivet.* Volda, Mreforsking.

Ezioni, A. (1995) *The Spirit of Community.* London, Fontana Press.

Flekkøy, M.G. and Kaufman, N.H. (1997) *The Participation Rights of the Child.* London, Jessica Kingsley.

FOR 1990-12-21 nr 1028. – Utlendingsforskriften

Freeman, M.D.A. (1983) *The Rights and Wrongs of Children.* London, Frances Pinter Publishers.

Frønes, I. and Brusdal, R (2000) *Pa sporet av den nye tid.* Oslo, Fagbokforlaget.

Giddens, A. (1998) *The Third Way: The Renewal of Social Democracy.* London, Polity Press.

Hareide, B. (1972) *De første elevrådene i Norge.*, Oslo, Aschehoug and Co.

Haugli, T. (1998) *Samvræsrett i barnevernssaker.*, Oslo, Universitetsforlaget.

http://odin.dep.no/bfd/norsk/barn82og82ungdom/demokratiforum/p10001903/index-b-n-a.html
http://www.lovdata.no/for/sf/jd/hd-19901221-1028.htm (13th November 2000)
http://www.ssb.no/emner/00/02/30/sa15/sammendrag.html (23rd May 2000)

Kingsley Publishers.

KUF (1996) *Læreplanverket for den 10-årige grunnskolen.* Oslo, Nasjonalt læremiddelsenter.

Lindboe, K. (1998) *Barnevernrett.* Oslo, Tano Aschehoug.

Nolet, R. (2000) *LEV VEL – Evaluering av kriminalitetsforebyggende skolepakke.* Volda, Møreforsk.

Norwegian NGO Coalition on CRC. (1999) *Supplementary Report to the UN Committee on the Rights of the Child.* Oslo

NOU 1995:26 *Barneombud og barndom i Norge*

NOU 2000:12 *Barnevernet i Norge*

Næss, S., Havik, T., Offerdal, A. and Wærness, K. (1998) *Landsomfattende undersøkelse om erfaringer med barnevernloven i kommunene.* Notat 148/april 19918, Oslo, Senter for Samfunnsforskning.

Oppedal, M. (1999) *Rettssikkerhet ved akutte vedtak etter barnevernloven.* Institutt for offentlig retts skriftserie nr 6/1999, Oslo.

Sandbæk, M. and Tveiten, G. (Eds.) (1996) *Sammen med familien: arbeid i partnerskap med barn og familier.* Oslo, Kommuneforlaget.

Skimmeli, M. (2000) *Medvirkning fra barn og unge i lokaldemokratiet.* Trondheim, NTNU.

Smith, L. (1980) *Foreldremyndighet og barnerett.* Oslo, Universitetsforlaget.

Smith, L. and Lødrup, P. (1998) *Barn og foreldre.* Oslo, Lødrup and Smith.

Statistics Norway 2000, http://www.ssb.no/emner/02/barn82og82unge/ (22nd May 2000)

Sti Tonje. (2002) *Database over Ungdomsråd/Ungdommens kommunestyrer i Norge 2002.* BFD.

Stortingsmelding nr 39 (1995–1996), *Om barnevernet*

CHAPTER 12

Children's Parliaments in Slovenia

Bojan Dekleva and Sonja Zorga

Introduction

Children's Parliaments represent an innovation in the process of implementation of children's rights in Slovenia. The first Children's Parliament took place in the same year as the constitution of the 'real' (adult) Parliament of the independent Slovenia. In the intervening years the governmental (schools, government) and nongovernmental structures have succeeded in integrating Children's Parliaments into their working and conceptual structures in a productive way. So Children's Parliaments have become 'traditional' and their structure expanded. This paper presents the history, the content and the functioning of this innovation.

Country sketch

Slovenia is one of the smallest transitional countries, bordering two Western European countries (Italy and Austria) on one side, and on the other two Eastern or South European transitional countries, Hungary and Croatia. Being once a part of Yugoslavia and gaining its independence early (in 1991) and in an almost non-violent way, the starting position for its path through the transforming 1990s was relatively good. With its 2,000,000 inhabitants and a rather decentralised pattern of urbanisation, Slovenia consists of a lot of small towns and villages. As in the majority of other (Western) European countries it is also a country which is ageing. The number of births has been falling and the GDP, which is about 10.000 US$ per capita and has been growing since 1995, cannot satisfy the quickly growing needs of the health, retirement and social security sectors. All the same, Slovenia is one of the two countries in South Eastern Europe in which the

investments in education, in proportion to its GDP, is larger than it was in 1989. The investment in the social welfare sectors are still meeting the needs to such a degree that, according to the UNDP Human Development Index, Slovenia ranks 37th among the world's countries (Rights, 2000). But besides these relatively positive socio-economic indicators Slovenia shares with other transitional countries similar (negative) trends in unemployment, poverty and income inequality (Gini's coefficient for earnings has grown by 40 per cent in the period 1989–1997; ibid.). In this context the growth of juvenile crime rates has not brought about any corresponding growth in juvenile criminal sentencing and institutional care. Due to the changing trend in the professions of child and youth care and social work, and due to the changing provisions in juvenile criminal justice, new alternatives to institutionalisation and sentencing have been developed and the number of sentenced and institutionalised children and young people has actually fallen in the last decade (Dekleva, 1995).

Implementation of children's rights

Slovenia inherited the treaty on the Convention on the Rights of the Child together with other international obligations from the Yugoslav Federation, which had ratified the Convention in 1990. The initial report on measures adopted by the Republic of Slovenia in implementing the Convention on the Rights of the Child was submitted to the UN Committee on the Rights of the Child in 1996 (Zacetno, 1997). Among the shortcomings of the Slovenian implementation of the Convention two were emphasised in the process of the evaluation of the initial report (Zacetno, 1997); the implementation of the Article 12 of the Convention and the question of lack of co-ordination of professional services dealing with child abuse and neglect. Since then some institutional adapatations and changes in these two fields have been implemented (Drugo, 2001), while many of the important problems and recommendations still wait to be resolved and implemented (e.g. institution of the family court).

Slovenia has been one of the 23 countries participating in the ISPA's (International School Psychology Association) cross-national children's rights research project. Data was collected from pupils between 12 and 14 in age and their teachers, who represented their significant adult persons. Results from this project can be taken as a basis of comparison and evaluation of the children's rights situation in Slovenia. Zoran Pavlovic, the Slovenian national researcher in this cross-national study, mentions (among others) two general findings. While average scores of Slovenian children (12–14 years old) are close to the gross average of the other 23 countries, some interesting characteristics can be seen from the specific structures of the average answers. The first finding shows 'relatively strong orientation of Slovenian children towards family and adults and rather less orientation towards their peers' (Pavlovic, 2001). At the same time children 'foster great expectations of the social functions of the school' (ibid.). The second finding is that teachers (at the upper part of the primary school level, which in Slovenia covers the age group of 14–15 years) 'mostly continue to treat students as "children" ' (ibid.). The same is the case if attitudes of teachers in secondary school (which covers the 14–19 years age group) are analysed. 'The overall impression is that the "average child" in Slovenia is relatively well cared for as an object of protection and less so as the subject of his own rights' (ibid.).

These research findings, and the perceived shortcomings of the implementation of the convention, both point to the issue of children's participation. In this field many innovations have been developed; many of them in the framework of Slovenian primary schools (covering the 7–15 age group). Maybe a contributing factor in this innovative process was the fact that every Slovenian primary school has its own school counselling service, consisting of one or more school psychologists, or pedagogues (educational specialists, social workers or child care workers).

The Children's Parliament and How it Functions

'Democracy without children is not inclusive', claims Pavlovic (1996) in his analysis of the Children's Parliament in Slovenia. Societies 'should foster persuasive and inclusive rather than exclusive myths', where we can understand myths as 'ideas and stories, that enable human beings to co-operate and work together as a society' (Pavlovic, 1996). The Slovenian Children's Parliament is an attempt to develop and implement a specific structure of children's participation, which should cover many levels between the school class and the state. This form of participation was developed with the idea of both exercising the powers of dialogue with children in the environment of everyday life at school, and of being heard and seen at the national level, and through that, symbolically promoting the concept of children's rights. In that sense the idea represents an inclusive myth. However the implementation of the idea cannot escape being limited by the existing cultural, economic and political conditions of each particular society.

The Slovenian Children's Parliament has been working for over ten years. The first Parliamentary session, which took place in the year 1990, when for the first time the Slovene multi-party 'adult' Parliament was constituted, did not as yet carry today's name. Then it was only a 'meeting', of 105 representatives of children from different Slovenian local communities with important politicians and government officials. Due to the success and significant media response to this first meeting, it was decided to continue with the preparation of such meetings in the future, to name the event the Children's Parliament, and to prepare the whole process more systematically and with greater care.

The Children's Parliament meets once a year at the state level. It is attended by approximately 100 pupils' representatives from the majority of more than 100 Slovenian communities. For the most part, these children are students of higher grades of primary school, of 13–15 years of age. Each year the session is dedicated to a specific topic chosen in advance. Depending on the topic, the ministers competent for the specific area are invited (among them the Minister of Education and Sport most frequently) or other high government officials, presidents of important bodies of the 'adult' Parliament and representatives of the press. The preparation and organisation of the Parliament is carried out by the organising group of the Association of the Friends of Youth in Slovenia (AFYS) and by invited outside experts.

In recent years the preparation process for Children's Parliaments has proceeded in several stages:

1. At each Parliament session, the children suggest topics for the next Parliament.
2. On the basis of these suggestions, the AFYS organising group decides the theme for the next Parliament session.
3. In September, the AFYS organises a public round-table discussion in Ljubljana, the capital of Slovenia, where experts from the specific area participate as introductory speakers, with the audience of (mainly) primary school staff members who will, in the mentor's role, carry out the preparations for the next Children's Parliament in individual primary schools. In recent years this phase of preparations has regularly included 24 hours of lectures, presentations and group discussions.
4. In October, individual primary schools organise various activities for their pupils (school round-table discussions, school surveys, visits to different organisations, discussions on relevant movies, projects, pupils' research work, etc.) connected with the theme of the coming Parliament. These activities are offered mostly to higher grade students, but they can also be carried out in lower grades of primary school, provided they are suitably prepared and within the possibilities of the school. Activities at this level are mostly focused on individual classes which represent – in the school setting – the most 'natural' organisational framework for organised group work.
5. It is above all the students of higher grades who then attend the meeting of the School Parliament, where they discuss the theme, form opinions and resolutions of their school and finally choose representatives to meet at the Community level Parliament meeting (local communities usually include about 3–10 primary schools).
6. The meeting of these representatives is then organised at the Community level. Here again they form several resolutions and choose representatives who are to take the messages to the meeting of the State Children's Parliament.
7. In some parts of Slovenia (mostly in towns consisting of more than one community), the fifth stage is repeated at this intermediate, one could say, regional level.
8. At the state level, the Children's Parliament usually meets in December. The meetings take place in the plenary room of the real national Parliament. The Parliament elects the chairman, which is actually an adult 'technical' aide (a youth worker or an expert for the specific topic). The session usually begins – after all the guests have been welcomed – with a short performance by some popular figure (a pop singer, for example), which is then followed by a

report from the Ministers who explain how successfully the demands or resolutions of the previous Parliament have been realised. Then a discussion about the theme of the current Parliament is opened. Individual speakers present their contributions, in which they try in their own words to reflect on the viewpoints of their home environment. This presentation is followed by open-ended questions and demands that the Ministers or State Secretaries endeavour to answer. In the majority of cases, they try to explain the circumstances responsible for the existing situation or present the policies and activities of their Ministries in connection with the Parliament's theme or questions asked. Sometimes the Parliament Chairman summarises the draft resolutions arrived at during the discussion. This is followed by the suggestions or voting for the theme of the next Parliament meeting, which brings the session to a close (lunch is served in the restaurant of the 'real' Parliament).

9. On the basis of tape recordings of all the discussions, the AFYS representatives collate the suggestions and resolutions of the Children's Parliament.

10. After some time, AFYS publishes a journal with all the expert papers (sometimes including also the discussions of the audience) of the autumn round table (and sometimes these papers are prepared before that round table), with taped transcripts of all the debaters at the Children's Parliament, including their suggestions and resolutions.

In the last two or three years two important changes in the process of the Children's Parliament have been introduced, developed and implemented:

First, the importance of the regional level parliament meetings (point 7 above) has been emphasised and formalised. Seventeen regions have been determined and in each of them a group of facilitators (mentors) selected and trained.

Second, from 2000 onwards a new executive body of the Children's Parliament has been instituted – the Children's Government. It consists of 17 delegates coming from the 17 regions. Also the regional and community/school level parliament may and do elect their Government, whose two most important roles are to control the implementation of the previous Parliament resolutions and to participate in the preparations for the next Parliament. The National Children's Government is supposed to have meetings four times a year. In May they discuss the resolutions of the last Children's Parliament and plan the next Parliament. In September they participate in the organisation and implementation of a 24-hour educational seminar (and round-table) for mentors. In October they meet regional co-ordinators (mentors) and local Children's Governments. In November they participate in organising and preparing the next National Children's Parliament.

The most important role of the National Children's Government is perhaps to control and follow-up the implementation of the resolutions of the previous Parliaments. They should not be concerned only with the last year's Parliament resolution; it was taken as an agreement that resolutions from the last three-year period should be taken into account.

Themes of Children's Parliament

The thirteen Parliaments have so far discussed the following themes:

- 1990/1991: Healthy and safe environment for children.
- 1991/1992: Leisure time.
- 1992/1993: Child-friendly school.
- 1993/1994: For friendship without violence.
- 1994/1995: Power of the friendly word (originally: relations between students and teachers).

- 1995/1996: How to say 'no, thank you' to alcohol, nicotine, drugs and all kinds of intolerance.
- 1996/1997: I have the right – you have the right (on what the new guidelines on school rules are bringing into school life).
- 1997/1998: I am you and you are me (peer relations, with an implicit emphasis on bullying).
- 1998/1999: Youth and mass media.
- 1999/2000: You and me – we are in love.
- 2000/2001: I want to do it, so I can do it!
- 2001/2002: My leisure time.
- 2002/2003: Childhood without violence and abuse.

In 1996, after the first six years of the Children's Parliament, an attempt was made to deduce trends from the chosen themes, which could point to a possible process of development of the Parliament over the years. The author of the paper (Dekleva, 1996) concluded that, in general, it could be established that all the themes were related to school and the life connected with it. This should really not seem strange, since all the attending child representatives were schoolgoers, and since the organisation of the Parliament was at the lowest possible (school) level – in the hands of school people (sometimes teachers, more frequently school counselling workers).

A way to assign meaning to the developmental process of themes would be to determine whether from the first to the fifth Parliament a shift in focus from the more 'external' themes (environment) to the more 'internal' ones (relations within the school) can be observed. Another hypothesis could tackle the question of the relations and balance of adults' and children's responsibilities, as they could be deduced from the discussions and resolutions of the Parliaments' meetings.

On the basis of tape recording analysis, Pavlovic gave his understanding of the fundamental (deep) messages from the children at the five Parliaments up till that time, in the following way (Pavlovic, 1996):

- 1990 'We want to have a future, but we do not seem to have any.'
- 1991 'Take care of us. We are entitled to it!'
- 1992 'If you [as adults] are fair, then we can do our part. We can live together well!''
- 1993 'Protect us!' This, however, does not only mean: 'You, the good people, protect us, the good children, from bullies, drugs and alcohol!' but it also means: 'Protect us, the good and the bad children, from yourselves. Change your ways!'
- 1994 'Adults, change your ways!' (adults again!) 'We may be able to help you!'
- The sixth Parliament's theme was drugs, an issue which had for some time beforehand been very topical in the Slovene media. In this connection Pavlovic (1995) implies that by accepting and discussing this parliamentary theme, the grown-up AFYS organisers actually delegated their problems and views to the children, or rather endeavoured to reflect their dilemmas and worries in their statements.

The themes of the following four Parliament meetings – children's rights, peer violence, mass media, and love and sex, which were chosen on the basis of children's suggestions, at the same time reflected four of the important topics which have been for some time in the focus of general public attention. In this sense the themes did not represent the specific and separate children's concerns, but to a bigger degree the concerns of the public which also concerned children, and relations between them and adults. Among these themes only one (peer relations) was mostly school-related, while the other three were related to general questions of children's living conditions and contexts.

The last three themes were concerned with (respectively) self-image and problem-solving, leisure time and violence. The fact that two of the themes appeared for the second time reflects the lasting concerns of children (and adults alike,) and probably also the quickly changing social contexts of these issues, which should be 'put on the table' again and again.

Functions and range of Children's Parliaments

The most obvious and inherent functions of the Children's Parliament could be those of *formalising decision-making, making legitimate confrontation and finding solutions to conflicting interests*, etc. But in fact the Children's Parliament cannot fulfil these functions, because child representatives do not possess much real social (political) power. Nevertheless the Children's Parliament, to a certain extent, functions as a pressure group, because it is strongly reported in the media. The fact that the annual themes of Children's Parliaments are discussed at all levels (from the school level to the state), represents a certain mobilisation of the wider social interests and perhaps even a certain pressure on changing the priorities of the relevant Ministries.

Because Children's Parliaments started to function in the same year as the adult ones, they could be assigned the role of 'introductory school' or *a foundation course for parliamentary democracy*, a mechanism which could enable children to learn about parliamentary principles and practice. Some speeches of adult Parliament representatives bear witness to this possible function, but on the other hand one must be aware of the fact that the Children's Parliament lacks several essential elements of the 'adult' Parliament, namely, they can only partly act as independent political subjects as they are not elected in a formalised way.

The third possible function is a symbolic one. Organising Children's Parliaments, and meetings of child representatives, with some of the most influential persons of the adult Parliament on a formally equal basis, means *a symbolic recognition of the utmost importance of children's interests*, and the *promotion of the children's rights concept*, which can all have a symbolic effect beyond the immediate time and space framework of Parliaments

themselves. Children's Parliaments can also play the role of mediators in the process of legitimising and supporting current political trends and projects in the field of child care and the educational system (for example: our Ministry of Education's project of the 'Child Friendly School').

The fourth function of Children's Parliaments seems to be the most pronounced. This is the function of the *educational treatment of children's rights*, which means that, for the treatment and 'education' of recognising one's own rights, typically school or educational means are applied, implying that it is the teacher who knows what the 'real' rights are, how to understand them properly, how to 'correctly' enforce them, which people and groups are already in advance defined as 'good' or 'bad'.

With Children's Parliaments and above all with the methodology behind the preparation, which was developed by AFYS, schools gained a new curriculum and also partly – new methods of educational work. This curriculum and these methods have partly replaced the former work with so-called 'school pupils' communities' in the framework of their national organisation (so-called 'Pioneers' organisation from the times of the previous political regime). This project of Children's Parliament has also enabled AFYS to develop from a semi-state organisation into a more credible non-governmental and independent organisation.

The importance of the 'educational' function can also be reflected in the fact that in the five years of Children's Parliaments the focus of attention and activities shifted from the state level to the more local one. This means that, at the beginning, the general symbolic function of Parliaments was of greater importance, but now it is the framework offered by the State Children's Parliament which enables a more meaningful organisation of the process of preparing school-level Parliaments. The symbolic function of the State Children's Parliament now serves as a strong support (or lever) for organising educational work in individual schools and school communities (partly also in the local environment of respective schools). The educational function is also mentioned as the most important one in many documents of the AFYS (Otroski Parlament, 2003) which declares that 'Children's Parliament is a program of education of children and youth for democracy'. In other documents and papers a similar idea is pronounced as the need for asserting Children's Parliaments as a form of civic education (Pavlovic, 2002).

Fifthly, Pavlovic, in his latest writing on Children's Parliaments (2001) mentions four types of problems with such kind of children's participation:

1. The first is the problem of all 'democracies by representation'. Children's Parliaments are directly and inclusively participative only at the class levels, while Parliaments at the following levels (the whole school, at community and state levels) consist of represented children – representatives of classes, school and communities.
2. The second problem refers to the tendency that children sometimes become too 'self-critical' and tend to 'produce socially desirable responses' (ibid.).
3. The next problem is that sometimes it seems as if 'adult political messages are being delivered to the Slovene government through the children's mouths', although Pavlovic (ibid.) adds that 'an authentic children's voice (always) does come through'.
4. The last of the four problematic aspects is that the lack of some formal, obligatory links and feed-backs are missing regarding the duty of adults to respect the conclusions of the Children's Parliament.

Pavlovic is, in describing these four problematic aspects, which should be addressed in the future, in fact referring to the third of the functions which were described above: it is the symbolic function, which is extremely important (in the symbolic cosmos) but could be too weak to tackle or change the very concrete conditions of the material world.

Sixth and finally, by stating four possible functions of the Children's Parliaments, of which the latter three are rather ambiguous or could (in the case of the implementation of children's rights) even be seen as fulfilling regressive roles, we have not wished to assess the Children's Parliaments as negative in any way. While representing a kind of a surrogate in the realisation of real changes in the situation of children, they can actually make people aware, or in other words, 'set the stage' for a possible future situation which will be more favourably inclined to listening to the children and considering their needs.

The decisive question in connection with the Children's Parliament is, whose views and interests are publicly being presented at these Parliaments, who speaks in the name of whom, or which symbolic divisions are here being constituted? In this connection we have to establish that the process of Children's Parliaments scoops up above all the 'good' children from 'normal' schools and that the less school-adaptable children, and children in care, to a large extent remain outside of the process. In the same way the influence of mentors, organisers and other mediators involved in forming parliamentary discussion is quite pronounced, which goes hand-in-hand with the earlier mentioned theme of 'educational treatment'.

Conclusion: empowering children

Empowering children is not only (nor above all) a question of a formal procedure, but is also a question of economic, political and cultural situations and processes. As a country in transition, Slovenia meets with several typical problems, though perhaps not in the most acute form or stage): underdeveloped legal culture, rather high unemployment and a generally unsure economic future, with rising economic and social competition, rising political centralisation with a potentially rising intolerance towards everything that is different. Alongside these phenomena and trends, greater importance is ascribed to knowledge, social mobility and appreciative value of the skills of public political engagement.

In such a context the process of Children's Parliaments can have several different (sometimes even contradictory) functions, and in the context of limited possibilities it offers rather ambitious visions. This chapter on the one hand tries to emphasise mainly the function of the 'new' educational treatment, corresponding to the new political times and new public rhetoric, and supporting new ideologies (above all, ideologies of the 'new' educational and child-oriented work). On the other hand it can, as a new form of activity, also offer new opportunities of empowerment and emancipation. These opportunities are not radical, and are not sufficient for overcoming the many mechanisms of exclusion on individual and systemic levels which still exist as a significant part of the realities of children's lives.

Note and acknowledgment

A shorter version of this chapter appeared in the materials of the Glasgow Conference *Realities and Dreams* in 1996, and another one in the journal *Social Work in Europe* (1999). The present chapter includes updated, additional information, and an analysis of Slovenian Children's Parliaments.

References

Dekleva, B. (1995) *Nove vrste vzgojnih ukrepov za mladoletnike (Alternative educational measures for juveniles*. Ljubljana, Institute of criminology.

Dekleva, B. (1996) The Slovenian Children's Parliament. in Macquarrie, A. (Ed.) *Realities and Dreams*. Plenary papers from the International conference on child care held at the University of Strathclyde 3–6 September. Glasgow, Centre for Residential Child Care.

Drugo (2001) *Drugo poročilo Republike Slovenije o sprejetih ukrepih za uresničevanje konvencije o otrokovih pravicah (delovno gradivo)*. Ljubljana, Vlada Republike Slovenije.

Pavlovic, Z. (1995) *Kako reci ne, hvala nesvobodi in da zivljenju (How to Say 'No, Thank You' to Non-freedom and 'Yes' to Life)*. Solski razgledi 1995/15 (p.11).

Pavlovic, Z. (1996) Children's Parliament in Slovenia, in John, M. (Ed.) *The Child's Right to a Fair Hearing*. London, Jessica Kingsley Publishers.

Pavlovic, Z. (2001) *Cross-cultural Study on the Rights of the Child in Slovenia: The First 10 Years*. School Psychology International.

Pavlovic, Z. (2002) *Participacija otrok (Participation of Children). In Reader for mentors and organizers of Children's Parliaments – Childhood without violence and abuse*. Ljubljana, AFYS.

Otroski parlament (Children's Parliament). (2003) April 21st http://www.zveza-pms.si/

Rights (2000) *Rights in Crisis and Transition. Developing a Children's Agenda for South Eastern Europe*. South East European Child Rights Action and Save the Children Draft Policy Platform, unpublished material.

Zacetno (1997) *Zacetno porocilo Republike Slovenije o sprejtih ukrepih za uresničevanje konvencije o otrokovih pravicah. (The Initial Report on Measures Adopted by the Republic of Slovenia in Implementing the Convention on the Rights of the Child)*. Ljubljana, Vlada Republike Slovenije.

Index

abuse 59, 72
Achenbach T. 67
Adults, role of 2, 8, 16, 20–21, 42, 50, 142
adult-child relationship 18,
adult-centred 55, 64
adult world 113
adult barriers (to participation) 42, 113
advocacy 70
Albermarle Report (1960) 15, 30, 70, 71
Alderson P. 15,
Alexander Foundation 112, 114, 117, 121
alienated 73
Altieri L. 101, 107
Andenæs J. 125
Arnstein S. 3, 15, 34, 50, 57
Article 12. 29, 44, 47, 72, 87, 124, 131, 139
Ascoli U. 105
Aster-X (Agenzia di Servizi per il Terzo Settore) 99
Astill J. 2,

Badman B. 5
Baker J. 30, 77
Bangladesh 5, 17, 20
Barnett A. 12
Bassanini S. 102
Boccaccin L. 105
Boyden J. 50
Britton L. 44, 45
Bruggeman D. 122
Brusdal R. 128, 133
Bulger James 7
Burrell G. 21
Busse M. 86

Cape Verdian 115
Care 9, 59; care institutions/residential care 101, 114, 115–117; young people resident in 112
Castellani A. 100, 108
Cavalli A. 101
Centro nazionale di documentazione e analisi per l'infanzia e l'adolescenza 102
Chakrabarti M. 60
Charter see Youth Charter

Childhood 11, 24, 48, 53, 91, 110; nature of 108; status of 85,
ChildLine 59, 62, 66
child-to-child programme 17
Child and Youth Services Act, 1991. see KJHG
capacity building 74
Childrens' Commissioner for Wales 73
children's committee 84
children's councils (see youth and children's councils)
Children's Hearing 60, 62–63, 66
children's lawyer 84, 87, 88, 89
children's offices 84, 88–89, 90
Children's Parliament 7, 56, 73, 74, 85, 88–89, 94, 95–96, forms of 89–90
children's representatives 84
Children's Rights Alliance for England (CRAE) 33
Children's Rights Office 31
Children's Rights Officers 59, 62,
Children's Rights Commissioner 33, 88, 90
Children (Scotland) Act 1995. 59, 64
Children and Young Person's Unit (CYPU) 28
citizenship 1, 2, 5, 7, 10, 11, 15, 21, 22, 99, 103; active citizenship 109; promotion of children's citizenship 106; citizen status 107; young citizens 113
Cohen S. 7, 44
Coles B 43, 44
Combe V. 32, 33, 76
competence 4, 9, 85
complaints (independent systems of making) 116, 118
Connexions 28, 45, 70; principles of 43
Connexions Service 37
Connexions Service National Unit (CSNU) 44
Connexions Partnerships 39, 41
consultation 5–6, 9, 38, 49, 52, 53–56, 103
Convention on the Rights of the Child (CRC) 1, 15, 23, 27, 31, 34, 44, 47, 51, 60, 72, 84, 85, 87, 92, 99,102, 124, 127, 128, 129, 138
Coopers & Lybrand Deloitte 72

Council of Europe (CoE) 9, 112
Cousins J. 50
Crawford A. 43
Crimmens D. 5, 28, 43
Cuninghame C. 14, 34
Cutler D. 6, 31, 32

Dahl T.S. 125
Dal Lago A. 108
Dalla Mura F.
Davies B. 76, 78
Davies E. 72
de Ambrogio U. 102
decentralisation 64, 100
decision-making 6, 8, 9, 16, 18, 19, 32, 62, 71, 73, 74, 77, 85, 86, 93, 103, 105, 143; instruments of 109; in residential institutions 119
de Lillo A. 101
Dekleva B. 142
democracy 5, 12, 23, 70, 73, 74, 84, 86, 96, 96, 133, 139; training for 124; foundation for parliamentary democracy 143; education for 144
democracy-learning 6, 84, 85, 87, 95
Department of Health (DoH) 30
Department for Education and Skills (DfES) 30, 34, 37
Detrick S. 85
Deutscher Verein 86
Deutsches Kinderhilfswerk [German Children's Aid] 87
Deutsches Kinderschutzbund [Society for the Protection of Children] 87
devolution 32
de Winter M. 15
disability 102
disaffected 73
Donati P. 105

Edwards L. 32
Electoral Commission 32
Ekeland T-J. 132
Elder G. 85
emancipation 86, 145
employment 7, 27
empowerment 7, 21, 22, 50, 70, 78, 81, 145; empower 113, empowering 144
enfranchisement 79
Ennew J. 50

ethnic issues/ ethnicity 4, 18, 101; diversity 104; background 114; origin 117
evaluation 104, 115, 117, 118; processes of 107
European Convention on the Exercise of Children's Rights 10
European Convention on Human Rights 31
EUROARRCC (the European Association for Research into Residential Child Care) 66
European Commission (Youth) White Paper 10, 11, 30
European Union 5, 9
EURONET 10

family – life 8, 15, 47, 48, 51, 128; family policy 92; promotion of 101; role of 102; mediation services 109; court 139; foster families 101, 102, 109
Family Group Conferencing 61
Flekkoy M. 33, 125, 133
Fondo Nazionale per l'Infanzia e l'Adolescenza (National Children's and Adolescent's Fund) 101
forums – for children 8; young people 65; children and young people 90–91, 94, 103; youth 70–74, 75–76.
Frädrich J. 94
France A. 108
Franklin B. 3, 15, 50, 55
Freeman M. 50, 133
Freire P. 70, 78, 79, 82
Frisanco R. 105
Frnes I. 128, 133
Frost D. 72
Fuchs W. 86
funding 101, 103
Funky Dragon 74, 81

Garrett M. 43, 45
Garelli F. 101
gender 1, 4, 18, 20,93
Giddens A. 128
Gilligan R. 49
governance 38–39
Gruppo Tecnico Territoriale 104
Gurumurthy 6

Haage B. 121
Haarsma L. 106
Hager H. 85

Hareide, B. 126
Hart R. 3, 5, 7, 9, 15, 34, 50
Haugli T. 132
Hayes N. 48
Hayter S. 34
Hazekamp J. 122
Hendrik H. 43, 44
Hogan D. 49
Holmes J. 75
Honig M.-S. 91
homeless 73
Howe D. 21
human rights 23, 61
Human Rights Act, 1998. 31
Hurley L. 21

Ireland 47
Irish Society for the Prevention of Cruelty to
    Children (ISPCC) 49

James A. 1, 15
Jean d'Heur B. 84
Jeffs T. 80
Jeleff S. 10
Johnson V. 15, 44
Jones B. 78, 79
Joseph Rowntree Foundation 32
Jovine N. 105
Jumelet H. 116, 121
Jurrius K. 122

Kahan B. 59, 62
Kasse M. 85
Kaufman N. 33, 125, 133
Kayser T. 115
Keesom J. 120
Kent R. 59, 60, 64
Khan S. 17
Kilbrandon C. J. D. Shaw, Lord, 60
Kinder und Jugendhilfegesetz, 1991 (KJHG)
    86–87
Kirby P. 16
Klaushofer A. 77
Klimmer A. 122
Knutson K. 9, 10
Koekkoek E. 121
KUF 127

ladder (of participation) 3, 15, 55
Lange A. 91

Lansdown G. 10, 15
law, number 285/97, 99, 106
Leigh M. 79
Levy A. 59, 62
Lindboe K. 132
Llais Lfanc (Young Voice) 73, 81
Local Government Information Unit (LGIU)
    31
Lødrup P. 132
looked after children 9, 63

Manchester Youth Council 24
Mantell H. 3
media – representation of children and
    young people 134–135
Melandri V. 105
Milson/Fairbairn Report. (1969) 71, 76, 78
Minister for Children 29
Molloy D. 32, 33
Morgan G. 21
Morris S. 62
Myklebust V. 132

Naber P. 115
Næss S. 133
National Children's Bureau 31
National Children's Government (Slovenia)
    141
National Children's Office (NCO) 55
National Children's Strategy (Ireland) 7, 47,
    49, 51, 52–53.
National Youth Agency 33, 71, 76, 77
Neill A.S. 3
Neresini F. 100
Neubauer G. 92
Newell P. 33
New Labour 27, 33, 37, 43; and panopticism 43
Newport Young Peoples Council 72
Nolan B. 48
Nolet R. 127
Northern Ireland Education Board 80
NOU 126, 127, 133

obligation 4, 51
Office hours at the mayor 85, 89
OFSTED 79
Oliver B. 34
Ombudsman for Children Act (Ireland,
    2002) 56
ombuds(wo)man 89, 124, 127

Oppedal M. 132
Ortmann F. 86
Ostermann H. 95

participation, training for 16; types of 17;
  purpose of 20; frameworks for 21–22,
  40–41, principles of 29, promotion of 39;
  process of 15, 50; levels of 50; and
  inter-agency work 43–44; models of 79, 86,
  92, 95; barriers to 76; in practice 93; culture
  of 30, 95; in school management 100;
  hybrid types of 103; in institutions 107;
  legal rights to 129; opportunity for 136
partnership 10, 50, 113
Pasquinelli S. 105
Pavlovic Z. 139, 142
peer education 15, 17; peer educators 119
personal advisors (Connexions) 37, 43, 45
Pinkerton J. 48
planning 100, 101; process of 104, 105;
  procedures for 106; for children's policy
  106
political inclusion 103
power 34, 44; balance of 38; power-sharing
  18, 77; structures and systems of 64
Pridmore P.
Progetto Giovani (youth project) 100–101
Prout A. 1, 15, 34

Quality Protects 28, 29
Quortrup 89, 91

Ranci C. 100, 105
recreation, promotion of 101
representation 88
research projects 59, 66, 79, 91; child-led
  research 9, 15, 23; focus groups 75; youth
  112–113; sharing research and
  consultation expertise 114; and legal
  theory 132
residential care homes 15, 59, 63; young
  people living in 64
rights 32, 51, protection of 60; promotion of
  101, 106, 143; and citizenship 103, culture
  of 106; legal 128; right to be consulted 125,
  132; implementation of 144
Rosenbaum M. 33
round tables 91
Rose J. 79, 80
Russell B. 82

Ruxton S. 10

Sandbæk M. 133
School 8, 15, 19, 27, 48, 54, 91, 95, 102, 108,
  112
school councils 7, 74, pupils councils 126
Schormann M. 87
Scottish Parliament 64
Scottish Institute for Residential Child Care.
  65
self-determination 128, 136
Simpson G. 40
Siza R. 100
Skimmeli M. 126
Skinner A. 60, 61, 67
Slovenian Children's Parliament 139–144
Smith L. 132
social education 71, 85, 101
Social Exclusion Unit 27, 28, 37, 44
social inclusion 27, 43, 74
social services 102, 107
South Lanarkshire 63
Stampfl K. 121
standards (for good practice) 3,
Stanzani S. 105
Strathclyde Regional Council. 62
street children 5,
street work projects 103, 104
subcultures 108
Sünker H. 85, 92
surveillance 43
Swiderek T. 85

Tayside Regional Council 62
Treacy D. 21
Thailand 24
theatre work 19
Thompson Report (1982) 30, 71, 72
Tisdall K. 48
Torti M. 108
training, experiential 4; for participation
  16–17, 27; professional 71; in research
  114Treseder P. 4, 15, 72, 79
Turco's law 99, 101–102; 104, 105
Tveiten G. 133

Unicef 99
United Nations Committee on the Rights
  of the Child 52, 124, 131–132, 133, 136,
  138

United Nations Special Session on Children
    (2002), 12
Utting Sir W. 59

Veldman F. 115
Verhellen E. 4, 85
viewpoint 41
voluntary organisations/third sector 10, 64,
    105, 106; NGO's 22, 51, 112
voluntary sector 8, 15
vote (right to) 6, voters/voting 23–24
Vriens G. 121

Wade H. 33, 39
Wainwright M. 32
Wales Youth Agency 70, 71, 76
Waterhouse R. 59, 72
Webb M. 48
Wellard S. 15
Welsh Assembly Government (WAG) 70, 73,
    76, 79
Welsh Association of Youth Clubs (WAYC)
    72, 78, 81
White C. 32
White P. 5
Who Cares? Scotland 59, 63–66

Willis P. 7
Willow C. 5, 15, 31, 34
West A. 5, 14, 16, 24

young mothers 115
Young People's Partnerships (YPPs) 75
Young Voice (Llais Ifanc) 73–74, 81
youth charter 41, 70, 73, 76
youth clubs 15, 78
youth consulting teams 121–122
youth (and children's) councils 9, 14, 23, 52,
    72, 114, 121, 128; in residential institutions
    116
youth forums (see forums)
youth inspection team 121
youth parliament (see Children's
    Parliament)
Youth Service, marginalisation of 75, 79,
    history of, in Wales 81, 86, 94
youth work 7, 8, 15, 70, 78, 79, 80
youth workers 78, 79

Zacetno 138
Zeiher H. 85
zero measurement 117–118